'Joy Gravestock's work remains a guiding star for music therapists engaging with the adoption community. She writes with a clarity that belies the depth of thought, expertly expanding her psychoanalytic foundations to draw on existential philosophy and her own lived experience as an adoptee.'

Ian Grundy, *Lead Creative Arts Therapist, Coram Creative Therapy London*

'This book is essential reading for all of us involved in the experience of the adoptee and adoption – whether music or arts therapists, talking therapists, or adoptees. The depth of exploration in Joy Gravestock's tenderly-held single case studies brings her cross-modality formulations on clinical practice off the page, giving us a visceral sense of the live relationship and play between therapist and client.'

Serena Jenks, *Attachment-based psychoanalytic psychotherapist and supervisor to Music Therapists*

'This book will not only be of value to music therapists working with adoptees, but to any practitioners who want to understand more about the relevance of psychoanalytic concepts in a relational, improvisational approach.'

Dr Luke Annesley, *Course Lead Music Therapy MA, University of Western England*

Music Therapy and Adoption

Operating at the leading edge of music therapy, *Music Therapy and Adoption* provides an in-depth examination of one single case study then compares this to a wider range of examples of the author's practice to identify four repeated 'adoption themes' that arise in therapeutic work.

Chapters guide readers through the rationale behind an adoption-specific music therapy and the psychoanalytic approach taken by the author. The book then approaches each of the adoption themes (feeling dropped and dropping things, lullabies and their meaning, the dynamics of hide and seek and the baby with the broken head), demonstrating how readers may identify similar themes and then appropriately develop music therapy practice for positive experiences within their own clinical work. Grounded in a needs-led collaboration within the adoption community, the author also navigates her dual position as a therapist with lived experience of adoption and how this relates to her therapeutic practice and clinical research.

As a non-verbal modality, music therapy is particularly well placed as a creative intervention for work with adoptees and their families. Accessibly written and informed by lived experience, this is an essential read for music therapists, other mental-health professionals and, most importantly, adoptees themselves.

Joy Gravestock is a freelance music therapist working with child adoptees, funded by the Adoption Support Fund and adult members of the adoption community. Her adoption-specific approach in music therapy draws upon psychoanalytic, relational, attachment and trauma-informed theories and modalities. Her Ph.D. highlighted attunement within adoptive families. She is currently training to be an attachment psychotherapist.

Music Therapy and Adoption

Co-creating Therapy Centered on Adoptee Lived Experience

Joy Gravestock

Routledge
Taylor & Francis Group
LONDON AND NEW YORK

Designed cover image: © Getty Images

First published 2027
by Routledge
4 Park Square, Milton Park, Abingdon, Oxon OX14 4RN

and by Routledge
605 Third Avenue, New York, NY 10158

Routledge is an imprint of the Taylor & Francis Group, an informa business

British Library Cataloguing-in-Publication Data
A catalogue record for this book is available from the British Library

ISBN: 978-1-041-22663-5 (hbk)
ISBN: 978-1-041-22662-8 (pbk)
ISBN: 978-1-003-73339-3 (ebk)

DOI: 10.4324/9781003733393

Typeset in Times New Roman
by Taylor & Francis Books

Rise up singing!
Remembering Lily, with gratitude.

Contents

Acknowledgements

Nick: in Buddhism, it is said, you can form a community of two in order to practise love. Through learning this, you learn to express your love for the whole of humanity and all beings. Thank you for enabling this.

Frances: for friendship that teaches me that planting a garden really does hold hope for a future.

Chris: I think I have internalised something of all our years of work together and am grateful.

Serena: wise as you are, full of experience . . . thank you for travelling to Ithaca with me! I hope our journey together continues long, full of adventure, full of discovery.

Dr Nour and the Rheumatology Team, especially Carly Durrow, Speciality Nurse, Royal Derby Hospital: you are continually working to help me live the life I want to, despite rheumatoid arthritis. Thank you for not giving up and believing I can do this stuff!

To the University of Western England for granting me the study time to shape my research of practice into this book.

Chapter 1

Continued development of an adoption-specific music therapy

'Jaden'

Jaden has been running rapidly and noisily around my music-therapy room for thirty minutes. He is in a hyper-aroused emotional state and has been picking up any and every instrument, attempting to play each one briefly then dropping it and moving swiftly on to another, then another, and another . . . His indiscriminate bashing and banging often results in inadvertent damage to instruments in the process. I feel exhausted. My ear is very tired of the relentless noise. I have tried running after him, but as soon as I get close, he is off again. All is chaos, and I am finding it hard to think at all. His adopted mum, Sarah, has been talking consistently. She keeps urging Jaden on: 'That's it, Jaden, show the music lady what you can do with all the instruments!' while providing me with a constant narrative of his play. She also is emotionally unregulated, speaking rapidly and in a high-pitched voice. As I am desperately wondering how to provide containment for them both, Sarah is encouraging Jaden to do yet increasingly more. I cannot get a word in and feel caught up in this high-energy enactment between Jaden and Sarah which also serves to exclude me.

What am I to do, I wonder. I decide that rather than matching and mirroring such intense play and embodied expression, I will offer a very different embodied presence in the room as a means of emotional regulation. I sit down on the floor, stilling my body first. Then I gently begin to play, almost inaudibly, glissandos on a child's xylophone. My hand softly and slowly sweeps from the bottom to the top of the two-octave instrument. I feel myself settling into another state; however, I also feel hopeless in the face of the noise and chaos around me. I wonder if my feeling state could be like Jaden's, who also cannot 'get a word in edgeways' and whose vitality affects in the room might arise from a desire to please his mum. Gradually, however, Jaden begins to hear the xylophone. In a rare moment of silence that occurs, he is listening, and suddenly I realise he is attuning to something different. He becomes stilled also.

I find myself saying, 'Perhaps Jaden and Mummy can just do nothing here if they want.' Jaden sits down on a sofa, drawing a blanket around himself.

DOI: 10.4324/9781003733393-1

Mum follows, after first discouraging him as she said he would 'just go to sleep'. Gradually she relents and sits down on the sofa alongside him. I continue to play soft glissandos on the xylophone. Jaden lies down now on the sofa, placing his head into Sarah's lap. He cannot see her face, but I notice immediately that her eyes have filled with tears. I continue to play, and Sarah begins to stroke Jaden's hair. (It is only later, watching back the video of this session, that I become aware that she and I shared an exact timing of movements, me in my xylophone glissandos and she in her hair-stroking.) Jaden picks up a beater and begins to make the softest of sounds on my xylophone, playing it from the opposite side to me and reaching down to it from the sofa in a languid manner. He beats the xylophone with a steady and assertive rhythm and picks out an interval of a fifth. He seems to anticipate an answering phrase from me, and I take the fifth, repeat it and extend beyond it into the tune 'Twinkle Twinkle Little Star'. The three of us are sitting now in calm; Sarah is stroking Jaden's hair, I am playing, and Jaden is snuggling into Mum while half playing the xylophone. He reminds me of a baby fighting against going to sleep. I think that now Jaden can safely regress, allowing the nursery song that we play together, along with the regular rhythmic sensorial stroking of his head by his mum, to provide some emotional regulation.

Four-year-old Jaden was fairly new in this adoptive placement with his single-carer mum. Sarah had herself spent her early years in the care system before eventually being adopted. Music therapy was happening for them as a parent–child dyad because Sarah had expressed what she described as 'an inability to attach' to Jaden. She thought this was due to his pre-adoption experiences of physical abuse which resonated with her own. The referral I received spoke of fear that the placement might 'fail'.

From the very start of our work, in the transference, I had felt as if I had two children who were impossible to hold on to in the room. Each time I found a thought arising in my mind to possibly interject into the situation, I would hear Sarah's pressured speech; 'Show the music lady . . . Show her the song you learned at school . . . Show her how you play piano . . . Show her your shoes . . . Show her your schoolbook . . .' etc. Supervision had helped me to realise that attempts to work verbally with Sarah's verbal material were failing as she could never allow space for thought. I hypothesised that Sarah feared her own emotional needs, which might be echoed if Jaden ever had space to express his.

After the session described above, I met with Sarah on her own. She told me how her personal traumatic early memories of physical abuse were being evoked by Jaden. Her trauma had to be defended against and so all potential space in the room had to be filled with what she described as 'noise' and 'fun'. She feared if Jaden expressed other feelings then she would also begin to feel things she did not want to. We negotiated that she should have individual therapy for herself (within adoption support services) as I recognised that in order to bear Jaden's trauma with him, she must first bear the extent of her own early lived experience. Sarah was able meantime to take something from the musical encounter we had all experienced and interpret it for herself and her situation. Feeling grounded in the music provided emotional regulation for her as much as for Jaden. The embodied musical experience, created and shared between the three of us, gave Jaden a reparative maternal experience in his interaction with me on the xylophone. He could now sense this and additionally know that his adopter was also safely being held and thought about.

This relationship difficulty which I have just described, occurring between Sarah and Jaden, was referred to me in my first year of practising as a music therapist in adoption. I am able now to theorise and make sense of the work as my description above shows, but to do so has taken time and many such therapeutic experiences. As I have developed my practice over almost twenty years, I have brought my own training as a music therapist, my earlier training in child psychiatry and family therapy, and my lived experience of adoption to this work. Additionally, I have sought out new ways of thinking, seeking explanations that can help me to make sense of the presentations of children, young people and their families, who present as referrals for adoption support through music therapy.

Music therapy remains a small (but growing) profession in the United Kingdom (UK). It is a profession that has much to offer the adoption community. The Adoption Support Fund advocates for music therapy as a creative arts modality that is recommended and funded. Adoption support teams have increasingly learned the value of non-verbal therapies for people who have experienced early trauma. This second book of mine situates both practice and research in the context of an historical, theoretical and philosophical frame, leading on to a discussion of why I have come to think that an attachment and adoption-trauma-specific, psychoanalytically informed music therapy is well placed for adoption work.

This book will describe the emerging theory base for what I have come to describe as my adoption-specific music-therapy practice, which has arisen directly out of the work in a needs-led way. I will discuss a theoretical and philosophical frame for how my practice has developed and evolved; I situate my practice in the context of historical and current music-therapy approaches described in the literature. I shall focus on the literature of psychoanalytic music therapy leading to my formulation that a psychoanalytically informed music-therapy approach is best placed for working with adoption-specific trauma. I define what adoption-specific music-therapy practice might look like, drawing on examples from the limited literature. Finally, I describe potential conflicts between the music therapist and researcher roles I have taken on situating these in a context of lived experience of adoption.

My Ph.D. thesis described a single case study of music therapy with an adopted child. Single case studies are validated as a research method in the writings of Hinshelwood (2013) and Yin (2018) and have been the mainstay of psychoanalytic research for decades. I hoped that a single research case might bring forth material that could more deeply illustrate the value of music therapy for adopted children and their families than my first book did, possibly connecting with themes from my previous work and generating thinking about future work. In this book, I also share additional case narratives to enable the reader to get a sense of how research informs practice.

Having gained ethical approval for my Ph.D. research, I invited families who were new music-therapy referrals to me to participate. One family was eventually identified as my research case. By thematically analysing this case at a micro level, I intended to capture moments from the therapy with therapeutic significance for the child concerned. Having generated case-study data (Stake, 1995) from therapeutic sessions, video of sessions, session notes and clinical supervision, I extrapolated themes arising to see if these tallied with general themes I previously defined as adoption themes. Three identified adoption themes are discussed in depth in this book which speak specifically to adoption trauma. I show how I have developed a theoretical understanding for why these themes were pertinent, how they were expressed in music therapy and what impact they had upon a child's life beyond the therapy room (especially within their adoptive placement).

My research investigated whether what I was defining as micro-moments of attunement were happening within music therapy. I assessed my hypothesis that such moments might affect a child's relationships beyond the music therapy room, potentially increasing positive relational experiences within their adoptive family.

I have come to understand attunement as being a shared relational process or event occurring between two individuals, resulting in one feeling understood by the other. I draw upon Stern's (1977) work pertaining to his recording and subsequent sense-making of interactions between an infant and mother. Music therapists such as Trondalen (2016) argue that what happens between music therapist and client is akin to mother–infant attunement because the musical and relational experience of music therapy is rooted in the proto conversation of mother and infant.

I wanted to explore in depth whether musical, relational attunement might be significant when experienced within music therapy and could it lead to potential change beyond the music therapy room, ultimately positively impacting adoptive families. This book will contain examples of attuned, intersubjective, musical, relational experiences which music therapy provides, offering a child opportunities to explore new ways of relating. Such opportunities might be experienced as less threatening for an adopted child than verbal therapies as music provides a symbolic language and symbolic distance from difficult experiences. Experimentation with new relational repertoire, in the here-and-now therapeutic musical relationship, engages adoptees in ways that can impact upon the development of their internal working model. As an adoptee trusts the music therapy relationship, new relational moments happening regularly can offer some reparation for their early lived experience. Music therapy cannot undo early experience but may reshape its affects.

I have previously described my practice as a music therapist specialising in post-adoption support therapy and how this evolved. In this book I will examine literature that has shaped and informed my practice and research. This provides a basis for my argument that psychoanalytically informed music therapy offers a modality for work with adoption-specific trauma. Psychoanalytic music therapy, rather than other music therapy methods, forms the core of my sense-making of therapeutic practice. I will consider the impact of both therapeutic and academic supervision on my work and finally shall conclude with a consideration of diversity issues when working within a paradigm of white Western music and adoption processes in the UK.

In my previous book, I discussed post-adoption support and what types of therapies are sought after and funded by the Adoption Support Fund (ASF). I will explore more in this text what sort of post-adoption therapists are desired from within the adoption community and the value placed on lived experience. I shall discuss implications for music therapists bringing lived experience to their practice, critiquing whether this is always helpful. I have previously referred to my own lived experience of adoption and the inevitable presence and implications of such, focusing especially upon embodiment and the music therapist's expression of such and explore this more here.

The main theorists and concepts I drew upon both in my first book and thesis are introduced. Using Winnicott's (1971) concept of play, again I shall describe how music can, as a temporal experience, offer something akin to play occurring in time that Winnicott writes about. Other Winnicottian (1971) concepts such as 'potential space' are introduced, and I will describe how music might itself become a potential space. I shall discuss similarities in the work of Ogden (1989), particularly his idea of 'the third' and explain how co-created improvised music might become a 'musical third'. In this book I am also working more with Stern's (2010) concept of 'moments of change' and 'now' moments which, like music, are temporal. I will describe how moments of meeting and musical moments of attunement might arise in music therapy and how these contribute to an intersubjective relationship with shared musical language. Finally, in this book I will turn to the world of philosophy, drawing on the work of music therapist Sami Alaane (2010) and particularly his use of Heidegger. I have found that Heidegger's (1959) concepts of both 'worldhood' and 'releasement' have been useful in my own sense-making of my work. Heidegger may seem a long way from the average music-therapy practice, but it is interesting to see how his ideas around being and presence especially can be helpful for us.

Winnicott's writing on the value of play has long been valued by music therapists. Playing music together is the creative modality we use to facilitate our clients' psychological development. A major psychoanalytic premise of my approach to working within adoption is that music therapy can reveal unconscious worlds and communicate inner early experiences. This is because musical relating, in temporal affect-laden form, is somewhat like the ways in which early mother–infant communication happens. Music therapy has historically similarly drawn upon Stern's (1995) concept of proto conversation, Trevarthen's (1979) descriptions of features of early mother–infant relationships, and Malloch and Trevarthen's (2009) concept of communicative musicality. I argue from my research that all of these can be repeated in the music therapy relationship, giving an adopted child a different relational experience, wherein music helps to regulate and shape emotions.

In this book, I shall elaborate more on concepts of Winnicott's 'potential space' and Ogden's 'third', giving case-study examples of theory in practice. I compare Winnicott's (1971) concept of 'mirroring' with Stern's (1998) concept of attunement, exploring similarities and differences between mirroring and attunement, linking both with Pavlicevic's (1997) concept of 'dynamic form'.

In Chapters 5, 6 and 7, I draw upon case material, referring to actual sessions of music therapy with 'Jack', my research client. Adoption themes take precedence here. The theme of 'dropping' is one which has been present in the music therapy of other adopted children and which viscerally encapsulates their felt sense of being relinquished or removed for adoption. Additionally, I use the work of Sinason (1992) in relation to learning disability. This is because Jack had a learning disability, but also a great majority of adopted children I work with have significant disabilities and have been relinquished because of this. I argue that music therapy is well placed for working with these children as music can become a 'first language' for the non-verbal child.

I illustrate from practice how Jack and other clients have used the musical form of lullaby in music therapy and discuss the meaning and function of this. Embodied musical relating is explored more deeply, recognising that sounds made in music therapy are made by bodies using instruments. Sharing embodied music-making together in music therapy can evoke prelinguistic stirring and as such seems relevant to working with early material in an adoptee's experience. Lullabies have clear musical structures (such as *ostinato*) that can act as holding forms which are evident from the work with Jack. Reflecting on the music of the case study, I argue that Bion's (1962) 'reverie' might have been experienced within the musical relating providing Jack with a means for accessing early experience. I link this with work by the music therapist Lawes (2019) and what he defines as 'dreaming' states. This further develops thinking around both Winnicott's potential space and Ogden's third. I describe how free improvisation in music therapy can act as free association might in psychoanalysis. This has implications for working with powerful experiences of transference and countertransference.

The case study of Jack analysed in such detail shows how music has elements like those of the core elements required for attachment relationships. Returning to Stern's concept of attunement, I show from practice that something akin to this is provided musically and relationally for the adopted child in music therapy. Stern's (2010) cross-modal attunement, as it could be being manifest in music therapy, will be explored. His writing helps me understand the usefulness of music as a temporal modality, offering fluidity in the moment, which enables it to become like Winnicott's (1960) concept of the 'adaptive mother', or Stern's (2010) concept of continuous feeling tone.

My final case-study chapters more deeply explore symbolic play which happens *within* the music but is also simultaneously held *by* the music. I discuss the significance of unrepresented early trauma manifest within a musical relationship. This thinking evolved from the case study, showing how symbolic play in music therapy provided a means of accessing preverbal unconscious material. This can be manifest in musical enactments, and I focus especially on Freud's (1920) notion of *Fort! Da!* Sinason has similarly used descriptions of clients playing out hiding and seeking in her learning disability work, and, drawing upon her ideas, I infer that issues of disability, damage and difference can all be bought symbolically to music therapy, as Jack evidenced. There is a double loss in disability and adoption when clients are aware of their disability and how this was implicated in them being relinquished and subsequently placed for adoption. (See the case study of Lily from my first book.) Winnicott's (1965) writing about hiding and finding helps to explicate this idea further, and I relate it to the adopted child's sense of absence and presence that can be rekindled in music therapy.

I shall go on to explore how 'here-and-now' play in the music-therapy room can provide a way for adoptee clients and music therapists to become aware together of the clients' previously unrepresented early experience. All adoptees have experienced the fundamental adoption trauma of being removed from their birth mother. At whatever age this happens, there is resultant enduring trauma. Many children will then enter the care system and may experience being in one or more foster homes prior to being placed for adoption. Some will have accrued further traumatic experiences such as physical or sexual abuse, either while still living with their first family or, sadly, also within foster families and indeed adoptive families. These experiences can be revisited and taken from 'then' to 'now'. In other words, the clients' trauma, when witnessed with the therapist, offers the safe vantage point of the here and now where the past can be safely thought about, held and given meaning.

Music therapy is discussed in this book as being an 'available object' for the adoptee-client, and musical objects can become transitional objects. Music and instruments and bodies and minds playing together function simultaneously in many ways to hold the intersubjective relating occurring between client and therapist. One example is the significance simply of the gaze when often children relinquished or removed at birth or soon after will never have known a maternal gaze. I have come to describe my work as providing an 'audible gaze' and will explain this idea and how it might be experienced.

Songwriting with clients is also explored in this book, with suggestions on how this way of working can also become a way of containing symbolic material. Songs can also be taken out of the music-therapy room and into the client's life and therefore act as transitional objects. This has been a way of working with adult adoptees that I have been using in recent years, especially since the pandemic. Music therapists are aware of how tricky it can be to work musically and relationally online. With adult adoptees in therapy, I have often used verbal relating in the first instance to enable the telling of a narrative and some initial sense-making. Then either the client or I have started a process of songwriting. Not all clients will be able to create music alone, though some can, and have indeed brought completed pieces of work to music therapy. Others have written words which I have been able to write music to. Either way, the song can be sung live as I listen or can be produced in other ways. Clients' stories are then contained within musical structures and witnessed by the listener.

Throughout this book, I continue to develop the body of theory I have been drawing on to date. I explain how Winnicott's (1960) 'holding' and 'playing' can be provided musically. If music therapy is to be used safely by the adopted child, then states of 'holding' must precede states of 'playing', in Winnicott's terms. Only when a child is safely held might revelation of early unconscious experience be safely shared and thought about, leading to meaning-making which impacts on relational difficulties. Music therapy thus becomes a modality for re-experience, which can lead to change, potentially contributing to the strengthening of the adoptive placement and preventing breakdown. Stern's attuned intersubjective relationship might then develop, through client and therapist utilising musical 'vitality affects' together in intersubjective relating. Heidegger's (1959) concepts of 'waiting' and 'releasement' are newer to me but have provided a philosophical base for my music therapy approach, enabling me to shape descriptions of the therapeutic presence I consider is necessary for an undergirding of this work.

When therapeutic presence is made available to an adopted child, opportunities arise for them to re-experience 'motherese' (Newport, 1974). Within therapeutic re-representations, music has a holding maternal function. Because of its temporal nature, music can offer an ongoing 'musical-ness', engendering a state of attention and presence within a flow of time, providing what Winnicott (1941) calls the full course of an experience. Examples of such experiences are evidenced in the case study of Jack. The music therapist and the client can become like an infant and a mother in experiences where unconscious affective memory can be manifest, witnessed, held and integrated. Music regulates both emotion and affect non-verbally, providing safe holding for an adopted child as they revisit traumatic early experience.

These early experiences can be revealed in free improvisation. In musical interactions then, it is important that the music therapist provides a state of being without reacting, so the child might reveal, in Winnicott's (1965) terms, their true self. Authentic musical intersubjectivity, utilising transference and countertransference can then be experienced. Drawing on Heidegger's (1959) concepts of 'waiting' and 'releasement', I have come to understand that if the music therapist can offer an attitude incorporating these concepts, then states defined by Winnicott (1960) such as 'being with' and 'going on being' might occur. Once the adopted child can safely 'be' with the music therapist, there are then opportunities for experiencing Winnicott's 'moving along' state and changes and reparation.

I connect Winnicott's 'moving along' concept with Stern's (2010b) concept of 'vitality forms' which similarly focus on movement, time and space. Within the case study, I demonstrate how sharing musical elements such as rhythm, tempo, time and pulse, provides experiences of reciprocity and resonance that can lead to intersubjective attunement. Both attunement and relationship happen in time, through the flow of musical vitality forms. The music therapist Trondalen's (2016) work on embodied improvised intersubjectivity is employed, illustrating similarities with my research. This leads me to revisit my position as an 'insider researcher' music therapist, with lived experience of adoption, working within post-adoption support.

This book concludes with a discussion about how both my previous book and my research might offer conclusions that potentially could impact upon future adoption-specific music therapy and indeed other post-adoption supports. I clarify from both experience in the clinical field and recent research that music therapy is a well-placed creative arts modality for the adopted child. As a non-verbal modality, it has now been used by many adoptive families, who are funded by the Adoption Support Fund, and it is important that as music therapists we understand more deeply how and why it may be helpful.

References

Alaane, S. (2010). *Music psychotherapy with refugee survivors of torture: Interpretations of three clinical case studies.* Picaset Oy.

Bion, W. R. (1984). *Learning from experience.* Karnac. (Original work published 1962.)

Freud, S. (1953–1973). Beyond the pleasure principle. In *The standard edition of the complete psychological works of Sigmund Freud*, 24 vols, Ed. and Trans. J. Strachey (vol. 18, pp. 1–64). Hogarth Press. (Original work published 1920.)

Heidegger, M. (1982). *On the way to language.* HarperCollins. (Original work published 1959.)

Hinshelwood, R. D. (2013). *Research on the couch: Single-case studies, subjectivity, and psychoanalytic knowledge.* Routledge.

Lawes, M. (2021). Trend of differentiation and integration in UK music therapy and the spectrum of music-centredness. *British Journal of Music Therapy, 35*(1), 4–15.

Malloch, S., & Trevarthen, C. (Eds.). (2009). *Communicative musicality: Exploring the basis of human companionship.* Oxford University Press.

Newport, E. L. (1974). *Motherese: The speech of mothers to young children* (Doctoral dissertation, University of Pennsylvania).

Ogden, T. H. (1989). *The primitive edge of experience.* Routledge.

Pavlicevic, M. (1997). *Music therapy in context: Music, meaning and relationship.* Jessica Kingsley.

Sinason, V. (1992). *Mental handicap and the human condition: New approaches from the Tavistock.* Free Association Books.

Stake, R. E. (1995). *The art of case study research*. Sage.
Stern, D. N. (1977). *The first relationship: Infant and mother*. Karnac.
Stern, D. N. (1995). *The motherhood constellation: A unified view of parent–infant psychotherapy*. Karnac.
Stern, D. N. (1998). *The interpersonal world of the infant*. Karnac.
Stern, D. N. (2010a). *Forms of vitality: Exploring dynamic experience in psychology, the arts, psychotherapy, and development*. Oxford University Press.
Stern, D. N. (2010b). The issue of vitality. *Nordic Journal of Music Therapy, 19*(2), 88–102.
Trevarthen, C. (1979). Communication and cooperation in early infancy: A description of primary intersubjectivity. In M. Bullowa (Ed.), *Before speech: The beginning of human communication* (pp. 530–571). Cambridge University Press.
Trondalen, G. (2016). *Relational music therapy: An intersubjective perspective*. Barcelona Publishers.
Winnicott, D. W. (1941). The observation of infants in a set situation. *International Journal of Psychoanalysis, 22*(2): 229–249.
Winnicott, D. W. (1960). The theory of the parent–infant relationship. *International Journal of Psychoanalysis, 41*, 585–595.
Winnicott, D. W. (1965). Ego distortion in terms of true and false self. In *The maturational processes and the facilitating environment: Studies in the theory of emotional development* (pp. 7–22). Hogarth Press.
Winnicott, D. W. (1971). *Playing and reality*. Tavistock Publications.
Yin, R. K. (2018). *Case study research and applications: Design and methods*. Sage.

Chapter 2

The modality

Psychoanalytic adoption music therapy

Introduction

Psychoanalytic and psychodynamic music therapy was the theoretical position in which I was initially trained, and the modality which I continue to practice, and which subsequently informs my writing and research and ever-evolving meta-theory. Therapeutic practice, accompanied by research, has led me to the development of an approach which I have previously described as contemporary relational, psychoanalytic, trauma and attachment informed, music therapy practice.

Why psychoanalytic music therapy?

In the UK/Europe there is a long tradition of psychodynamic music therapy since the 1950s. The first psychodynamic pioneers of music therapy included Juliette Alvin in 1968 (with her model of free improvisational therapy) and Mary Priestley in 1975 (with her analytic music therapy). Early models of psychodynamic music therapy purposed to be therapy models in themselves, but contemporary psychoanalytic work recognises that any theory offers but one contribution to and perspective on psychoanalytic music psychotherapy theorising (Alanne, 2010). Mary Priestley's 1994 text 'Essays on Analytical Music Therapy' was the first to describe a psychoanalytic methodology and proffered examples of what might constitute a psychoanalytic music therapy practice. She describes evolving predominantly Kleinian techniques in practice but in essence stated that analytical music therapy was the name she preferred to describe analytically informed improvised music with symbolic meanings by the music therapist and client.

In a much later book edited by Searle and Streng in 2001 (in her chapter titled 'Music Therapy and Its Relationship to Psychoanalysis'), Odell-Miller suggests that free improvisation in music therapy can be likened to the aspect of free association and free-floating attention in verbal psychoanalytic work. She also recognises that psychoanalysis defined two major terms that almost all music therapists currently will be familiar with and use, namely

DOI: 10.4324/9781003733393-2

transference and counter transference. Odell-Miller argues that these terms are common to almost all because the concepts of transference and counter-transference are taught on every UK music therapy training. They will therefore at least be in the vocabulary of music therapists who may not define themselves as psychoanalytic.

The basic premise underlying contemporary psychoanalytic music therapy is that music may express emotions, thoughts and unconscious conflicts even when they are not accessible with words (Alanne, 2010). A music therapist works with clients presenting with difficulties, using improvised musical interactions as the prime mode of communication, and meaning is made together from the shared music emerging. In essence, a psychoanalytic music therapy approach broadly proposes that musical material emerging from sessions might be processed verbally using psychoanalytic concepts so that the unconscious experience might become conscious. This approach also pays special attention to the symbolic aspects of musical play. The music therapist may not interpret meaning in situ with the client and might rather allow the symbolism to do its work without being translated back to verbal language.

For these two reasons, I see psychoanalytic music therapy as a most useful way of working with and understanding material that adopted children bring to sessions in musical playing. This is because much of what is enacted within a music therapy relationship between an adopted child and their music therapist will have its roots in the child's earliest experiences. Early life experiences are likely to remain unknown cognitively to the child who will have been too young (most likely preverbal), at the time of living them. Such experiences though, especially when traumatic, stay embedded in the adopted child's internal world, and although remaining unconscious they will be impacting upon the 'here and now' of adoptive family relationships. Music therapy offers a space where such unconscious material might be revealed and literally 'played out' within the transference and countertransference of the therapeutic relationship. Also, such material is likely to be additionally played out in the symbolic use that an adopted child makes of the instruments, the music and the therapist. Usually in a verbal psychoanalysis there would be an attempt to think about symbolic use in words after the experience has been had. However, this book will go on to explore how, for children, symbolism can often do the work, and it does not need 'decoding'.

Why not other music therapy approaches in adoption?

There has historically been, and continues to be, debate about what sort of music might 'work' and why, with different client groups, and this debate still resonates throughout the music therapy profession. The debate might be most succinctly summarised in the differences between the Nordoff–Robbins model (eclectic, humanistic and 'music-centred') and the psychoanalytic/psychodynamic schools. These two groups are often presented as the most polarised (though there are now a plethora of varying approaches and eclectic models within these groupings). They have often been set in opposition in the literature and discussion. Later work by Annesley (2019) takes issue with the perceived falsity of this polarity, arguing that music therapy can be at once music-centred *and* psychoanalytic. There is no definite detraction or devaluing of the musical content if it is thought about through a psychological frame. Indeed, this can enhance understanding of the music.

The Nordoff–Robbins approach describes applying music itself as the 'therapy', i.e., the various elements of music such as rhythm or timbre and so on have qualities that evoke a response. As such, a Nordoff–Robbins music therapist will avoid (and even discourage) the use of verbal language within sessions. This is a significant area of difference from psychoanalytic music therapy because a psychoanalytic music therapist will work with music as a sort of pre-language which can be thought of as a communication of unconscious material. It is the latter use of music that has seemed most relevant to my own therapeutic practice. Finding a balance between both musical thinking and psychological awareness is essential for understanding what is 'going on' in the music therapy relationship, and it is certain that some musical elements do seem to be significant when working with adoptees. The specific value that music therapy has is that these elements may not be found in other therapeutic modalities. However, musical thinking alone (as the pure Nordoff–Robbins model argues) might not be robust enough to underpin all aspects of the therapist–client relationship, especially when there has been a wealth of psychological thinking in the adoption arena that music therapists can additionally draw upon. For example, recent psychoanalytic music therapy developments draw on concepts such as 'relational knowing' from contemporary relational psychoanalysis (Trondalen, 2016), and I think it is incumbent upon music therapists to avail ourselves of such ideas to the benefit of our clients. Dialogue and debate are still prevalent throughout the profession and are likely to remain so.

Using psychoanalytic concepts outside of the realm of the psychoanalytic clinic

Frosh, in his text *Psychoanalysis Outside the Clinic*, writes that psychoanalysis has 'migrated elsewhere and become one of the most significant tools available to those who wish to understand the social world' (Frosh, 2010, p. 5). Psychoanalytic music therapy could be said to be one of the places psychoanalysis has 'migrated' to, as essentially it uses psychoanalytic ideas outside of their original realm of the traditional clinic. It has been criticised for this reason, both by other schools of music therapy (who argue that the music itself is enough without requiring the addition of a psychological frame to think about it) and from within traditional psychoanalysis itself (where the argument is that music is not verbal and therefore is a completely different domain to work in). Freud himself, the father of psychoanalysis, is reported to have disliked music with a passion. He was much more positive about other creative-arts modalities which he thought had 'an intuitive grasp of the unconscious that could be used to provide evidence for psychoanalytic claims' (Frosh, 2010, p. 42). Yet, music is about feeling, emotion, passion and the irrational, all of which are the stuff that psychoanalysis aims to engage with and explore. Conversely, Jung is known to have himself experienced one session of music therapy after which he is reported to have said that music should form a part of all therapy for individuals (Darnley-Smith, 2018). Jung felt that music could be a valuable aspect of psychoanalytic treatment as it had potential to hold together conscious and unconscious opposites. Psychoanalysis has certainly moved on from the time of Freud and Jung, and yet the core concepts of early psychoanalytic thought would still seem to translate well to thinking about music therapy when working with adoption material.

Core terms from Freudian psychoanalysis have become common parlance in Western culture. Words such as 'unconscious', 'ego', 'transference' and so on are heard in ordinary conversation so pervasive are these terms. Psychoanalytic thought more specifically has provided a framework or model for thinking about what is going on in music therapy and pervaded other music-therapy models, not just the psychoanalytic. For my work in adoption, the psychoanalytic concept of a personal unconscious that contains early repressed experience has become core. I also argue however for the relevance of music-as-therapy because as music is non-verbal, it has a capacity to connect with and evoke unconscious material. Two fundamental goals of both psychoanalysis and psychoanalytic music therapy are (1) to bring repressed unconscious material into awareness; and (2) to move towards corrective emotional experiences through processes of transference and countertransference occurring between therapist and client (Bruscia, 1998). It is these experiences I have when working with adoptees that seem to be of most importance in leading to reparation of early trauma.

Frosh accepts that psychoanalysis is being used outside of the clinic setting but questions what the effects are when it is used in other domains. He identifies positives and negatives, recognising that new insights might be gleaned from different arenas but also warning that there are dangers arising from potential distortions of what he calls the true practice. Potentially, psychoanalysis has something to offer the world, and the world has something to offer to the development of psychoanalysis. Similarly, I find in my own clinical work that music itself might be opened up by psychoanalytic enquiry and, likewise, psychoanalysis impacted by what might be learned from research in the creative-arts therapies regarding possible manifestations of the unconscious through arts processes. I agree with Frosch that 'something dwells between representation and the unrepresentable' (2010, p. 122) which manifests symbolically in music therapy and which is most helpfully thought of using psychoanalytic ideas. To this end, the effects of taking psychoanalytic thought beyond its traditional confines and into the practice of music therapy has provided the most useful frame for sense-making about my work I have to date found.

Practitioner research

I did not come to writing and research as either a writer or researcher. Rather, as a practising music therapist, I desired to make sense of my work from the ground up. I wanted to embark on meaning-making about what adoptees were doing in music therapy and how they were using it. When I began the work, my main motivation was to find a way to express what was happening in music therapy and its perceived value within the adoption community. I wanted to ensure adoptee voices were heard and their therapeutic needs understood. Researching the work provided a way of giving it value and of enabling other music therapists to be able to access what I had learned from my clients and how this had been theorised. This was especially important as adoption music therapy has to date been relatively unexplored.

There are many positives of being a practitioner-researcher. For example, it is rarely possible for an external researcher to gain the closeness to the clinical work that is required to gain the data that music therapists researching their own work can. For this book, only by being immersed in the music therapy and directly experiencing a therapeutic relationship with Jack was it possible for me to have the trust that generated research and writing material. I cannot imagine how a researcher observing my sessions might have picked up on all the musical and embodied communications that are only experienced directly in relationship with another. However, the insider practitioner position can, if used without self-awareness, honesty and reflection, produce a biased report of limited use (van Heugten, 2004). It is therefore important that music therapists find ways to subject our own personal experience utilised in professional practice to the rigour and protocols of more conventional social-scientific research.

There were inevitably complex issues that arose in researching my own work. Some are obvious, such as the very fact of it being my own practice and my inevitable immersion in it. Potentially, this meant it might be difficult to have any degree of objectivity in analysing it. I also had a commitment to my clients and was in relationship with them, which meant I wanted the research to 'work'. It was important that Jack and his family did not feel his music therapy with me was contingent upon him becoming also a research subject (and we hoped that the robustness of the consent procedures I have described helped to mitigate against this). My blurred roles of therapist-researcher needed ethical consideration due to power differentials in the relationships that ensued and the potential risks associated.

Additionally, my own lived experience adds another layer of complexity to this practitioner research. Although lived experience can be valuable (and certainly is seen as such when adoptees describe what they need from a therapist), it can also increase unhelpful subjectivity. I was an 'insider researcher', as both a therapist researching my own cases and as a member of the adoption community attempting to make sense of the therapeutic needs of that community. It was imperative that I was alert to a potential reduction of objectivity and an increase in bias. This was partially managed by ensuring both rigour and transparency in every aspect of the research process, from design through to data reporting and discussion.

Later in this book, I describe my supervisory processes for both the work and the research. Choosing academic supervisors carefully is one way that music therapists seeking to become researchers can use to mitigate some of the complexities of the dual role as therapist-researcher. My team of research supervisors were not music therapists and indeed had limited knowledge or experience of music therapy. I hoped this would mean my work would be subjected to greater scrutiny, interrogation and criticism, as none of my team had any vested interest in my profession or indeed my clinical work. My academic team encouraged my constant self-reflection and deep examination of my preconceptions. At times I was challenged about my thinking and construction of theoretical concepts. My team did not share assumptions about the work with me and were able to provide objectivity, especially when digging beneath intrinsic value judgements I held but was unable to recognise. I had sought out, and therefore welcomed, this challenge and rigour because I wanted to have my assumptions challenged, so that my thinking could become more robust. As a freelance practitioner, I was not working for any institution or organisation so there were at least no complexities regarding any commitment to an employing body. Thus, overall accountability was to the research itself and to the voices of those who contributed to it.

Thematic analysis

Before I commenced my case-study research with Jack, I had much experience of the music therapy of other adoptees. From this experience (over a decade), I had seen various themes occurring in the work. Prior to researching my case study, I had not conducted any formal analysis of themes and was simply aware that material seemed to arise specifically in work with adoptees that differed from work with other client groups. I had kept a list of this thematic material and was aware after working with Jack that similar material had arisen in his sessions. I therefore needed to find a way of analysing the data from Jack's session and seeing if this connected with my previous work with other adoptees.

From my work with Jack, I had obtained differing types of data. First, there was video footage (as each session had been recorded in full). Second was my process notes written immediately after the session. Additionally, I made notes from my clinical supervision and academic supervision. All of these comprised data about the case study. I then needed to think how adoption themes might be thought about.

I was aware that the time I had been immersed in adoption music therapy could mean that what I thought were adoption-specific themes arising within both the case study and previous music-therapy work were simply my preconceptions and theorising about my work (part of my practitioner-researcher potential bias). How could I include all the musical, verbal and embodied elements of my music-therapy approach that I thought may have relevance. Adoption-specific themes were recognised, developed, reviewed and refined before finally an analysis report was written (Braun & Clarke, 2022). Four of the most prevalent themes were analysed in depth and thereby were able to 'provide a more detailed and nuanced account' (Braun & Clarke, 2006, p. 83).

It was not possible to analyse the data of all my previous adoption music-therapy work in this much detail for my research, and I was not therefore able to adopt as rigorous a thematic analysis of it, as per the Braun and Clarke model. Instead, I searched more generally through notes, reports and supervisions on previous case work. All of the themes that I identified in my research case study of Jack were evident from work with other adoptees (discussed in my first book). I was therefore able to position the case study 'Jack' within the body of my earlier work and make sense of what might be adoption-specific themes in his case, drawing on the fact that such adoption themes had in fact been evident in earlier work.

Relational research and the relational 'turn' in psychotherapy

Finlay and Evans (2009, p. 1) describe relational research as a 'considered type of qualitative approach . . . a facet of the qualitative diamond'. Relational researchers engage in reflexive processes in ways that I also have (for example, in my exploration of the conscious and unconscious intersubjective dynamics between myself and Jack). Relational researchers also recognise that they are inevitably a part of the relational field they study and give value to this involvement. The approach differs from traditional research that 'constructs a world in which there are separate entities, typically related to each other through cause and effect' (Gergen, 2009, p. 234). My work has to date foregrounded 'relational dimensions between researcher, participants and their wider social fields' (Finlay & Evans, 2009, p. xi) and in some sense must qualify as relational research, even largely unknowingly at first!

Relational research then in definition forms part of a qualitative interpretative methodology that seeks to investigate 'the meanings people give to particular forms of social action and the social worlds and cultural forms these actions help to constitute' (Fujii, 2018, p. 2). Relational research involves the researcher engaging participants in a two-way dialogue which is inevitably shaped not only by the context in which the interview occurs but also by the interests, beliefs and backgrounds that *each party* brings to the exchange. From a relational-research perspective, then, the idea of a detached researcher is not especially important. Gergen

(2009) has critiqued the idea that any research method can be neutral, totally objective and detached. He writes:

> Methods of research are scarcely value neutral. They are saturated with assumptions . . . they do not reveal the contours of an independent phenomenon but create the phenomenon in their terms . . . It is important to explore limitations . . . add resources for alternative futures . . . breathe life into the promise of relational being.
>
> (Gergen, 2009, pp. 234–5)

Central instead to the relational research process is researcher reflexivity, which involves 'careful consideration of how issues of positionality . . . shape the research process' (Fujii 2018, p. 1). The data that is generated in relational research is often described as 'narratives' or 'stories' that people tell about themselves and others in the world. Narratives and storying that also happen within music therapy, i.e., an adopted client's story of themselves might come to be differently understood as a new narrative about their experience is co-produced with their music therapist in the therapy room. By playing with narratives and stories of the self within music therapy, adoptees can challenge previous self-conceptions and in a sense then re-author their understanding of their lives (McLeod, 1997).

However, there are major differences between psychotherapy and research. Relational-centred therapists highlight the core importance of the therapeutic relationship. The term 'relational' was first applied specifically to psychoanalysis by Greenberg and Mitchell in 1983. Relational psychoanalysis arose out of interpersonal psychoanalysis (Sullivan) and object-relations theory (Klein), also incorporating perspectives such as feminist theory. A significant change in thinking occurred for those embarking on what was to become described as relational psychoanalysis, as Finlay writes: 'Ideas from traditional psychoanalysis that innate drives were the basis of psychic development were partly dropped in favour of the view that the individual developed in relationship with other people' (Finlay & Evans, 2009, p. 33).

Significantly also, relational psychoanalysis argues

> against therapist neutrality as an a priori given. Instead, the therapist is acknowledged as being a major influence impacting on the clients conscious and unconscious experience . . . both client and therapist are seen to affect one another as they 'co-mingle' and mutually share a range of emotions generated in the therapy process
>
> (Finlay & Evans, 2009, p. 34)

It could be said that this idea is nothing new as Jung in the late 1800s and early 1900s was writing about 'alchemy', and his belief was that it was inevitable because *both* therapist and client were active participants in a relationship and would impact one another resulting in change of both. Also, Winnicott in the 1960s was describing the individual as inseparable from others, showing in his work how human beings from birth are in relation to the mother, and then others.

Those coming to describe themselves as relational psychoanalysts argued that learned patterns of interaction are,

> inevitably enacted in the therapy situation, and so careful attention needs to be paid to what is happening in the therapy relationship . . . special attention is given to regression and transference as powerful unconscious manifestations of early trauma, while the relational analyst tries to find the best mix of safety and challenge . . . to help the client construct new meaningful narratives . . . Focusing on the immediate therapy relationship is thought to impact on the client's way of being in wider relationships.
>
> (Finlay & Evans, 2009, p. 34)

This essentially is a core belief of my therapeutic practice: that early trauma might become more conscious, and thought about, for new relating to emerge in the therapy, which hopefully will be transposed into the clients' relationships beyond the therapy room. This belief seems to be useful when working with adoptees who bring complex internal worlds to music therapy, based upon early experience, and how interaction based upon these worlds might be modified. Most importantly for me is the idea that new relational styles might be taken out into an adoptee's adoptive context and life so that new ways of relating can be experienced in the 'real' world. Interestingly, it is Gergen (a research professor, and not a therapist) who I think best sums this up:

> We are invited to view the therapist and client as engaged in a subtle and complex dance of co-action, a dance in which meaning is continuously in motion, and the outcomes of which may transform the relational life of the client.
>
> (Gergen 2009, p. 282)

Relational psychoanalysis has however been much critiqued by other schools of analysis. It has been described by Mills (2005) as the new middle group of American psychoanalysis. However, Mills argues that this group has been lacking a proper critique. He describes how relational psychoanalysis challenges the orthodoxies of classical analysis, especially regarding the use of the analyst's self, and to self-disclosure. Additionally, traditional ideas of interpretation and insight flowing from therapist to client are much less significant when psychoanalysis is viewed as a relational process. A text written in 2018, edited by Aron, Grand and Slochower, counteracts Mills's claim by providing critique from the inside of the movement. Clearly then the 'relational turn' in psychotherapy has not been without considerable criticism. However, aspects of it have been relevant to my work in adoption music therapy, focusing as it does on attempting to understand early relational experiences and how these might 'play out' in later life. Relational psychoanalysis also offers to me a sense of hope for therapy in its view that the therapeutic relationship might offer something new that may, at least in part, mitigate against early experience and enable new relating for adopted children in their adoptive families.

Narrative in practice and research

A narrative carries meanings, first for those who create it and then for those who come to understand it. Exploring an adoptee's narrative of experience then involves working with the differing ways in which human beings create their narrative material, to tell their stories. As an example, my research drew directly upon data from videoed music-therapy sessions. Narrative research 'involves analysing that material, trying to categorise or interpret it' (Squire et al., 2014, p. 7). All narratives will reveal something of the person who is sharing their story and their world(s). There will be an 'I' who is sharing the narrative and the 'other' ('you') who listens to and receives it; therefore, an intersubjectivity.

Approach to data was significant for me as the researcher of an adoption narrative. My aim was always to start from the data and build theory up from it rather than coming to it with any preconceived ideas. It is the same way that I have approached all my adoption music therapy clinical work prior to researching it, i.e., attempting to understand therapeutic relationships from the ground up, as it were. Clinical work happens within sessions, wherein narratives have been somehow presented by adoptees. I have, over time, formed my theoretical therapeutic understandings of these narratives once I have reflected upon video and notes from sessions. This can to an extent also be described as an articulation of the voices of adopted people about what sort of therapy they need. It is not correct, however, to state that narrative 'gives voice' to people but rather that people give their voices to the music therapist-researcher. Regarding emancipatory social practice however, and the centering of the adoptee voice, it is my hope that this book contributes to some representation of the collective voices of the adoption community.

I shall now explain how I use the idea of narrative within therapeutic practice. I will introduce Jack and discuss the multiple narratives that he bought and explored in sessions. Jack came to adoption music therapy immersed in the narratives of others. There was a story told of him by his referring social worker, which detailed his early life and reasons for coming into local-authority care and subsequent adoption. Jack's adoptive parents told me their narratives about him, how he acted within their family and how they understood his behaviour. Within music therapy, I hoped to give space wherein Jack's story *about himself* might emerge. Additionally, I anticipated (from experience in earlier work) that Jack's stories of his experiences within his first family would be implicit in the way he had come to be in the world, and that this would likely emerge in music therapy. Riessman (2008, p. 8) describes the importance of narrative in the excavation and reassessment of memories that may have been 'fragmented, chaotic, and/or scarcely visible before narrating them'. As a music therapist, incorporating relational psychoanalytic ideas, I hoped to be able first to hear how Jack had come to make sense of his world, from his early experience. I would simultaneously work within our relationship, deliberately offering new opportunities for relating. In other language, I would co-create with him new narratives that he could begin to tell about himself. The work was explicitly offering Jack opportunities for re-narrating his life because the current narrative that had brought his family to seek help was impacting in ways that did not serve him well.

Diversity issues

To date, throughout my work and writing on music therapy and adoption, I have employed a Eurocentric musical language. This is in part inevitable as I draw upon the language of, first, my own musical training and, second, my music therapy training. I am a classically trained violinist but have a broad spectrum of arenas in which I perform professionally, including musical theatre, folk, rock and pop. I acknowledge that these arenas, though diversifying from my classical world, are still largely white and Western musical genres. I have little experience of playing within other genres from other cultures. As such, I think it would be at best inauthentic, and at worst appropriation, if I attempted to draw upon musical languages of other cultures both in my work and in the describing of my work.

As a music therapist, I have been asked to take tabla to play with an Asian adoptee, but I did not comply at the time as this felt tokenistic (especially as tabla is an incredibly sophisticated drumming that without any experience I could not possibly hope to replicate for a client). This chimes with a similar decision I have made not to write about transcultural adoption. As a white working-class female (albeit with lived experience of adoption), I do not feel able to offer comment on the experiences of transcultural adoptees which are complexified by intersectionalities of race and culture. Transcultural adoption is a matter of much critique within the adoption community (Ali, 2013), and there is both research and narrative currently being written. To date, it has revealed levels of challenges related to identity and discrimination, with many adoptees feeling disconnection from their cultural heritage and racism (Richards, 2025).

Essentially, adult adoptees with lived experience of transracial adoption are arguing that therapists without experience should not be doing therapeutic work with them (Harris, 2014). This raises issues more broadly than for the practice of adoption music therapy. Few enough music therapists are properly trained in adoption music therapy and fewer still with lived experience (which, the adoption community argues, is crucial for therapists to possess for them as clients to feel truly heard and understood). The British Association of Music Therapy is currently waking anew to degrees of privilege that are held within our profession. Training has to date largely been within a classical paradigm and inevitably attracted predominantly white middle-class students. As training becomes more focused on equality and diversity, it is hoped that practitioners will be emerging who will be much better positioned to take on necessary work. In the meantime, I endeavour to keep myself alert to the privilege inherent in my own musical practice and writing. I consider my work to still have relevance while recognising that my view of the 'realities' I describe is shaped and interpreted by my cultural context. Psychoanalysis itself has been challenged by a view through a race-centred lens, and I acknowledge that it may not be the chosen approach for many.

References

Alanne, S. (2010). *Music psychotherapy with refugee survivors of torture: Interpretations of three clinical case studies.* Picaset Oy.

Ali, S. (2014). Multicultural families: Deracializing transracial adoption. *Critical Social Policy, 34*(1), 66–89.

Alvin, J. (1974). Music as a means of projection and protection. Paper presented at the Conference of the British Society for Music Therapy, Birmingham.

Annesley, L. (2019). Two kinds of music therapy: Exploring 'genre' in the context of clinical practice. *British Journal of Music Therapy, 33*(2), 74–79.

Aron, L., Grand, S., & Slochower, J. A. (2018). *De-idealizing relational theory: A critique from within.* Routledge.

Braun, V., & Clarke, V. (2006). Using thematic analysis in psychology. *Qualitative Research in Psychology, 3*(2), 77–101.

Braun, V., & Clarke, V. (2022). *Thematic analysis: A practical guide.* Sage Publications.

Bruscia, K. E. (1998). An introduction to music psychotherapy. In K. E. Bruscia (Ed.), *The dynamics of music psychotherapy* (pp. 51–70). Barcelona.

Darnley-Smith, R. (2018). Jung and the transcendent function in music therapy. In S. Wilson (Ed.), *Music – psychoanalysis – musicology* (pp. 136–151). Routledge.

Finlay, L., & Evans, K. (2004). *Relational-centred research for psychotherapists: Exploring meanings and experience.* Wiley-Blackwell.

Frosh, S. (2010). *Psychoanalysis outside the clinic.* Palgrave Macmillan.

Fujii, L. A. (2018). *Interviewing in social science research: A relational approach.* Routledge.

Gergen, K. J. (2009). *Relational being: Beyond self and community.* Oxford University Press.

Greenberg, J. R., & Mitchell, S. A. (1983). *Object relations in psychoanalytic theory.* Harvard University Press.

Harris, P. (2014). 'I started to feel not ashamed of who I was': Transracially adopted adults and adoption support. *Adoption & Fostering, 38*(4), 346–360.

McLeod, J. (1997). *Narrative and psychotherapy.* Sage.

Mills, J. (2005). A critique of relational psychoanalysis. *Psychoanalytic Psychology, 22* (2), 155–188.

Priestley, M. (1986). *Music therapy in action*. MMB Music. (Original work published 1975.)

Priestley, M. (1994). *Essays on analytical music therapy*. Barcelona.

Richards, S. (2025). The politics of biological otherness in intercountry adoption. In L. Magalhães (Ed.), *Otherness in communication research* (pp. 195–207). Palgrave Macmillan.

Riessman, C. K. (2008). *Narrative methods for the human sciences*. Sage.

Searle, Y., & Streng, I. (Eds.). (2001). *Where analysis meets the arts: The integration of the arts therapies with psychoanalytic theory*. Karnac.

Squire, C., Davis, M., Esin, C., Andrews, M., Harrison, B., Hydén, L.-C., & Hydén, M. (2014). *What is narrative research?*Bloomsbury.

Trondalen, G. (2016). *Relational music therapy: An intersubjective perspective*. Barcelona.

Van Heugten, K. (2004). Managing insider research: Learning from experience. *Qualitative Social Work*, *3*(2), 203–216.

Verrier, N. N. (1993). *The primal wound*. Gateway Press.

Chapter 3

Literature, practice and research informing an approach

Prior to training as a music therapist, I worked for many years in Child and Adolescent Mental Health Services (CAMHS), first as a psychiatric nurse then as a specialist child-mental-health nurse before later qualifying as a family therapist. Further training on trauma and attachment developed my knowledge and therapeutic experience. Before training as a music therapist, I worked as clinical lead for adoption in an East Midlands mental-health trust. On qualifying as a music therapist, I was invited back to work within the adoption community. Professionals were requesting music therapy as a form of creative-arts therapeutic intervention for adoptive families.

When I began this work, there was no established practice, model or approach within the music-therapy profession specifically for adoption. My first referrals were of adoptive placements in jeopardy. The severe difficulties that were being presented as identified referral problems meant children faced a real risk of being placed back into the care system (Palacios et al., 2019) if the adoption did break down. How specifically music therapy might help was uncertain, although referring social-worker colleagues felt a creative non-verbal modality may help children who had been unable to access talking therapies (McCarthy, 2008). I sensed music therapy might have value for this specific client group, though I was uncertain what the work might look like. I was certain that I could not save failing placements and wondered if some needed to end where adoptees were continuing to suffer. Referring colleagues had previous positive professional experiences of music therapy and were themselves highly experienced with extensive knowledge and experience of adoption trauma and potential resulting difficulties enacted in adoptive family life.

In my previous work experience, and that of my social-work colleagues, many children referred for post-adoption support did not engage with traditional CAMHS services (if offered verbal therapies only). Adopted children expressed that they simply did not want to talk, or that they did not know what to talk about. I suggest this was because their adoption trauma occurred at a pre-verbal stage of life so was inaccessible to their conscious memory (White, 2014). I shared a working premise with the referring social workers

DOI: 10.4324/9781003733393-3

that pre-adoption early lived experience remained with these children but was buried and unconscious. Memory was held in the body, not the mind, and therefore was inaccessible to cognitive knowing (Van der Kolk, 1994). Creative-arts therapies are said to be a means of contacting such unconscious material as they do not require verbal language or cognitive knowledge to engage (Bannister, 2003). Drama and dance-movement therapy had not been explored by the referrers. Art therapy had been received positively and was ongoing for some children. It was felt, however, that music had something special to offer. I sensed what this might be, from my previous adoption work and from reading which elements of music (such as its forms of rhythm, timbre, melody, harmony, etc.) might be significant (e.g., Robarts, 2014). Music therapy also felt relevant for this client group, from the psychoanalytic premise that early lived experience sets up enduring relational patterns (Beebe & Lachmann, 2014) and that it might be possible to work with such early experience non-verbally.

I accrued more referrals from the local authority and adoption agencies providing post-adoption support to families 'in crisis' with 'a risk of adoption breakdown'. In 2015, the national Adoption Support Fund (ASF; now the Adoption and Special Guardianship Support Fund) was established to provide therapeutic support for families post-adoption. This recognised that adopted families had previously struggled to access supports they said they needed. Previously, services were reported as being patchy and inconsistent nationally as they were managed locally. The ASF promised national consistency, also allowing families to apply themselves for therapies they felt would be beneficial. Creative-arts therapies were recognised by the ASF; therefore, families could obtain funding to receive non-verbal therapies, within which music therapy was included. I have been providing long-term psychoanalytic music therapy since 2015 (with a minimum duration of one to three years and currently a maximum of six years) that has been ASF-funded. Ways of accessing the ASF for both families and other professionals are fully detailed in my first book.

From these beginnings, I evolved the approach that currently informs my practice of music therapy with adoptees and their families (see Gravestock, 2021). I use the term 'approach' because this is not a fixed, prescribed method I advocate. Instead, an ever-evolving organic approach is regularly reinformed and adapted by new knowledge or theory I either encounter myself or which the work urges me to seek out to make sense of a client's lived experience (Hart & Lucock, 2004). Working in a needs-led way means not limiting the client to the extent of any method. Rather, music therapists should reach beyond the parameters of their knowledge when working in new therapeutic specialisms, seeking out that which might most help us make sense of our client's presentation (Kendrick et al., 2006; and Mitchell et al., 2020).

I shall now describe various elements of my practice that have emerged and evolved over time as I have learned from my clients and sought out therapeutic theories and modalities that may help me to help them make sense of their experience.

Emerging: A practice, some theories and meaning-making

To make sense of adoption material emerging in music-therapy sessions necessitated engagement with theoretical positions that seemed polarised sometimes, yet which I somehow needed to synthesise to enable me to adequately describe what was happening in the therapeutic setting. I have been applying psychoanalytic thinking to my adoption practice since the beginning. It has felt extremely relevant, given its attention to the significance of early life experience.

Also fundamental to my ontology has been an understanding of adoption as a specific trauma. Adoption is the only socially sanctioned removal of an infant or child from one family into another whereby all legal contact is severed with the family (and subsequently society and culture) of origin (Wadia-Ellis, 1996). However, a client's adoption experience is not their entire narrative, and I have learned, as Ringstrom writes here, to work with the whole person:

> I do not work with trauma victims. I work with patients who among many things have likely suffered some trauma in their lives. Calling a patient a trauma victim ironically invokes a great deal of reductionist thinking as well as objectification.
>
> (Ringstrom, 2014, cited in Kuchuck, 2014, p. 58)

This then is an example of one polarity I need to draw together: that an adoptee has experienced a specific trauma that affects them at the deepest levels, yet they are also much more than this experience.

While still coming to understand the sort of adoption music therapist I am emerging into, I have also been describing for myself and others the sort of music therapist that I think adoptees can make use of. This description needs to be adoption-specific without being adoption-limited. Essentially, my approach seems simply about coming alongside the adoptee on what is after all their journey and learning from them how to play together. Gradually then, a jointly evolved sense of meaning arises in the relationship between us. Winnicott's concepts of both play and the adaptive mother have been useful regarding this as has Stern's work on intersubjective relating. (Their relevance will be discussed in detail later.) At times, some aspects might be verbalised. At others, the meaning-making may be implicit, remaining held in the music and therefore unspoken. An adoptee may share the sense I am making of things, or not, and in this relational to and fro between us new truths and ways of relating can emerge. Contemporary relational psychoanalysis has much to offer to this work. I consider this in detail in later chapters, exploring how such theory makes sense of practice, focusing especially on the part the music therapist contributes to an intersubjective relationship (this being an aspect that has rarely been written about before in the music-therapy literature).

The following quote of Winnicott's about a patient resonated for me early in the work: 'She exists in the searching rather than in finding or being found' (Winnicott, 1971, quoted by Bjorklund, 2014, p. 11). I have inevitably been engaged in a meaning-making searching journey which has been significant alongside what has been found out from research results. This can be compared to the search of an adoptee for meanings and an organisation of narrative form. In effect, it has been a parallel process. Bjorklund continues: 'sometimes the act of searching can be an act of freedom and agency that can enliven lost or disavowed selves. However, what we find may not be what we thought we were searching for' (2014, p. 11).

My music-therapy practice and subsequent research of it might well represent a parallel process for my own adoption journey, and I have certainly found things not necessarily sought which have required my own supervision and personal psychotherapy. Like Glassman and Botticelli (2014), I know my work to have been 'a testament to the complex and deeply personal purposes to which our patients may put us, purposes undreamt of in the mind of the evidence-based treatment researcher' (quoted in Kuchuck, 2014, p. 175).

Jaenicke (2015) describes how he has also learned to search in uncertainty, allowing meaning to emerge through relating. He argues, 'I don't believe therapy is something that I do to you, but rather that we change and become who we are through one another' (Jaenicke, 2015, p. 5). I concur with his view and for this reason often feel uncomfortable with methods that define aims and objectives for music therapy, delineating from the start what an outcome measure should be for a client. (I recognise I am fortunate as a self-employed freelance music therapist to not be hindered or restricted by organisational aims, which do necessarily impact many of my colleagues.) Jaenicke continues:

> the idea that the clinician unilaterally, uni-directionally heals the patient is medical model thinking, a natural science outlook that doesn't apply to psychoanalysis . . . maybe now we can get a first inkling of how to view cure . . . it is in some sense a mess, but a mess from which we can extract meaning.
>
> (Jaenicke, 2015, p. 7)

Often, my emerging practice and subsequent theorising of practice have felt like Jaenicke's 'mess'. In early sessions with a new client, even now, I still feel tentative about shaping any sense or meaning about what is happening to and for them in the music therapy. My approach embraces uncertainty as I never plan what will happen in sessions. I come to each client ready to freely improvise and co-create music together, not knowing how this will work out. Yet I hold to Darnley-Smith's (2018, p. 143) assertion that 'a good improvisation is concerned with 'care for others', in this case, care for the therapeutic quality of the relationship'. I certainly cannot guarantee outcomes such as that placements will endure (despite the referrer often wanting music therapy to prevent breakdown happening). I see what emerges in the musical relationship and gradually find meaning in the messiness because, as Darnley-Smith (2018, p. 142) writes, ‘a therapeutic practice of free improvisation has intersubjective meaning also’.

Love (2007) argues for this non-directive stance, writing that therapists need to approach their work from a position of ‘not knowing’, thereby allowing the client’s experience to lead the way. This is so we can first hear the client’s experience, without needing to fix it. Glassman and Botticelli (2014, p. 175) write that:

> to a therapist’s ear, [Love’s] quiet acceptance of this circumstance jangles, grating against our therapeutic ambitions, our will to repair, and wishes for our patients (and our own) progress. Yet with some people it may be all we can do, all we’re allowed to do, to be a witness to injury.

Music therapist Pavlicevic (1990) writes that the therapist’s first goal is to meet the patient’s music as this emerges. My approach then needs to be revisited afresh with each new client that I witness, meeting their music and obeying Darnley-Smith's (2018, p. 146) edict to ‘follow the client’ because ‘in following our clients’ direction, we have the greatest hope of gaining understanding of their inner worlds’.

In my first year of Ph.D. study, I ‘discovered’ elements of Heidegger’s philosophy that resonated with this approach, and that have since informed it (discussed later in depth). Heidegger's (2002, p. 44) statement that ‘In waiting, we leave open what we are waiting for’ chimes with what I recognise myself doing in this music therapy approach. Open expectancy to both my client and to our improvised music seems to be about such ‘waiting’. This process is far from inactive, however. While I wait, a supportive presence is made available to the client. This apparent simplicity of waiting and supporting a client is in fact extremely complex relationally and feels profoundly alive and responsive. Alanne (2010) interestingly draws on Heidegger’s notion of releasement to describe his music-therapy practice. Releasement is defined as contemplation and wondering without calculating and analysing and interpreting things. Alanne describes how releasement becomes both his attitude and method of music therapy. He argues that releasement for a music therapist means trusting our capacity to be with, witness and bear our clients’ suffering while we patiently wait, either silently, or attentive, listening, playing. Presence provided is more about what is not done rather than any technique used for doing. This is a gradual slow work, and these philosophical concepts now resonate in my approach.

Eigen similarly writes about experiencing the ‘slow, hard drudge of daily practice’ in therapy work (quoted in Kuchuck, 2014, p. 129). He describes not just the sensitively attuned moments, which will be highlighted in this book, but also the more gradual, regular working through of material. (I suggest a sort of 'going on being' in Winnicott's terms.) I argue for my approach that a 'waiting' attitude of releasement offers clients something they rarely find elsewhere. As a music therapist, I become present to, attend to, witness and then 'simply be' consistently with whatever the client needs to bring. Occasionally, this might manifest in dramatic musical enactments, but at others the musical play can feel boring, yet it is this very music that an adopted child may be calling forth from the deepest level.

Latterly, I have continued to encounter ideas that impact upon and inform my approach, which I know will continue to evolve. Within this book, other contributing theories will be evidenced and explored, all of which enable me to make meaning of micro-moments of music therapy. I shall now set my approach in the broader context of music therapy more generally.

Historical and current music therapy approaches

Music therapy is a relatively young profession yet has nonetheless experienced profound splits and conflicts. For example, I have already discussed the apparent major differences between psychoanalytic music therapy and Nordoff–Robbins' music-centred music therapy. Yet many music therapists work bridging this gap and using elements of both.

I had knowledge and awareness of differing therapeutic positions because of my varied training prior to music therapy and therefore made an informed choice to train in psychoanalytic music therapy. Other influences inform my choice of paradigm, and I am reassured by the work of Jaenicke (2015) who argues that our subjectivity influences our choice of theories and our approach to therapeutic practice.

I shall now briefly explain the emergence of my profession regarding the establishing of music-therapy training and provide a short literature review. Professional training for music therapy began in 1968, 'when Juliette Alvin was invited to introduce music therapy into the Guildhall School of Music and Drama in London' (Bunt & Hoskyns, 2002, p. 12). Since those early days, music therapists have been trained to work with diverse client groups, developing a body of knowledge arising from professional lived experiences generated with clients within various settings. Academic papers began to emerge, but it was only in the 1990s that music therapy texts 'proliferated' (Bunt & Hoskyns, 2002, p. 19). Several music therapists contributed chapters on music therapy to other specialist texts such as Robarts (1996) on autism, Sloboda (1996) on psychotic violence, Loth (1996) on forensic psychotherapy and Odell-Miller (1997) on caring for older people. Also, Sobey and Woodcock (1999) outlined the specific psychodynamic orientation to the music-therapy training at the Roehampton Institute, clearly delineating a psychoanalytically informed training (cited in Bunt & Hoskyns, 2002).

In the later 1990s, complete texts appeared focusing entirely upon music therapy. Lee's (1996) case study of a man living with AIDS is referred to by Ansdell (2001) as being at the forefront of this musicological perspective in music therapy research. Pavlicevic's (1990) text 'developed a broad range of theoretical concepts to a more sophisticated level than had previously been attempted in British writing' (cited in Bunt & Hoskyns, 2002, p. 22). Hers is one of the first syntheses of the theoretical connections between musical processes and the observations and theories of Stern and Winnicott and, as such, has informed my practice. Clinical material, amassed over the previous 30 years, was now at this point allowing 'for more concentration on discussion of effective theory' (Bunt & Hoskyns, 2002, p. 22).

Bunt and Hoskyns go on to describe a contested debate highlighting pronounced differences in the profession, summed up in Streeter's (1999) writing that 'finding a balance between musical thinking and psychological awareness was essential for understanding the music therapy relationship' (cited in Bunt & Hoskyns 2002, p. 24). Streeter critiqued the view that musical thinking and theorising alone was adequate to account for all aspects of the musical therapeutic relationship and that additionally some sort of psychological framework was required. Her paper in turn was critiqued by others who argued that all that was necessary could happen within and be explained through music alone. This apparent dichotomy of music-centred versus psychodynamically informed music therapy continues to be debated within the music therapy profession. However, Annesley (2019) argues that these apparent polarities of being either purely musically based or only psychologically informed are false constructs and that music therapists can be, and indeed often are, working in a way that is both music-centred and psychoanalytically informed.

At the time of writing this book, a multiplicity of music-therapy models exists in the UK. This list includes some, though by no means all, and shows that music-centred and psychoanalytic approaches are now two of many approaches:

- behavioural (or educational)
- cognitive
- systemic
- psychoanalytic/psychodynamic
- Community Music Therapy (CoMT)
- Nordoff–Robbins/creative
- humanistic
- integrative/holistic
- Helen Bonny's method of Guided Imagery and Music" (GIM)
- biologically orientated (psychoacoustics)
- neurologic.

Psychoanalytically informed music-therapy approaches

Psychoanalytic theory, originated by Freud, developed through the 1900s, with the primary assumption that people possess unconscious thoughts, feelings, desires and memories. The aim of psychoanalytic therapy, therefore, is to make the unconscious conscious, releasing that which has been repressed. Early models of psychodynamic music therapy purposed to be therapy models in themselves, but contemporary psychoanalytic work recognises that the purpose of theory is to offer 'one contribution to and perspective on psychoanalytic music psychotherapy theorising' (Alanne 2010, p. 21).

In the UK and Europe, there is a long tradition of psychoanalytic/psychodynamic music therapy since the 1950s, whereas in the USA, only 2.3 per cent of music therapists identify with this theoretical orientation (Alanne, 2010, p. 22). The first pioneers of psychoanalytic music therapy included the previously mentioned Juliette Alvin (1974) with her model of free improvisational therapy, and Mary Priestley (1986), with her analytic music therapy. Nygaard Pedersen from Denmark advocated for a psychodynamic approach and 'analytically orientated music therapy' (AOM), establishing the first psychodynamic music-therapy master's degree training programme in Scandinavia (at Pedersen/Aalborg University in 1982).

Priestley's *Essays on Analytical Music Therapy* was the first text to describe a methodology of what might constitute psychoanalytic music therapy and practice examples. Chapter 1 begins:

> I have privately thought that there is no such thing as analytical music therapy. What I mean by this is that as soon as you think it is this or it is that you have reified it, concretised it, put it lifeless and inert into a box of words and thus taken it out of the realm of sensitive, spontaneous, empirical creativity which characterises the therapeutic dyad, and killed it – stone dead.
>
> (Priestley, 1994, p. 1)

She perceived danger inherent in describing musical happenings in verbal terms yet nevertheless attempted to do so. She wrote that:

> analytical music therapy is the name that has prevailed for the analytically informed symbolic use of improvised music by the music therapist and client. It is used as a creative tool with which to explore the client's inner life so as to provide the way forward for growth and greater self-knowledge.
>
> (Priestley, 1994, p. 3)

Also, she advocated that analytical music therapy should be: 'an orientation training to a certain way of working using one's whole life experience, together with one's own analysis or analytical psychotherapy as a skeleton on which to hang ideas about what developed between the therapist, patient and the music' (Priestley, 1994, p. 3). This is a premise that I apply to my work now, as this book shows.

The literature of psychoanalytic music therapy

Odell-Miller describes music therapy's relationship with psychoanalysis with a historical, theoretical and clinical context (Searle & Streng, 2001). She argues that free improvisation can be seen as like free association/free-floating attention in psychoanalysis. I concur, having experienced in my work how free improvisation offers potential for engagement with the client's (early) unconscious material. Odell-Miller also recognises that the terms 'transference' and 'countertransference' have become core concepts for most music therapists.

Eschen's (2002) collection, *Analytical Music Therapy*, describes the origin and development and theoretical basis of the term. Case-study chapters discuss its usefulness with specific client groups. Areas such as analytically informed music-therapy supervision, music-therapy students in an analytic training and basic training methodology are covered. The existence of this complete text, defining a training and an approach, indicated the strong presence of psychoanalytic thought within the music therapy community.

Hadley's (2003) edited text of case studies provides first an overview of psychodynamic music therapy. The terms 'psychodynamic music therapy' and 'analytic music therapy' are used interchangeably, although their practices had considerable differences. Hadley (like Priestley) argues that theorising should offer useful constructs not absolute truths. Her framework is therefore theory-informed rather than theory-led and draws upon musical creativity as an innovative practice to enable clients to lead a healthier life.

Garred's 2006 text sets analytic music therapy in the context of other music therapy approaches. He enters the debate started by Streeter (1999) between the music-centred approach and approaches that incorporated psychological thinking. Streeter (like Odell-Miller) proposed that musical improvisation was likened to free association but was met with objections by others who argued these were not quite the same. The debate continues throughout Garred's text, incorporating more recent analytical developments, such as relational knowing which draws on contemporary relational psychoanalysis.

De Backer and Sutton's (2014) more definitive text described psychodynamic music therapy across Europe, evidenced in clinical, theoretical and research approaches, with ideas for continuing professional development. Cohen's (2018) text posits that analytic/psychoanalytic/psychodynamic music therapy is an advanced form of music therapy requiring additional training.

This text, however, is American, and in most parts of the United States, music-therapy training happens at undergraduate level. In the UK, 'advanced' refers to the master's level training of student music therapists. Cohen asserts that Priestley's original analytic music therapy is in decline because, she argues, psychoanalytic theory is no longer fashionable and cannot survive in a time-limited culture when it requires longer-term work. I disagree with this as in my practice I know long-term psychoanalytic work can be coherently argued for, valued and have evidenced this is in successfully gaining funding over years for adopted clients through the ASF.

Wilson's (2018) text also offers a more optimistic evaluation of the contribution of psychoanalytic music therapy, describing a growing interest (rather than something on the wane) in what psychoanalytic theory brings to music. Authors draw on classical psychoanalytic writers such as Freud, Lacan, Jung, et al. Darnley-Smith's chapter describes Jung's concept of the 'transcendent function' and its application within music therapy. Acknowledging Jung did not mention music, Darnley-Smith argues that his proposal can extend to all creative arts practice because: 'Jung suggests moving away from "intellectual clarification" . . . into the domain of art, whereby the "emotional disturbance" might be given a different kind of clarification through the act of giving it "visible shape"' (Darnley-Smith, 2018, cited in Wilson, 2018, p. 138). She cites Priestley, writing: 'the patient explores new pathways symbolically in the world of the imagination but with the bodily expressed emotion in sound which gives her a safe toe-hold in the world of everyday life' (Darnley-Smith, 2018, cited in Wilson, 2018, p. 139). This idea of music as embodied expression informs my work and is discussed in more detail later.

Clearly, then, the relationship between psychoanalysis and music therapy remains complex, and dialogue, debate and disagreement still prevail throughout the profession. Music therapy informed by psychoanalytic thinking can help with understanding what is going on, especially in complex crisis/breakdown situations. Hindle and Shulman (2008) argue that an adoptive placement will be shaped by unconscious processes from the child's internal world (and, I would argue, by the internal worlds of adopters also), and therefore I conclude that psychoanalytic music therapy is well placed for work with adoption. I shall now define what I understand by adoption-specific music therapy and provide a literature review of the limited work in this area.

Defining adoption-specific music therapy

Over a decade ago, little was offered, nor was indicated, specifically for adoptees as a clinical population. Now, music therapy is a recognised creative therapy identified and funded by the ASF. Few therapists, however, seem to develop expertise in adoption as a speciality because, generally, adoption work sits alongside work with fostered children or those in kinship care. This broader work with children in the care system fails to recognise adoption as a discrete qualitatively different experience. Adult adoptees, however, argue for adoption-specific services, including therapies. This is because common to every adoption experience is the (usually early) permanent separation of mother and child (and consequent loss of all family and community). Many adoptees have described this experience as resulting in a sense of an internal hole (Verrier, 1993). Additional trauma occurring within the birth or first family might result in a decision to remove a child for adoption (such as neglect, or emotional, physical and sexual abuse). However, I argue that any experience of early loss, internalised by the child, will be manifest in definitive and distinctive ways which adoption-specific psychoanalytically informed music therapy can work with.

There is plenty of literature available on music therapy with attachment difficulties, likewise with trauma (Roberts, 2018) and its effects, yet little addresses the specific adoption experience. The republished updated *Oxford Handbook of Music Therapy* (Edwards, 2017) contains no reference to adoption in its subject index (though does have three subject links to attachment). Most music-therapy literature describing work with adoption is found as single chapters in edited collections. My first book (Gravestock, 2021) was described to me by the British Association of Adoption and Fostering (personal conversation, January 2021) as being the only single-authored creative-arts therapies text solely focused on adoption. If music therapy is to be relevant and desirable for the adoption community, I have learned that it must take account of the specific nature of adoption trauma and the lived experience of adult adoptee voices.

I will now discuss the contribution of three chapters on adoption to the scant literature on adoption-specific music therapy. The lack of literature highlights a significant gap which slowly is being addressed. Music therapists might want to investigate this gap further, both in terms of providing specifically informed therapeutic work and in making further contributions to the literature and research.

Music therapy and adoption-specific literature

Robarts' (2014) single chapter resonates closely with my own work. She describes her 'synthesis of musical, developmental and psychodynamic processes . . . with the focus on use of musical form as central to integrative processes of music therapy with young people whose foundations of self have been damaged by early relational trauma' (Robarts, 2014, p. 67).

Throughout her chapter, Robarts uses clinical vignettes strikingly like those which I used in my first book. Interestingly, she identifies repeating aspects of practice arising in her work that I have also frequently witnessed (some of which I understand as being adoption-specific). From each of our observations on children in music therapy, we both have noted the following themes (which I have termed 'adoption themes'):

- building musical instruments into a house/tower, as protection/defence rather than being able to play musically with them
- presenting a false happy self
- needing always to be perceived as 'good'
- imagining hauntings, and ghosts being sung about (I suggest possibly in adoption this refers to the 'ghostly' birth family remaining ever-present as well as 'haunting' remembrances embodied in the inner world)
- creating musical games of hide and seek
- needing to reject and control the therapist
- searching for safety in rhythmic relating.

Robarts identifies, as do I, that the music therapist needs to use simple, even banal, musical forms to engage with early inner-world material. Despite similarities in our approach and experience, there is still nothing in this chapter or Robarts's other trauma work that speaks specifically to adoption.

Hasler previously worked in adoption in the UK. Her single chapter (in Hendry & Hasler, 2017) refers to adoption but focuses more on adoptive parent work. Her approach differs enormously from mine. She addresses adoption as developmental trauma but without reference to the adoption experience having a specific quality.

Elefant's chapter (2017) describes a single case study of music therapy. Elefant draws on the work of Drake (2011), which described how unregulated, erratic and anxious adopted children were in the music-therapy room, leading them to demonstrate avoidant, controlling or withdrawn behaviours. This chimes with my therapeutic experience, as does Elefant's experience of her client engaging in what she calls dropping behaviours (which I will discuss later). Elefant does not interpret the possible symbolic meaning of the dropping behaviour or connect it with early experience, however. She does write similarly to me about attunement, arguing that musically attuned experiences with her client led to the beginnings of their intersubjective relationship. Like Robarts and I, Elefant describes her client playing hide and seek and needing to have a musical experience of being both 'lost' and 'found'.

Adoptive families' music therapy in the literature

Adopted children have complex multi-peopled inner worlds, carrying an internal working model of both their birth and adoptive families. Adopters too have internal worlds. Both can be thought about within an adoptive family music therapy, where internal worlds of both children and parents might be revealed. Sometimes, I do work with entire adoptive families where indicated (and indeed the case study of Jack describes some instances of working with him together with his adoptive mother).

Salkeld advocates working with child adoptees and adopters together. She argues:

> in order for any kind of attachment behaviour to be biologically useful both parties in the bond need to be interested in one another. Working together in therapy clearly enables both the child and the parent to feel that they are jointly interested in one another.
>
> (Salkeld, 2008, p. 143)

A case vignette illustrates her working in a way that enabled adopters to respond to their child's innate musical language. She concludes, 'interactive music making became foundational to the development of their relationship with their adopted son' (Salkeld, 2008, p. 156).

Similar work is described in Jacobsen's (2017) chapter. She argues that experiences of attunement are lost in families where there may have been emotional neglect. These are not adoptive families necessarily, but her hypothesis is similar: 'Parents and their child in music therapy can re-engage in early developmental forms of non-verbal interaction and experience these intimate connections in a new way' (quoted in Daniel & Trevarthen, 2017, p. 228).

I have argued similarly in previous writing that musical interactions between an adopted parent and adoptee can provide fresh opportunities for attunement experience previously lost to the adoptive couple.

Examples of adoption family work are encouraging to read about, and music therapy can be a way of playfully encouraging new sorts of relational bonding. Future research could focus the lens even more narrowly on specific work with adoptive families or on work with individual children within those families.

Conclusions from the literature

The literature available shows how music therapy can offer children (who have been separated from their birth mother by adoption) a way in which they can communicate this loss and integrate it into their experience within an adoptive family. Trauma for many adopted children occurred before they had language; therefore, their recollection of it is not likely to happen through verbal language. Music, however, can do psychic work for an adopted child because it provides a symbolic language and symbolic distance from these most early, unworded lived experiences. Adoption trauma that remains incommunicable is likely to impact often negatively on relationships because of its shaping of the internal working model that a child develops. Implicit to psychoanalysis is the notion that what happens to people in early life is significant and matters because it will continue to impact upon relating in the future. There is therefore a reparative role especially for psychoanalytic music therapy, which offers adopted children possibilities for (non-verbal) musical 'talking' and listening in relationship with a therapeutic other, which can provide access to unconscious early memories.

I conclude this chapter by very briefly examining the difficulties of being both therapist and researcher in and of adoption work. Also, I have researched within what is described as the 'adoption community' (Gravestock, 2021), of which I am myself a member. I will therefore consider implications for the 'insider researcher' (Le Gallais, 2008). These complexities of being a member/therapist/researcher within the adoption community are more fully explored later.

The music therapist-researcher roles and lived experience

Although there is value in my single case study, the limited resources for such research must be acknowledged. I am one music therapist and one researcher. Not only have I researched my own therapeutic practice, I have also researched a community of which I am a member. The music therapist Sami Alanne (2010, p. 16) writes, 'there should be no denying or excusing that I, as researcher/therapist have continuously been in interaction with my patients and therefore have affected their world'. He recognises that the music therapist/researcher assesses phenomena not just from outside it but also belongs to the research that is created within it, with the client. I consider this of particular significance for my research within the adoption community of which I am both personally a part of and professionally work within.

The adoption community accepts and welcomes professionals with lived experience of adoption; however, there is no real sense of what it is that such lived experience might contribute to adoption work. I have critiqued the notion that all lived experience is valuable and can be made of use in therapeutic work (Gravestock, 2021). It is essential that we have done all that we can to process our own lived experience before attempting to draw on it in the work. Interestingly, the psychotherapist Peter Wilberg (2002, p. 63) argues that therapists might gain benefit as much as their clients when working in areas of their own lived experience: 'No matter how little we were heard in our early years, one way that we can overcome the psychological deformations or disturbances that may have resulted is by learning to listen to others.'

I argue against Wilberg's position because in my opinion the music therapist must have had their own therapy and processed their own trauma (in as much as this is possible) before becoming truly able to listen to others. We must safeguard against conscious or unconscious exploitation of the client or using the work to our own ends or gratification. Lived experience in itself is not necessarily therapeutically useful but rather what has been made of such experience might become so. The more the music therapist's material becomes conscious, the less likely they are to be caught in enactments with clients or, as and when occasions do arise, they are better resourced to manage them.

To conclude this chapter then, I have trusted that my personal psychoanalysis enabled me to become sufficiently aware of material that may become activated in transference and countertransference in my music therapy practice with adoption. Nonetheless, I anticipate some difficulties will inevitably be encountered, and these are at least partly mitigated by my own clinical supervision. It has been especially important to me to have a clinical supervisor who is appraised of my own lived experience and with whom I feel safe to discuss the possible impacts (both positive and negative) of such upon my work. Additionally, for my research, I was supervised by a team of non-music academics, and my team enabled me to step back from my work and become more critical of it. This, in turn, enabled me to be less assumptive about my practice and to develop a second-order perspective on it.

I shall in the next chapters describe how my practice as a music therapist in adoption support 'works'. Research was rooted within practice and arose directly out of experiences I had with clients, out of which my subsequent thinking has developed, deepening this discussion.

References

Alanne, S. (2010). *Music psychotherapy with refugee survivors of torture: Interpretations of three clinical case studies.* Picaset Oy.

Alvin, J. (1974). Music as a means of projection and protection. Paper presented at the Conference of the British Society for Music Therapy, Birmingham.

Annesley, L. (2019). Two kinds of music therapy: Exploring 'genre' in the context of clinical practice. *British Journal of Music Therapy, 33*(2), 74–79.

Ansdell, G. (2001). Musicology: Misunderstood guest at the music therapy feast? In D. Aldridge, G. di Franco, & T. Wigram (Eds.), *Music therapy in Europe.* ISMEZ/Onlus.

Bannister, A. (2003). *Creative therapies with traumatized children.* Jessica Kingsley.

Beebe, B., & Lachmann, F. M. (2014). *The origins of attachment: Infant research and adult treatment.* Routledge.

Bjorklund, S. (2014). How Betty and Vincent became Sally and Scott. In S. Kuchuck (Ed.), *Clinical implications of the psychoanalyst's life experience: When the personal becomes professional* (pp. 3–17). Routledge.

Bunt, L., & Hoskyns, S. (2002). *The handbook of music therapy.* Brunner-Routledge.

Cohen, N. (2018). *Advanced methods of music therapy practice: Analytical music therapy, the Bonny method of guided imagery and music, Nordoff–Robbins music therapy and vocal psychotherapy.* Jessica Kingsley.

Daniel, S., & Trevarthen, C. (2017). *Rhythms of relating in children's therapies: Connecting creatively with vulnerable children.* Jessica Kingsley.

Darnley-Smith, R. (2018). Jung and the transcendent function in music therapy. In S. Wilson (Ed.), *Music – psychoanalysis – musicology* (pp. 136–151). Routledge.

De Backer, J., & Sutton, J. (2014). *The music in music therapy: Psychodynamic music therapy in Europe: Clinical, theoretical and research approaches.* Jessica Kingsley.

Drake, T. (2011). Becoming in tune: The use of music therapy to assist the developing bond between traumatised children and their new adoptive parents. In J. Edwards (Ed.), *Music therapy and parent-infant bonding* (pp. 22–42). Oxford University Press.

Edwards, J. (2017). *The Oxford handbook of music therapy.* Oxford University Press.
Elefant, C. (2017). From cocoon to butterfly: Music therapy with an adopted girl. In S. Daniel & C. Trevarthen (Eds.), *Rhythms of relating in children's therapies: Connecting creatively with vulnerable children* (pp. 100–113). Jessica Kingsley.
Eschen, J. T. (2002). *Analytical music therapy.* Jessica Kingsley.
Garred, R. (2006). *Music as therapy: A dialogical perspective.* Barcelona.
Glassman, N., & Botticelli, S. (2014). Perspectives on gay fatherhood: Emotional legacies and clinical reverberations. In S. Kuchuck (Ed.), *Clinical implications of the psychoanalyst's life experience: When the personal becomes professional* (pp. 162–179). Routledge.
Gravestock, J. (2021). *Music therapy in adoption and trauma: Therapy that makes a difference after placement.* Jessica Kingsley.
Hadley, S. (2003). *Psychodynamic music therapy: Case studies.* Barcelona.
Hart, A., & Lucock, B. (2004). *Developing adoption support and therapy: New approaches for practice.* Jessica Kingsley.
Hasler, J. (2017). Healing rhythms: Music therapy for attachment and trauma. In A. Hendry & J. Hasler (Eds.), *Creative therapies for complex trauma: Helping children and families in foster care, kinship care or adoption* (pp. 135–154). Jessica Kingsley.
Heidegger, M. (1982). *On the way to language.* HarperCollins. (Original work published 1959.)
Hendry, A., & Hasler, J. (Eds.). (2017). *Creative therapies for complex trauma: Helping children and families in foster care, kinship care, or adoption.* Jessica Kingsley.
Hindle, D., & Shulman, G (2008). *The emotional experience of adoption: A psychoanalytic perspective.* Routledge.
Jaenicke, C. (2015). *The search for a relational home: An intersubjective view of therapeutic action.* Routledge.
Kendrick, J., Lindsey, C., & Tollemache, L. (Eds.). (2006). *Creating new families: Therapeutic approaches to fostering, adoption, and kinship care.* Karnac.
Kuchuck, S. (2014). *Clinical implications of the psychoanalyst's life experience: When the personal becomes professional.* Routledge.
Le Gallais, T. (2008). Wherever I go, there I am: Reflections on reflexivity and the research stance. *Reflective Practice*, 9(2), 145–155.
Lee, C. (1996). *Music at the edge: The music therapy of a musician with AIDS.* Routledge.
Loth, H. (1996) Music therapy. In C. Cordless & M. Cox (Eds.), *Forensic psychotherapy: Crime, psychodynamics and the offender patient.* Jessica Kingsley.
Love, H. (2007). *Feeling backward: Loss and the politics of queer history.* Harvard University Press.
Malchiodi, C. A., & Crenshaw, D. A. (Eds.). (2006). *Creative arts and play therapy for attachment problems.* Guilford Press.
McCarthy, D. (2008). *Speaking about the unspeakable: Non-verbal methods and experiences in therapy with children.* Jessica Kingsley.
Mitchell, J., Tucci, J., & Tronick, E. (2020). *The handbook of therapeutic care for children: Evidence-informed approaches to working with traumatized children and adolescents in foster, kinship and adoptive care.* Jessica Kingsley.
Odell-Miller, H. (1997). Music therapy and the functions of music with older mentally ill people in a continuing care setting. In M. Denham (Ed.), *Continuing care for older people.* Stanley Thornes.

Oldfield, A., & Flower, C. (Eds.). (2008). *Music therapy with children and their families.* Jessica Kingsley.

Palacios, J., Rolock, N., Selwyn, J., & Barbosa-Ducharne, M. (2019). Adoption breakdown: Concept, research, and implications. *Research on Social Work Practice, 29*(2), 130–142.

Pavlicevic, M. (1990). Dynamic interplay in clinical improvisation. *Journal of British Music Therapy, 4*(2), 7.

Priestley, M. (1986). *Music therapy in action.* MMB Music. (Original work published 1975.)

Priestley, M. (1994). *Essays on analytical music therapy.* Barcelona.

Ringstrom, P. (2014) Becoming an analyst: A play in three acts. In S. Kuchuck (Ed.), *Clinical implications of the psychoanalyst's life experience: When the personal becomes professional* (pp. 146–162). Routledge.

Robarts, J. (1996). Music therapy for autistic children. In C. Trevarthen, K. Aitken, D. Papoudi, & J. Robarts (Eds.), *Children with autism: Diagnosis and interventions to meet their needs* (pp. 172–203). Jessica Kingsley.

Robarts, J. (2014). Music therapy with children with developmental trauma disorder. In C. Malchiodi & D. Crenshaw (Eds.), *Creative arts and play therapy for attachment problems* (pp. 67–84). Guilford Press.

Roberts, J. L. (2018). *Trauma and the ontology of the modern subject. Historical studies in philosophy, psychology, and psychoanalysis.* Routledge.

Salkeld, C. (2008). Music therapy after adoption: The role of music family therapy in developing secure attachment in adopted children. In A. Oldfield & C. Flower (Eds.), *Music therapy with children and their families* (pp. 141–159). Jessica Kingsley.

Searle, Y., & Streng, I. (Eds.). (2001). *Where analysis meets the arts: The integration of the arts therapies with psychoanalytic theory.* Karnac.

Sloboda, J. A. (1996). Music therapy and psychotic violence. In E. Welldon & C. Van Velsen (Eds.), *A practical guide to forensic psychotherapy* (pp. 121–130). Jessica Kingsley.

Sobey, K., & Woodcock, J. (1999). Psychodynamic music therapy: Considerations in training. In A. Cattanach (Ed.), *Process in the arts therapies* (pp. 132–154). Jessica Kingsley.

Streeter, E. (1999). Finding a balance between psychological thinking and musical awareness in music therapy theory. *British Journal of Music Therapy, 13*(1), 5–21.

Van der Kolk, B. A. (1994). The body keeps the score: Memory and the evolving psychobiology of posttraumatic stress. *Harvard Review of Psychiatry, 1*(5), 253–265.

Verrier, N. (1993). *The primal wound.* Gateway Press.

Wadia-Ellis, S. (Ed.). (1996). *The adoption reader: Birth mothers, adoptive mothers, and adopted daughters tell their stories.* Women's Press.

White, K. (Ed.). (2014). *Talking bodies: How do we integrate working with the body in psychotherapy from an attachment and relational perspective?*Karnac.

Wilberg, P. (2002). *Being and listening: Counselling, psychoanalysis, and the ontology of listening.* New Yoga Publications.

Wilson, S. (2018). *Music–psychoanalysis–musicology.* Routledge.

Winnicott, D. W. (1971). *Playing and reality.* Tavistock.

Chapter 4

Intersubjectivity and the sharing of lived experience in adoption music therapy

Introduction

> For those of us in a profession dealing with suffering, our own suffering plays an intricate, ongoing and irrevocable part in each of our encounters with our patients. It is not our patients who are called upon to understand or be responsive to our pain, it is we ourselves. Shame, that ghostly jailor, prevents us from accepting this as a matter of course.
>
> (Jaenicke, 2015, p. 4)

In this chapter, I explore how what I describe as micro-moments of attunement happen for adopted children in music therapy in the context of their relationship with myself as music therapist, within intersubjectivity. This term, originally used by the philosopher Edmund Husserl, describes the interchange of thoughts and feelings both conscious and unconscious, occurring between two people, or subjects. Daniel Stern (2005, p. 77) writes that intersubjectivity is 'the ability to share in another's lived experience'. Regarding psychotherapy, Stern (2005, p. 77) describes how intersubjectivity occurs, writing that 'psychoanalysis is the interplay of two subjectivities and the unpredictable material that is co-created by this encounter'. Stern's work on intersubjectivity is now taught on almost all music-therapy trainings in the UK. There is recognition given to the fact that music therapists always play music together with their clients (unlike, for example, art therapists, who do not necessarily make their own artwork alongside their clients, although this is increasing as a practice). It is in playing together, I argue, and in the sharing of something which I define as a 'musical gaze', that both therapist and client subjectivities are manifest in the music-therapy room. Then, opportunities arise for the co-creation of intersubjective relational states.

'Musical gaze' is something I have identified as an essential part of intersubjective relating for music therapists working in adoption. I root this idea in Winnicott's (1971) description of maternal gaze. Winnicott describes how a mother needs to truly see and recognise her baby:

> The mother gazes at the baby in her arms, and the baby gazes at his mother's face and finds himself therein, *provided that the mother is really*

DOI: 10.4324/9781003733393-4

> *looking at the unique, small, helpless being and not projecting her own expectations, fears, and plans for the child.*
>
> (Winnicott, 1971, p. 14; italics mine)

Gaze implies an emotional capacity in both the mother and the music therapist, who must be able to hold the client's experience without detracting from it or turning it into something else. If the music therapist has difficulty being there with the client's reality, a meta-message will be communicated that discourages further exploration. Detracting from the client's experience or turning it into something else are at risk of happening when the music therapist's own lived experience is not being held safely somewhere. For these reasons, I argue it is necessary to think how a music therapist such as myself, with lived experience of adoption, might work to ensure that my musical gaze does not project my material onto clients but rather provides a felt sense of holding.

Intersubjectivity has been written about regarding the part the client might play in relating, yet less so about the therapist's part. In my research, I have not come across any literature specifically pertaining to the part the music therapist (literally) plays in intersubjective therapeutic musical relationships. However, in recognising that both client and therapist do each contribute to the relationship, I argue that both need to be considered. Local authorities and adoption agencies often prefer therapists working with adopted clients to have some lived experience of adoption themselves, yet it does not follow that therapists without this experience will be somehow 'lacking' in their work or not be able to empathise. I do concur that therapists who have similar lived experience to their clients can use this advantageously, but it can conversely be enormously problematic (as discussed by Glassman & Botticelli, 2014). Stern argues that intersubjectivity requires an ability to share in the other's lived experience (via the interchange of thoughts and feelings, which may be conscious or unconscious). Therefore, both the client's and the therapist's lived experiences will be present somehow within the therapeutic encounter, whether this is consciously acknowledged or not.

Having then briefly outlined this chapter's themes, I shall now go on to define intersubjectivity and specifically how I understand this manifesting in a music-therapy relationship. Then I shall explore a consideration of the body/embodiment in intersubjective musical relating. This is essential to music therapy intersubjectivity, first because it is impossible to play an instrument other than through the body and second because the body is the site of enacted subjectivity. I shall attempt to quieten, if not totally silence, my feelings of shame (see the Jaenicke quote at the opening of this chapter), to own my subjective adoption narrative. Making my lived experience explicit feels necessary to this thesis because the intersubjective musical relationships I describe throughout this research are inevitably influenced by each party's lived experiences. I write later about musical intersubjective relating which requires the music therapist to own their lived experiences, especially when these might chime closely with their client(s). This will lead finally to some thinking about the complexities for music therapists of becoming researchers of our own work and how we might analyse our own therapist–client relationships, manage these complexities and write about the work as case studies. This is most important work if we are to learn from client experiences.

Defining and contextualising intersubjective experience

Central to his work in later life, Stern argued that significant moments of change can occur in an intersubjective therapeutic relationship. Stern's various 'moments' happen because, he argues,

> a 'real experience' emerges . . . between two people. It is about their relationship. It occurs in a very short period of time that is experienced as *now*. That *now* is a present moment . . . in which a micro-drama unfolds . . . This jointly lived experience is mentally shared . . . each person partakes in the experience of the other.
>
> (Stern, 2004, p. 22)

Inherent to Stern's argument of intersubjective sharing is the idea that a shared jointly lived experience can be grasped without it having to be verbalised. I infer then that intersubjective sharing can occur in the non-verbal modality of a music-therapy relationship. In fact, part of the value of the creative-arts therapies is that there is not necessarily a need to put words around symbolic creative experience. Rather, the now of that experience exists between therapist and client and is shared. This differentiates the 'now' from the client's 'then' (which was a non-shared experience).

Playing together

Playing music together is significant for intersubjective relating because play can draw on healthy creative parts of both the client's and therapist's selves. Music therapy can deceptively look like very simple musical play yet can be a highly sophisticated way of relating. Stern (2004, p. 20) describes how generally what seems to be 'just' playful relating has a tremendous potential for relationship: 'Here, we meet the other and both sense the mutual participating in the others experience . . . an interpenetration of minds – a new state of intersubjectivity.' Marks-Tarlow (2012, p. 89) agrees, writing, 'I suggest that play bears an important relationship to creativity, especially as it exists in the intersubjective space between the therapist and patient.' This seems to me to exactly describe the playful, creative space that music therapy offers. But both therapist and client must be able to play. This is why it is important to pay attention to the music therapist's capacity to play. Paraphrasing Winnicott (1971), if the patient can't play, he must be taught, and if the analyst can't play, no psychotherapy can occur . . . and if the music therapist cannot play then the adopted child certainly will not be enabled to do so.

Simultaneously co-creating music together in a music-therapy space brings into existence a new intersubjective relational field between client and therapist. Playing together within this field can alter the relationship, permitting both therapist and client freedom for experimentation to take different directions together. The new, intersubjective musical experience, occurring in the 'now' moment, contains opportunities to playfully and safely risk new forms of relating. This is significant for the client because it can hopefully lead to similar relational experimentation in their relationships outside of the therapy room. It is also significant for the music therapist who may likewise be changed. Tronick (1998) suggests that it is this expansion of the intersubjective field that is a potent experience for relational change for both. Stern (2004, p. 22) concurs, writing, 'the moment enters a special form of consciousness and is encoded in memory. And importantly, it rewrites the past.' This then is part of the hopefulness of music therapy as a modality of work with adoptees who have past trauma experience. Later, I discuss in detailed analysis of a session how this might have been happening within the transference with Jack, referring specifically to Freud's *après-coup*. As transference is worked through, the past, if not entirely being 'rewritten', can perhaps be understood differently.

Playing in time

For an adopted child, then, I argue that sharing a new intersubjective field with their music therapist can impact upon and even alter their relational styles that came into being via their early experience. Stern writes a lot about the temporal nature of intersubjective relating stating for example, 'therapeutic work *in the here and now* has the greatest power in bringing about change. That is where and when mutually aware contact between the minds of the therapist and patient takes place' (Stern, 2004, p. 3; italics mine). This is significant for music therapy, which can provide a re-experiencing of 'then' in the transference but reshape this experience into the 'now'. New relational 'now' moments are experienced in music therapy as temporal forms that can enter an adopted child's consciousness and be encoded in memory. Music exists in temporal form and in this way differs from other art products (such as a static image, created in a session but then existing as a fixed solid object). Music arises in time and space and is ephemeral. Musicians have nothing other than the moment to play in, yet, while it is being played, music exists. Music therapists especially are required to stay in the 'now' moment and be responsive.

In music therapy then, experiencing new musical, relational, temporal moments can offer a different perspective on the past as it is worked through in the transference. Transference is an opportunity for a repetition of the client's early material that can be untangled and thought about in the 'now'.

This fits with Winnicott's idea that the early trauma has already been lived through and survived and can now be safely shared and witnessed when replayed in therapy. As this happens, points of both convergence and divergence between client and therapist will arise. Working through transference provides new musical and relational 'repertoire' as it were for the child which can impact on their internal working model. Then they can continue to experiment and play with this in their adoptive family and beyond.

Aspects of Stern's writing on 'moments' clearly connect his ideas with music. He describes present moments as temporally dynamic, having 'a marked time dynamic, *as does a musical phrase* . . . these dynamic time-shapes are called *vitality affects*' (Stern, 2004, p. 36; italics mine). Stern (2004, p. 36) writes that vitality affects can be captured 'in terms such as accelerating, fading, exploding, unstable, tentative, forceful and so on'. Such descriptors are often applicable to music's temporal dynamic. For example, a pulsed rhythm can 'accelerate', a sudden loud sound 'explode', a steady rhythm can become 'unstable', a melody be 'tentative', or an insistent bass line 'forceful'. Stern's temporally dynamic perspective critically informs his thinking about 'moments', which he writes about variously as 'now moments, moments of meeting, temporal feeling shapes and shared feeling voyages' (Stern, 2004, p. 37). He specifically acknowledges how the 'present moment' or 'now moment' is something he considers can exist in music because 'the present moment is clearly situated in time phenomenologically' (Stern, 2004, p. 60). It is present/now moments then that I argue can be experienced within an intersubjective music-therapy relationship because, as Stern (2004, p. 38) writes, 'two minds share the same experience, at least as measured by the temporal shape'. In the 'here and now', moments arise that might share similarity with the adopted child's past (and these can manifest in transference) but which also diverge from the past, thereby creating different experience and diverging from being the 'same' as.

In an intersubjective musical relationship then, each subject has potential opportunities to become both one and separate as possibilities arise for subjective and intersubjective positions to be moved into and out of multiple times in one single session. The psychoanalytic music therapist Jos De Backer (in De Backer & Sutton, 2014, p. 276) has described how, for intersubjective relating to happen, both subjects need to be free and possess autonomy and independence while choosing to engage in a shared interdependence. The musical sounds themselves become a dialectical interplay. This thinking has helped me to conceive of what I have come to term 'micro-moments of attunement' in music therapy, and their significance for adoptive families.

Moments of meeting and musical micro-moments of attunement

Stern (2004, p. xiii) writes, 'the present moment I am after is *the moment of subjective experience as it is occurring*, not as it is later re-shaped by words' (my italics). Here he particularly describes the relational significance of moments occurring between a mother–infant dyad. However, many music therapists have applied his theories to music therapy as they fit so well to descriptions of significant therapeutic musical 'moments'. Stern's present moments contain moments of meeting which he defines as 'an emotional lived story . . . physically, emotionally, and implicitly *shared not just explicated*' (2004, pp. xvi and xvii; italics mine). Stern argues that it is the moment as it is occurring that is most significant. This matters for music therapy because, I argue, possible intersubjective moments of relating can exist within the present musical moments co-created between music therapist and client. Music therapists often spend time trying to explain the art of our practice in words, and I concur with Stern that words reshape the present experience into something other than that which existed alive in the room. Words then cannot really get to the essence of the moment of intersubjectivity in the way that I shall now continue to argue music might.

Music (of all sorts, not just that made within music therapy) happens in the 'space between' people. Marks-Tarlow (2008, pp. 225–6) has suggested that intersubjectivity also happens in that same space between:

> I view intersubjectivity as pattern that forms uniquely in the space between self and other. This pattern is both emergent and self-organizing, offering a degree of complexity not present at the level of constituent people . . . where what is inside versus outside one person versus another becomes unclear, and patterns appear to arise in the intersubjective space created by two interlocking psyches.

I explore this notion in depth later where I write about music becoming like both the potential space (Winnicott) and the third (Ogden), existent between client and therapist. For now though, I am focusing on the significance of Marks-Tarlow's idea of intersubjective merging and how this may manifest musically.

Moments of merging

The sense that things merge and become unclear within intersubjective relating is certainly something I have experienced in music therapy with adoptees. When playing music in early sessions with an adoptee, I have often felt musically merged with them initially. I suggest this merged state resonates something of the merging a mother and her newly born baby experience and has significance for working with early experience in adoption music therapy. Merging is a necessary state at first. Gradually, however, this merged state lessens as the client develops, realising they have permission to use their volition and shape musical play as they want.

Music therapist and client continue to play together over weeks, months, years, each contributing their own musical 'ingredients'. The music that is subsequently co-created contains elements provided by each, combining like a cake mixture, until individual ingredients are indistinct, merged and eventually become another form altogether. The form of music then exists in its creation, and co-created music becomes something other now, real and alive, existent in time between therapist and client. Buber (cited in Eberhart & Atkins, 2014, p. 77) describes how this might happen in a relationship, and I have adapted his words for music therapy usage, with the italicised words in brackets mine: 'It is in encounter [*intersubjective music therapy*] that the creation [*music*] reveals its formhood [*musical structure*]'. By this point, the client and music therapist have moved well beyond merging and will be playing as two separate individuals. Often the client will lead an improvisation, and the music therapist will attend to it, and perhaps follow, or even introduce new material.

Intersubjectivity in music

Jung was one of the earliest psychoanalytic writers to suggest that within a psychotherapy both client and therapist will be inevitably affected by each other and that this can be a useful thing to happen:

> For two personalities to meet is like mixing two different chemical substances: if there is any combination at all, both are transformed. In any effective psychological treatment, the doctor is bound to influence the patient; but this influence can only take place if the patient has a reciprocal influence on the doctor.
>
> (Jung, 1963: para. 163)

This resonates with my experiences within the musical play of adoption music therapy relating. Playing music together inevitably means participating in an intersubjective relationship. Music, co-created in free improvisations, might move, influence and continue to affect both parties. I emphasise the importance of free improvisation here, rather than structured, directed music-making, as this draws upon both participants' internal and unconscious worlds.

Because music is a wordless modality, feeling states are somehow heightened. We know this at its most basic when, for example, a tune playing on the sound system in a shop can suddenly stop us in our tracks, arousing strong feelings instantly. Therefore, there is a risk that co-creating music in music therapy might arouse the music therapist's own material unhelpfully. Yet we can only make sense of the client's early relational experience by entering a musical relationship where feeling states manifest. Marks-Tarlow (2008, p. 81) sums up the risk, stating, 'Too much personal identification during intersubjectivity always carries hidden potential for un-self-aware enactments.' However, if enactments are also part of what happens inevitably when transference gets going, then therapists need to work out what it is they are getting pulled into with the client. Somehow, the music therapist needs to openly enter musical relating and authentically play as themselves but not act out their material. Experiencing musical intersubjectivity is necessary to understand an adoptee's early experience because 'developmentally traumatic affective states can be understood only in terms of the relational systems in which they took form' (Jaenicke, 2008, p.103). Within intersubjectivity, it becomes possible to experience an adoptee's inner world material being literally played out. Then meaning may be gleaned about how this continues to impact their present life, relationships and adoptive placement.

Ultimately, however, the music therapist is responsible for holding the boundaries of the session, keeping a part of herself somehow outside enough of the experience. Entering intersubjective musical states requires the music therapist to decentre herself from the music, while remaining fully in touch with herself and continuing to play. Marks-Tarlow (2012, p. 2) again describes how difficult this can be in verbal therapy:

> My actual experience was nothing like what I had envisioned . . . The relationship took on a life of its own. This was my first taste of intersubjectivity, where what takes place in the space between two people has the momentum to carry both along.

I argue that music itself can provide the momentum of which she writes, and both therapist and client risk being 'carried along' in it. When this risk is well managed, the intersubjective experience works to the benefit of the client.

The music therapist Martin Lawes (2012) describes how, for this to happen, music therapists first must listen within to themselves before risking engagement in playing music, which involves unconsciously relating with the client in a musical flow or momentum. By allowing herself to be aware of her own lived experience, and having conscious access to her own trauma, the music therapist is neither swallowed nor destroyed by the client's reality but can remain humanly and affectively present. Additionally, the music therapist retains access to a meta-perspective. Then, freely improvised music engenders sharing in a felt responsiveness that moves back and forth safely between music therapist and client.

I conclude this section citing Wilberg (2004) who conflates the idea of intersubjective relating (in verbal psychotherapy) with a notion of relational 'music':

> The way she (the mother) handles the infant is not her music but her playing of this music. This playing can be mechanical and erratic or sensitively attuned – musical. If it is musical then it is based not simply on a listening receptivity to her own being, but on a sensitive attunement to the 'music' of the infant – its language of being.
>
> (Wilberg, 2013, p. 67)

There are echoes here of Winnicott's maternal holding and handling, and I find it hard to distinguish exactly what is 'music' and what is 'relationship' for Wilberg. He clearly believes that intersubjectivity is closely allied to the 'musical' experience described.

Like Wilberg's mother figure, I have also learned to play not 'my' music in therapy but rather 'this' music, which arises in relationship. The music that grows between myself and my client is shared, and therefore, I argue, is a joint language of being in Wilberg's terms: 'our music' then. He continues:

> Then the music that is played is not hers alone but a common music. The music of what Buber called the Between . . . Wording is the handling and shaping of our pre-verbal, bodily, or 'musical' sense of meaning. This felt sense is attuned to the Between. In listening to people's language . . . we hear the nature of their listening attunement to this Between – their way of hearing and playing its music.
>
> (Wilberg, 2013, p. 67)

My case study of 'Jack' describes in detail how such a 'between' (intersubjective musical playing) came into being for myself and Jack (as it has many times for other adopted clients). Forthcoming case-study chapters detail what both Jack and I experienced as we became attuned to one another through using music as a language of being, within our intersubjective relationship. I shall now discuss the significance of the body in such relating.

A brief consideration of embodiment in intersubjective musical relating

Winnicott (1969) writes that all psychotherapy is about people playing together. As music therapists literally playing music with our clients, it is impossible to do so without using our bodies. Whether we recognise it or not, our whole embodied subjectivity is brought to musical relating. A phenomenology of the body states that it is our 'primary source of knowledge and the subject of all our actions' (Merleau-Ponty, in 1962, cited in Trondalen, 2016, p. 5). Stern's concept of intersubjectivity has become so relevant to music therapy because he describes an embodied process of relating that intuitively makes sense to musicians. Lawes (2016, 2017) acknowledges the significance of the body as a source of retained musical memory upon which music therapists draw in free improvisation. Music therapists can, in his terms, 'dream' in music, meaning they can draw upon their internal unconscious reservoir of musical experiences retained in embodied memory to access music that the client is seeking.

Winnicott also turns to musical analogy to describe the embodied experience of therapeutic relating, which, I argue, is close to Stern's description of intersubjectivity. Both Winnicott and Stern draw upon the language of music to describe what they think occurs in shared relational space. Winnicott writes about the therapeutic relationship being: 'like the music of the spheres, absolutely personal. It belongs to being alive . . . the two extremes, explicit communication that is indirect, and silent or personal communication that feels real' (cited in Guntrip, 1985, p. 241).

Musical sounds are first created by the individual client and music therapist and are personal to each. Yet the jointly created music, existing when individual sounds combine, is felt by both, within and around both bodies. Sounds vibrate in the molecules of air between both, and within the eardrums of both, as well as resonating in other bodily parts. Music therapy is then inevitably a total embodied experience of intersubjective relating, thereby providing a place where the client's material can be revealed, addressed, survived and integrated.

I have recognised in this section that music therapy occurring between client and therapist is influenced by each party's lived experiences. My understanding of intersubjectivity, when expressed in embodied, therapeutic, musical relationships, leads me to argue that it is also inevitable that the subjectivity of the music therapist will affect intersubjective relating.

I shall now explore in more detail how I conceive therapeutically intersubjective relationships occurring within music therapy, and being of use to an adopted child, while also implicating the music therapist.

Adoption music therapy: Multiple intersubjective resonances

This chapter opened with a quote by Jaenicke, and I draw upon him now as a psychotherapist who pays attention to how closely subjectivity is tangled with our approaches and methods. How much more likely this is to be when we work with our own lived experience: 'How interwoven our subjectivity is with our choice of theories and with our clinical practice' (Jaenicke, 2015, p. 2).

As described previously, music therapists cannot observe phenomena occurring in therapy sessions completely objectively, as if from the outside (as Alanne, 2010, points out regarding his own practice and subsequent research). We are *in* the experience because *we play too.* I often liken this to having one foot in a river and the other foot on the riverbank when I try to explain to music-therapy students how intersubjectivity happens. Although both client and therapist are immersed in intersubjective music-making, the therapist must somehow retain part of themselves that is located outside of this experience. This section will describe the complex interplay of parts that a music therapist with lived experience in similar areas to her client brings to intersubjective music therapy.

Jaenicke's quote with which I opened this chapter highlights the shame he considers prevents professional therapists from discussing the inevitable involvement of their own material in the formation of an intersubjective relationship. If only shame can be silenced, then previous suffering and needs the music therapist brings from their lived experience might be given consideration as 'a matter of course' (Jaenicke, 2015, p. 4). Personal suffering often leads someone to seek therapy, and even later then perhaps to consider training as a therapist. The music therapist's personal suffering, or lived experience, will continue to be influential in therapeutic encounters, whether this is consciously or unconsciously acknowledged. Elfred (2013, p. 18) takes a strong position about this, writing that, 'If the psychotherapist wants to see themselves as a healer, then they must first acknowledge that they themselves are in need of healing.'

Some cultures expect that those who are perceived as 'healers' will also be 'sufferers' who 'possess some defect . . . that they had mastered . . . or come to terms with . . . What might seem to Westerners as a weakness was seen as evidence of the ability to communicate . . . and thus was conceptualised in positive terms' (Bennet, cited in Rippere & Williams, 1985, p. 6).

Music therapy training in the UK recognises the likely earlier suffering of students coming to training, and so student music therapists are required to undertake personal therapy. The training music therapist hopefully becomes sufficiently cognisant of their personal internal worlds and psychological wounds, which have the potential to become activated in professional musical relationships with clients This is particularly significant 'to avoid consciously or unconsciously exploiting or using the client for their own ends or gratification' (Driver, 2013, p. 18).

Intersubjectivity: Implications of lived experience within the adoption community

In this section, I develop my understanding of how the music therapists lived experience impacts upon practice. Later, I shall utilise an interrogation of lived experience as methodology along the lines that Scott-Hoy (2002, p. 276) suggests: 'a blend of ethnography and autobiographical writing that incorporates elements of one's own life experience when writing about others'. Such interrogation is essential for me to describe how my varying lived experiences of adoption are implicated in the musical intersubjective relationships I form in my work.

First, though, I will define what is known as the 'adoption community', as being the client group with which I work. In my previous book, I loosely described the adoption community as

> the shared networks of individual lives that are connected by the experience of adoption, in some way. Membership of this community is gained by being either an adoptee or an adoptive parent/grandparent/relative, but with the lived experience of adoptees being privileged.
>
> (Gravestock, 2021, p. 15)

The adoption community purports to value the lived experience of its members. Local-authority and charitable-body adoption teams with which I have worked have ideally preferred that their music therapists come either from within the adoption community and/or have lengthy experience of adoption-specific trauma work. Newly qualified music therapists with a desire to get involved in adoption music therapy describe being told they lack either experience yet struggle to know where experience can be gained, if not from within the work itself. My access to work with clients within the adoption community came about partly because I have a previous professional background in therapeutic adoption work. However, I also have lived experience of adoption.

I have been arguing that adoption lived experience has the potential for good and harm in therapeutic practice, depending upon how it is made sense of, and drawn upon. Therapeutic intersubjective relationships are not about the therapist coming to understand themselves; rather, the therapist's adoption experiences might become useful in helping understand client experiences. It is an ethical imperative for myself as a music therapist that I consider the impact of my lived experience. Malone (2018, p. 219) is clear that 'responsibility falls asymmetrically on the analyst not only to be mindful of how they participate, but also to reflect upon the implications of the interpersonal and intrapsychic processes simultaneously unfolding'.

I must therefore acknowledge that the adoption music therapy approach I have evolved at least partially has origins in my own lived experience, which is a deep seam running beneath my work. The intersubjective relationships I develop with clients affect them but also significantly affect me. It is clearly the responsibility of the music therapist to be able to hold her own experience safely so that the client's experience is central. To at least partially account for this, I now offer an interrogation of my lived experience in an account of becoming a music therapist in the adoption community, of which I am also part.

Interrogating lived experience

The methodology of autoethnography 'incorporates elements of one's own life experience when writing about others' (Scott-Hoy, 2002, p. 276). Ellis and Bochner (1996, p. 739) describe the process of how researchers create their autoethnography:

> they zoom backward and forward, inward and outward, distinctions between the personal and the cultural become blurred . . . Usually written in the first person voice, autoethnographic texts appear in a variety of forms . . . appearing as relational and institutional stories affected by our history, social structure, and culture, which themselves are dialectically revealed through action, feeling, thought and language.

I considered utilising autoethnography within this book; however, I decided to instead use interrogation of my lived experience. Although an autoethnography would have been an interesting and possibly enlightening way to write, I also felt it may reveal my lived experience in ways that may not be helpful to future clients and their families. I will now go on to describe some varied elements of my lived experience which cannot easily be separated from my work or research and therefore require interrogation.

Lived experience: Being adopted or being an adopter

The first lived experience I consider is that of my own adoption experience and how this may be present in my work. In 'How Betty and Vincent became Sally and Scott', Bjorklund considers her experience as an adoptee/psychotherapist. She enquired of a colleague how he felt her adoption coloured her work and records his response: 'He thought of how my practice has tended to be populated by people who operate primarily from schizoid defences, people who are hard to reach and hard to hold' (Bjorklund, 2014, p. 13). On reflection, Bjorklund realised she was drawing to herself clients who not necessarily had her adoption experience but who shared issues/difficulties around being contacted and being held. These would be issues that I recognise arise in my practice as carrying resonances of my lived experience. Bjorklund felt that she could remain with such clients, and her lived experience in fact enabled her to be creative and play within the psychological games clients engaged in which were familiar to her. I would argue that Bjorklund's capacity was known by her clients in the way she related to them. Lyons-Ruth (1998) describes this as implicit relational knowing, arguing that it offers a positive way in which therapists can connect with clients in intersubjective relating. Bjorklund's lived experience was therefore turned into a capacity to offer holding of clients who found it difficult to risk attaching in the therapeutic relationship. She writes (2014, p. 13), 'I have some ideas about how to play the hide and seek game that working with people who "aren't there" requires.'

However, in recognising that resonances of our lived experience will colour our work, it is important to address that experience in and of itself is not necessarily helpful. Bjorklund seems to recognise and argue for our own experiences engendering an openness and a patience within us to the experiences of others. I would argue that equally though, if I did not have lived experience of adoption, I would hopefully still be able to assume how adopted clients might feel. In situations where I work with a client I don't share lived experience with, I engage via empathy and listening to the client's experience. There is a mid-ground of identification to be found, it seems, between overvaluing the usefulness of lived experience or ignoring that it can have a therapeutic significance. Central to this is the prerogative that the client's experience must always come first and the therapist's experience can be useful in the way it might help to make sense of the client's experience. At all times, a therapist should be concerned with how they can be made most useful for clients. Being able to hold our own lived experience 'in parenthesis', as I suggested earlier, is imperative. This can only happen when the therapist has had their own experience of having been through therapy themselves and therefore worked through and processed their trauma – at least enough. Then such trauma is no longer repressed and unconscious but is made available and can be used in the service of clients.

Maybe, because of my own experience, I might have more capacity than the average clinician to bear the (sometimes) years of patience required for an adopted child to form an attachment to me. Like Bjorklund (2014, p. 15), I can admit that 'I think I really do get what is terrifying about depending on another, and the impossibility of living without attachments to people.' Later in this book, I describe the way in which many adoptees I have worked with have literally played hide and seek, both in the music and in enactments. In many cases of music therapy, clients have needed to play out this game over weeks or even months. Perhaps, like Bjorklund, I can bear the seemingly endless repetition of adopted children's games and give the necessary amount of time that is required for an attachment to form. Perhaps also this is why I have consistently argued for funding for long-term pieces of work for adopted children because I know from my lived experience that to really work through adoption trauma takes a long time.

A second author in Kuchuck's volume, Philip Ringstrom, is an adopter. He describes how living with his adopted children who had experienced trauma resulted in him changing his language to describe trauma: 'I reply on numerous occasions, "I do not work with trauma victims. I work with patients who among many things have likely also suffered some trauma in their lives"' (Ringstrom, 2014, p. 158). He describes how he wants to recognise that his children, his clients and himself are all open-ended subjects who are not constituted by a single label of experience. Ringstrom's own lived experience resulted in a reframing of the trauma that he met in his professional world, coming to view his clients as having many layers of lived experience that required using multiple other lenses to look with. Ringstrom, however, also writes about the negatives of having similarities in lived experience with clients:

> As I discovered, the process of witnessing (however limited, however failed) may engage us with a patient in deep and unwanted ways that implicate our own histories . . . I present my work . . . as a testament to the complex and deeply personal purposes to which our patients may put us, purposes undreamt of in the mind of the 'evidence-based' treatment researcher. Testament, too, to the way in which our own infantile material, if not worked through, may curtail our empathic responsiveness to our patients.
>
> (Ringstrom, 2014, p. 175)

His writing contains strong warnings about 'deep, unwanted' resonances that may occur with clients. If client material unexpectedly resonates with our own, we can be left feeling vulnerable and exposed and may, in response to such reverberations, withdraw the degree of contact we offer. Ringstrom argues that, in the worst scenarios, the therapist's personal history can reduce the degree of 'empathic responsiveness' they can offer their client. He argues that it is our 'unhealed wounds' that become problematic. I concur with his thinking but prefer to talk about this in terms of our unintegrated material rather than healing (which sounds absolute).

Professionals who are either adopted or adopters themselves do not routinely have supports to manage complex resonating feelings when working in adoption, and this can be destructive. I do not agree with the general sense in the adoption community that any personal lived experience of adoption is good and useful. This is why I argue the experience of having had one's own therapy is essential to the music therapist with lived experience of adoption choosing to work in this area.

Lived experience: Evolving an adoption-specific music therapy approach

My practice as an adoption music therapist commenced years ago. Therapeutic work has, varyingly over time, been informed by my psychoanalytic music therapy training, intersubjective theory, attachment theory, contemporary relational psychoanalysis and my own experiences both of supervision and psychotherapy. Aspects of the theories I choose to use to make sense of adoption experience may not entirely always seem to fit together. However, I argue for eclecticism as my approach has evolved. I have needed to make sense of varied presentations that have happened within the space of music therapy and have looked to theories that make the best sense of what clients bring 'here and now', even if such theories may not always be completely congruent with one another. I use the term 'approach' to describe the work that has emerged because I am not advocating a fixed prescribed method. Rather, an ever-evolving organic approach is regularly reinformed and adapted by new knowledge/theory I encounter, or which the work urges me to seek out to make sense of a client's experience.

My lived experience has been a resource that could hold both potential benefits and risks where it might resonate in this specialist area of adoption. I was alert to Driver's (2013) warning that unconscious material of my own might drive my choice of client group. To minimise unconscious complications that my lived experience might bring to the work, I provided myself with specific places set apart to think deeply about it, including increasing both my supervision and personal psychotherapy hours. This enabled me to recognise powerful experiences of transference and countertransference arising in intersubjective relationships, distinguishing them from my own experience.

Countertransference has been viewed in various ways within psychoanalysis. Freud recommended that analysts should somehow bracket their own emotional responses as a way of protecting themselves from the effects of transference. Countertransference was therefore regarded as problematic. However, since the 1940s, Heimann and Racker advocated that the countertransference could be useful as a means of understanding the entire analytic process. It is difficult teasing apart aspects of what may be considered 'countertransference' happening within music therapy from what might be arising in the client's experience that resonates the music therapist's experience. Some contemporary writers (e.g., Daly, 2016; Erskine, 2015; Romanyshyn, 2013; Slochower, 2014) argue it provides valuable insight into the intersubjective relational process that arises afresh with each client. Others remain more critical, arguing that countertransference is something to be addressed by the therapist away from intersubjective relating so that unresolved issues of the therapist do not colour the work. This might explain why more discussion of therapists' lived experience is absent from the literature:

> Countertransference sometimes tends to be thought of in the analyst's fantasy as impermissible, embarrassing or professionally damaging . . . Thus the analysts subjective experience with the patient, which may be the core of in-depth analytic work, has been less well attended to than the patients experience of the analyst.
>
> (Sedgwick, 1994, p. 1)

From my own experience of having analysis, I became aware of what is termed the 'relational' approach to psychotherapy (Charles, 2018), which pays attention to how the analyst's self is implicated in the co-constructed narrative that emerges in any psychotherapy. Driver (2013, p. 2; italics mine) writes:

> if we accept the premise that in therapeutic work the therapeutic relationship is vital then it is crucial to consider the client's *and also the therapist's* state of being and examine theories of being, or ontology, in relation to the client *and the therapist within the therapeutic encounter.*

Similarly, Kuchuck (2014, p. xviii) writes about theories of psychotherapy stressing the need for a 'fit' between therapist and client, yet how little attention is given to the therapist's self and what they contribute to such 'fit':

> It is the intersubjective fit and patient-therapist dynamics that determine the course of a treatment . . . The therapist's subjectivity, therefore, plays a significant role in the co-construction of the clinical fit and trajectory, though it is seldom examined as carefully as other elements of the work.

Kuchuck argues that it is impossible for any therapist to be truly opaque but also recognises the struggle that can ensue for therapists who attempt to openly acknowledge this. Opacity is not about being deliberately elusive, nor is it claiming some superior sort of neutrality, but it does mean the therapist puts parts of themselves in parenthesis for the sake of the client. If opacity can never be total, then anxiety is likely to arise because of the therapist's own issues around seeing and being seen, especially in therapeutic cultures that emphasise opacity. Being seen may lead to being judged, or at least a fear of being judged. This connects closely with the sense of shame Jaenicke identifies. I wonder how difficult it is for music therapists, working in our relatively small profession, to feel we are truly seen (first as students by our course leaders, then by our clinical supervisors). This is especially pertinent for those of us carrying trauma histories (which are often integral to adoption histories) as trauma depends upon shame if it is to be kept hidden: 'The fact that analysts are never really invisible – even if they try – and that patients often want desperately to know us, raises tremendous anxiety for those struggling with our own longing to be known and defensive temptation to hide' (Kuchuck, 2014, p. xix).

Despite recognising this anxiety, Kuchuck (2014, p. xix; italics mine) nonetheless argues that acknowledging shame beneath personal narratives is important because an acceptance of lived experience can lead to it being more openly acknowledged, explored and thought about:

> We are urging recognition of the *inevitability of inadvertent disclosure and influence* that is the cornerstone of working within a two-person psychology . . . As a profession, we attempt to overcome or at least address the shame, vulnerability, and antiquated theoretical prohibitions that prevent more widespread explorations of the therapist's subjectivity in the literature.

The value of integrated lived experience in adoption music therapy

How then might it be possible for the music therapist to integrate their subjective lived experience and utilise it for good? Integrating experience for me has meant becoming able to acknowledge what has happened and gradually fold it into the fabric of life so it is no longer controlling or dominating the present. Being in therapy can offer opportunities for such integration; however, no therapy can completely bring our unconscious fully to light. It can though enable us to fully acknowledge the reality of what has been forever lost to us and can never be retrieved. This necessitates work that is about mourning the past. Our losses cannot be restored (as the notion of 'healing' perhaps implies), but we can have the present experience of now sharing them with another.

The music therapist's own experience of being in therapy can hopefully then enable them to distinguish their own material from that of their clients. Gradually then we can recognise where the client's experience may echo our own but also explore difference. As Meltzoff and Decety (2003, p. 498) write:

> The adult human framework is not simply one of resonance. We are able to recognise that everyone does not share our own desires, emotions, intentions, and beliefs. To become a sophisticated mentaliser one needs to analyse both the similarities and differences between one's own state and those of others. This is what makes us human.

Integrating lived experience means becoming able to identify what is 'me' and what is 'the client'. Situations can still nonetheless arise for therapists when their own deprivations and lack of intimacy are reactivated in a present therapeutic situation, and such times are potentially difficult. No one is immune, and this is why our own supervision and therapy are required.

Guggenbuhl-Craig (1971) suggests that one of the most important mitigating factors for the therapist working with clinical groups that resonate their own material is for the therapist to know that they have a personal life that is being lived in the here and now, with its own fulfilment and potential. This reduces the risk for the therapist to be tempted into acting out being a saviour for clients. 'Only an analyst who is passionately engaged in his own life can help his patients live theirs' (Guggenbuhl-Craig, 1971, p. 56). One of the ways that music therapists can do this is to remain strongly engaged with their own music-making processes. It is insufficient to only play the music that we play in music therapy because such music is predominantly supportive, holding and containing. We need opportunities to connect with other aspects of our musical selves. For me, as a violinist, this has meant a continued playing/performing career where I am able to challenge myself musically and technically and engage in other sorts of musical relationships (such as orchestra, quartet, band or theatre pit). It is by feeding and nurturing ourselves that we can come to music therapy as complete and authentic human beings, able to then use our music in service of the client.

I have described why I think it is essential that music therapists working in specialist areas that resonate their own material need to have processed and integrated such material as far as is possible. I think that perhaps my own lived experience of adoption and trauma now adds subconsciously more positively to the sense of intimacy in the intersubjectivity between myself and my clients. Interestingly, without knowing any of my history, some clients have mentioned their feeling that I, too, might 'know what it's like'. One (adult) client did once state to me at a session's end, 'You know about this too, don't you?' A child also, while resting in almost a reverie state and gazing up at me, noticed a scar from a physical injury I have (resulting from childhood trauma). To my surprise, the child said, 'Did your birth daddy do that?' This child was implying that I too might have a 'birth daddy' as well as an 'adopted daddy' and, in their own fantasy about me, had come very close to my lived experience. Without clients having access to my personal narrative, then, it has become present in music therapy, either in their projections and fantasies about me, or resonating, unspoken but embodied, in the space between us.

Becoming a researcher of intersubjective relationships

Janesick (2000, p. 385) brings attention to how contemporary research methods within therapy allow for us to consider the inevitability of our subjectivity and lived experience: 'The researcher owns up to his or her perspective on the study.' Having considered the contribution of the music therapist's lived experience in an intersubjective musical relating with clients, I shall now address a further layer of complexity: that of how we come to occupy a dual position as both therapist and researcher in and of our work. I have drawn on supervision (both therapeutic and academic) to enable me to think about how I could become a research instrument of integrity for client 'Jack'. This additional layer needed important consideration in order to make sure that both he and I were protected and safe in all aspects of the work. I needed to think constantly about the impact upon Jack of his music therapist also being the same person who was researching his case.

There are obvious differences between the roles of music therapist and researcher. I have been enabled to think about these partly by having different supervisors for each role. My music-therapy supervisor had no vested interest in my research, and her role was to ensure the well-being of my clients and myself in the work. My research-supervision team enabled me to take a clear research position and to develop a second-order perspective on my own practice.

The process of getting my research approved through ethics caused me to think about how I might separate out aspects of these roles for myself. I was clear when seeking ethical consent that if a client or family chose to withdraw from the research, then this would in no way impact that child or family's ongoing therapy with me. I acknowledged internally that I would inevitably have strong feelings to manage if a research client I had done a lot of work with then chose to opt out of my study. I needed to be open about this potential occurrence, to prepare myself for it happening, in as much as I could.

Having now had the experience, I think that in some ways it may be better to be a music therapist doing research than a researcher researching music therapy. As a music therapist, I am at least used to examining my own internal processes and having to be mindful of their impact. It would have been more complicated, I think, to consider a researcher as a third party either needing to attend music-therapy sessions or view video and read notes of the therapeutic work. This would not offer the researcher the experience of being inside the music therapy, and therefore there would be less potential to discuss the felt lived experience and impact of a musical intersubjectivity.

In my role as music therapist, I continued to privilege the needs of any potential case-study clients while at the same time recognising that I needed their experiences in my role as a researcher. It was important that what my music therapist self thought of as potentially significant therapeutic moments should not become overinvested with my own desires as a researcher self. Marks-Tarlow (2008, p. 81) sums up the problem well:

> Therapist insights also carry dangers of over-identification or becoming too involved emotionally. Further, how do we know that such a moment is indeed a valid one, rather than springing creatively from our own desires and unconscious needs? With such intimate links between therapist and patient at multiple levels, many of which are not only unconscious but also inaccessible to consciousness, we must always be on guard to keep from exploiting patients in order to meet our own personal or theoretical ends.

I was much encouraged to read the thesis of Sami Alanne, music therapist, who had likewise struggled with this problem of becoming therapist-researcher. Alanne (2010, p. 34) identifies three potentially problematic issues for the music therapist-researcher, namely: (1) the dynamics in the work; (2) the therapist's own traumatic experience; and (3) the psychological dynamics arising particularly to the researcher role. Regarding dynamics in the work, Alanne recognises that unconscious material aroused in music-therapy sessions is not only the material of the client but also the music therapist. He refers particularly to transference and countertransference, seeing these as valuable, though requiring mediating through the music therapist's clinical supervision or psychotherapy. Relating this to the music therapist's own traumatic experience, Alanne is clear that this should not become a complicating feature of the music therapy. Therefore, the music therapist's experience must be processed enough that it can be held as it were 'in parenthesis' so that the client is foregrounded. Finally, Alanne recognises how psychological dynamics arising in the therapeutic work are likely to impact upon the research when the therapist and researcher are the same person. The music therapist works with the 'in the room' experience and will make sense of it, but then this material will be scrutinised from the researcher's perspective and interpreted differently on another level.

Having become aware of these issues, I hoped I was doing all I could to address Alanne's identified problematic points for the music therapist-researcher. Earlier in this chapter, I acknowledged that dynamics which my clients encountered in the intersubjective relationship would also likely be felt by myself and resonate with my personal material. To manage this, I had put in place what Alanne suggests is helpful, namely, I increased both my supervision and personal psychotherapy. By engaging with my own lived experience of adoption/trauma, I was ensuring (in so far as it is possible) that unconscious material of my own did not obscure that of my client. Thus, I was acknowledging that I am, as Alanne suggests, often being a research instrument that is in turn examined in my own work.

Alanne roots research of his own music therapeutic practice in Heidegger's (1927) concept of 'worldhood'. I shall later in this book discuss how I also have used Heideggerian concepts to describe core aspects of my approach). Worldhood is a description for how

> the researcher is not observing the phenomena from the outside, but belongs to the world with them, just as I, as a music therapist, have my history . . . knowledge and questions, which arise from my professional field, as well as my personal situation and the preunderstanding that related to my being-in-the-world.
>
> (Alanne, 2010, pp. 16–17)

In my research, I recognised a very specific sharing of worldhood with my client, i.e., the fact that both of us belonged to the adoption community. Alanne (2010, p. 16) also utilised another philosophical concept of Heidegger's, applicable to his becoming a music therapist-researcher: 'With research, this also means self-experiencing (pathos) and hence it comes near to Heidegger's concept of releasement; the researcher stops to see and listen to what is around him/her, and thus notices the interaction between the world and him/herself.'

Releasement is described as not only a method but also an attitude wherein some of the research material and topics remain open. Alanne (2010, p. 16) argues that the necessary work that is to be done both within music therapy and within the research of that therapy cannot be defined beforehand or determined afterward because 'what shows itself to us also hides from us simultaneously and thus requires an attitude of openness to the mystery'. Alanne's research evidenced that maintaining both an attitude of releasement and an openness to mystery belonged together and could 'provide new ground – soil – on which to stand while staying inside the technical world' (Alanne, 2010, p. 16). His experience of being a music therapist-researcher certainly chimes with my own. I realised I had always unknowingly approached each music-therapy session with what I could now call a stance of releasement and openness. Now I needed to come to research with the same attitude.

Conclusion

This chapter has explored the significance of the music therapist's lived experience when engaged in intersubjective relating with their client, especially when client and therapist share similar experience. My explorations lead me to argue that the notion that a therapist should always become opaque for their client is debatable. Opacity can be a desirable and valuable position for a music therapist to adopt; however, it is possible to be playful with semi-opacity also. To truly enter a state of musical intersubjectivity with a client necessitates the music therapist being able to acknowledge and own their personal history and to accept that this will in some way enter therapeutic work and impact upon client experience. I argue (based on instances from my therapeutic practice) that this happens whether the music therapist is aware of it happening or not. As Driver (2013, p. 6) writes, 'When therapist and client meet . . . they encounter, consciously and unconsciously, the being of the other or, as Heidegger would suggest, the "being of being" of the other in a way in which both are affected.'

Sedgwick (1994, p. 19) sums up the apparent choices for the therapist between 'neutrality' and relational transparency:

> After stating that Jung thought countertransference to be as valid therapeutically as transference, Moody (1995) asks how the analyst might use the inevitable subjective reactions constellated in treatment. A choice sometimes arises between a 'neutral' attitude and one where the analyst leaves his 'ego-stronghold' and lets himself be drawn into a relationship as an active participant.

In my own terms, I think that as music therapists we work at moving into and out of opacity. When the choice to be drawn into the musical relationship is acknowledged, it can then be safely thought about (for example in clinical supervision). Music therapists can then willingly place themselves and their musicking in the service of the client while recognising that this means becoming vulnerable. It is only by so doing that we might find ourselves capable of relating musically in an attuned state of being with our clients because 'empathy truly appears to be a mutual process of shared communicative attunement' (Norcross, 2011, p. 145).

When as a music therapist I attune to an adopted client in intersubjective musical relationships, I experience musical manifestations of my client's internal world. This enables me to gain insights which may well also lead to gaining a sense of what their early lived experience has been and how this may be impacting upon their relationships in an adoptive placement. Playing music with my client means I am involved in a shared embodied intersubjectivity where aspects of myself and my lived experience will become available to the client. While playing music, I must simultaneously listen to hear the client's music, which can then be witnessed, held and eventually played with in the context of new relational experience:

> The way we attune to another person sets a tone . . . Musical tones only speak to us if we really attune to them with our feelings – if we let them echo our feeling tones. We only really listen to music when we listen through the music to ourselves – for it is by attuning to it with feeling

> that it recalls us to our being. The feeling tones with which we attune to someone not only allow us to hear the music of our feelings – they recall us to our own being and echo its "toning".
>
> (Wilberg, 2002, p. 28)

I have recognised dangers inherent in working within intersubjective relating when the work resonates our own lived experience:

> The therapist's intimacy needs can easily come into play. It is, again, inevitable that the therapist working via himself will bring his whole self to the treatment. Needs must be known, fulfilled elsewhere if possible, or sometimes sacrificed. This is not fun.
>
> (Sedgwick, 1994, p. 147)

I have described ways I have found to meet my own needs (especially my musical needs) and mitigate such dangers. Additionally, I have spoken of the value of my own psychotherapy and supervision, which enables me to embrace my own life and live it fully, as well as teaching me when to rest or seek assistance:

> So, it becomes clear that I am still working on the issues . . . it takes a very long time to deal with psychological trauma both in ourselves and in our patients. The risk of relatedness for me was mirrored in the inherent emotional difficulties in facing unbearable affect – mine and his- and in the resistance towards my patient. . . . We go slow, we use a lot of rope and good ties on our way in, and we rest a lot.
>
> (Jaenicke, 2008, p. 102)

In the course of my work, I have often written poems about my experiences with clients, and I conclude this section using one such poem as an auto-ethnographic text. This poem speaks of my experience of first working with my lived experience so as to be able to become a container for my client's material. I use the image of a singing bowl, which is a bowl traditionally composed of seven metals, including gold and silver. The singing bowl originated in ancient Buddhist meditation practices. It can be hit with a (usually wooden) beater to create a resonant bell-like sound, or, alternatively, the beater may be gently pressed against the side and moved slowly and gently around the bowl in a continuous motion. This creates a resonant and contemplative tone around which a client may improvise. I liken myself to the singing bowl in the poem, thinking of the resonances of my lived experience and my capacity now to hold my clients. It is the significance and results of holding which I shall describe in the next three chapters on my case-study material of 'Jack'.

Singing bowl
Hollowed and hammered
To be hallowed.
The wounds which
Made me, structured me
Now burnished bronze
Each layer a resonance of things past
Dark brown melding
Blue copper healing
Now held safe and secure
This bowl becomes container,
Container now contained.
Here is space for your darkness
Your pain
Your life
And we resonate together
In this alchemy, where both are transformed.

References

Alanne, S. (2010). *Music psychotherapy with refugee survivors of torture: Interpretations of three clinical case studies.* Picaset Oy.

Bjorklund, S. (2014). How Betty and Vincent became Sally and Scott. In S. Kuchuck (Ed.), *Clinical implications of the psychoanalyst's life experience: When the personal becomes professional* (pp. 3–17). Routledge.

Charles, M. (Ed.). (2018). *Introduction to contemporary psychoanalysis: Defining terms and building bridges.* Routledge.

Daly, A. (2016). *Merleau-Ponty and the ethics of intersubjectivity.* Palgrave Macmillan.

De Backer, J., & Sutton, J. (2014). *The music in music therapy: Psychodynamic music therapy in Europe – Clinical, theoretical and research approaches.* Jessica Kingsley.

Driver, C. (Ed.). (2013). *Being and relating in psychotherapy: Ontology and therapeutic practice.* Palgrave Macmillan.

Eberhart, H., & Atkins, S. (2014). *Presence and process in expressive arts work: At the edge of wonder.* Jessica Kingsley.

Elfred, M. (2013). The healing relationship. In C. Driver (Ed.), *Being and relating in psychotherapy: Ontology and therapeutic practice* (pp. 9–22). Palgrave Macmillan.

Ellis, C., & Bochner, A. P. (Eds.). (1996). *Composing ethnography: Alternative forms of qualitative writing.* AltaMira Press.

Erskine, R. (2015). *Relational patterns, therapeutic presence: Concepts and practice of integrative psychotherapy.* Karnac.

Glassman, N., & Botticelli, S. (2014). Perspectives on gay fatherhood: Emotional legacies and clinical reverberations. In S. Kuchuck (Ed.), *Clinical implications of the psychoanalyst's life experience: When the personal becomes professional* (pp. 162–179). Routledge.

Gravestock, J. (2021). *Music therapy in adoption and trauma: Therapy that makes a difference after placement.* Jessica Kingsley.

Guggenbühl-Craig, A. (1971). *Power in the helping professions*. Spring Publications.
Guntrip, H. (1985). *Psychoanalytic theory, therapy and the self: A basic guide to the human personality in Freud, Erikson, Klein, Sullivan, Fairbairn, Hartmann, Jacobson and Winnicott*. Karnac.
Heidegger, M. (2000). *Discourse on thinking* (J. M. Anderson & E. Hans Freund, Trans.). Harper & Row. (Original work published 1927.)
Husserl, E. (1999). *The essential Husserl: Basic writings in transcendental phenomenology* (D. Welton, Ed.). Indiana University Press. (Original work published 1900–38.)
Jaenicke, C. (2008). *The risk of relatedness: Intersubjectivity theory in clinical practice*. Jason Aronson.
Jaenicke, C. (2015). *The search for a relational home: An intersubjective view of therapeutic action*. Routledge.
Janesick, V. J. (2000) The choreography of qualitative research design: Minuets, improvisation and crystallization. In N. K. Denzin & Y. S. Lincoln (Eds.), *The handbook of qualitative research* (2nd edn). Sage.
Jung, C. G. (1963). *Memories, dreams, reflections*. Fontana.
Kuchuck, S. (Ed.). *Clinical implications of the psychoanalyst's life experience: When the personal becomes professional*. Routledge.
Lawes, M. (2012–2013). Meaning, dreaming, relating and levels of consciousness in music psychotherapy: A psychoanalytic, developmental and transpersonal paradigm. *Journal of Music and Meaning*, *11*, 85–132.
Lawes, M. (2016). Perspectives on the real, the imaginary and the music in GIM. *Journal of the Association for Music and Imagery*, *15*, 93–124.
Lawes, M. (2017). Music as dynamic experience of unfolding wholeness in guided imagery and music (GIM): A psychoanalytic, musical, transpersonal and trans-scientific paradigm. *Approaches: An Interdisciplinary Journal of Music Therapy*, *9*(2), 275–299.
Lyons-Ruth, K. (1998). Implicit relational knowing: Its role in development and psychoanalytic treatment. *Infant Mental Health Journal*, *19*(3), 282–289.
Malone, J. C. (2018). Relational psychoanalysis: Not a theory but a framework. In M. Charles (Ed.), *Introduction to contemporary psychoanalysis: Defining terms and building bridges* (pp. 208–227). Routledge.
Marks-Tarlow, T. (2008) *Psyche's veil: Psychotherapy, fractals and complexity*. Routledge.
Marks-Tarlow, T. (2012). *Clinical intuition in psychotherapy: The neurobiology of embodied response*. Norton.
Meltzoff, A. N., & Decety, J. (2003). What imitation tells us about social cognition: A rapprochement between developmental psychology and cognitive neuroscience. *Philosophical Transactions of the Royal Society B: Biological Sciences*, *358*(1431), 491–500.
Merleau-Ponty, M. (1968). *The visible and the invisible* (A. Lingis, Trans.). Northwestern University Press. (Original work published 1964.)
Norcross, J. C. (2011). *Psychotherapy relationships that work: Evidence-based responsiveness*. Oxford University Press.
Ringstrom, P. (2014). Becoming an analyst: A play in three acts. In S. Kuchuck (Ed.), *Clinical implications of the psychoanalyst's life experience: When the personal becomes professional*. Routledge.
Rippere, V., & Williams, R. (Eds.) (1985). *Wounded healers: Mental health workers' experiences of depression*. Wiley-Blackwell.

Romanyshyn, R. (2013). *The wounded researcher: Research with soul in mind.* Spring Journal Books.

Scott-Hoy, K. (2002). The visitor: Juggling life in the grip of the text. In A. P. Bochner & C. Ellis (Eds.), *Ethnographically speaking: Autoethnography, literature and aesthetics.* AltaMira Press.

Sedgwick, D. (1994). *The wounded healer: Countertransference from a Jungian perspective.* Routledge.

Slochower, J. (2014). *Holding and psychoanalysis: A relational perspective* (2nd ed.). Routledge.

Stern, D. N. (2004). *The present moment in psychotherapy and everyday life.* Norton.

Stern, D. N. (2005). Intersubjectivity. In E. S. Person, A. M. Cooper, & G. O. Gabbard (Eds.), *The American psychiatric publishing textbook of psychoanalysis* (pp. 77–92). American Psychiatric Publishing.

Trondalen, G. (2016). *Relational music therapy: An intersubjective perspective.* Barcelona.

Tronick, E. Z. (1998). Dyadically expanded states of consciousness and the process of therapeutic change. *Infant Mental Health Journal, 19*(3), 290–299.

Wilberg, P. (2002). *Being and listening: Counselling, psychoanalysis, and the ontology of listening.* New Yoga Publications.

Winnicott, D. W. (1969). The use of an object. *International Journal of Psychoanalysis, 50*, 711–716.

Winnicott, D. W. (1971). *Playing and reality.* Tavistock.

Chapter 5

Psychoanalytic music therapy

Chapters 5, 6 and 7 are in the large part a narrative of sessions with 'Jack'. The detail provided of session content is intended to enable other music therapists (and other non-therapy professionals such as adoption social workers) to look extremely closely at what is 'going on' in psychoanalytic music therapy with an adoption-trauma-specific focus. These chapters elaborate adoption themes arising during music therapy with Jack.

Jack was a new case that was referred to me after my Ph.D. ethics approval. Therefore, the child and his family were asked at the point of referral if they would agree to participate in research, as well as coming to music therapy. Jack had only been seen in the context of being a research-client and had no prior experience of music therapy where I was only his therapist and not also researcher of the work.

Adoption themes were recurring thematic material that I previously observed arising within my music-therapy practice with adoptees. It became apparent that material in sessions with Jack had similarities with those of other adoptees I had worked with. Therefore, at the end of our work together, I examined both the video footage (full video recordings of every session) and my process and reflexive notes (written in the immediate aftermath of each session) for instances of the music therapy containing elements that might suggest a particular theme. By conducting a modified thematic analysis (explained in detail in the methodology of my Ph.D.), I identified eight themes in total. All eight had also arisen in earlier therapeutic work with other adoptee clients so I classified them all as adoption themes. Here, though, I will focus upon four themes that appeared most frequently, according to the thematic analysis. By narrowing my focus to four themes, I can analyse each in depth.

My hypothesis for my thesis was that something of particular significance for adoptees might occur within music-therapy sessions that were needs-led and collaborative. Such an approach could provide an adoptee with space in which they might experience empathic, unconscious, emotional resonances with their music therapist. In addition, shared musical and relational experiences could capitalise on the strengths of intersubjective dynamics which were

DOI: 10.4324/9781003733393-5

experienced in the music therapy rather than the music therapist attempting to fix or cure identified difficulties thought to reside with the client. Music therapy therefore could emphasise resonant, shared, communicative musical exchanges (or what I term micro-moments of attunement) which might have significance for an adopted child's relationships beyond the music-therapy room.

I conducted in total 23 sessions of music therapy with Jack which were all video-recorded. Sessions were each planned to last for 45 minutes and were held on the same morning at the same time at the special-needs nursery that Jack attended. Initially, Jack was accompanied by a teaching assistant and later for some sessions by his adoptive mother. He attended later sessions unaccompanied. All sessions were totally comprised of free musical improvisations arising between Jack and myself and were client-led. This meant that I did not set any specific musical agenda but instead offered a space wherein I hoped Jack might be able to reveal himself in his music-making. I hoped that aspects of his internal world constructions might be revealed within both the music and our relationship and that meaning could be made from what was presenting. Making sense of the internal world of an adopted child such as Jack is essential to gaining insights into their early experience. Modifying the impacts of early traumatic experience upon an adoptee's internal world is the only possible aim of this music therapy approach.

These case-study chapters then provide an in-depth description and analysis of micro-moments from sessions. Such micro-moments may have a feeling tone of attunement about them as they occur in the music and relationship. In these chapters, I make sense of the micro-processes occurring in a music therapy relationship; by drawing on experiences shared between Jack and myself in the music-therapy room and thinking about what such experiences might mean within and beyond the therapy room. There is enormous value in single case-study research, offering an opportunity to dive deeply into musical therapeutic processes.

Introduction to the case study Jack

Jack was referred to music therapy with me when he was three years old. His history, received via his adoption social worker, informed me that Jack had been adopted at a few months old by a family who had fostered him for some months before taking steps to secure a permanent place for him in their family through adoption. Although Jack's adoption was ostensibly going well, his adoptive mother had reported feeling that Jack was difficult to get close to. She was curious about what impacted on his capacity to attach and relate within his adoptive family.

Prior to coming into the care of the local authority, Jack had lived briefly with the family he was born into. There were reports of apparent neglect of Jack's care; however, it was unclear whether this had been wilful neglect or whether Jack's parents had similar learning difficulties to him, leaving them unable to care for him adequately. Jack has a rare genetic disorder which is caused by a chromosomal fault (not unlike a condition such as Down Syndrome) which results in a specific learning disability. It seemed likely that one of his parents would also have had this disorder.

Jack's adoptive family consisted of his mum and dad and three older sisters (the birth children of his adopters). His elder brother from his family of birth (therefore a full sibling) was also adopted into this family. Both boys were described as having significant learning difficulties, but paediatricians felt that the full extent of these would only become apparent as each child developed, so complete diagnoses were still to be confirmed. Jack's brother, aged five, had an autism diagnosis, but not the rare genetic disorder Jack had. Their adoptive parents were regularly in touch with a national association for people who shared Jack's genetic chromosome fault and were informed that only six other people worldwide had a similar condition. In the past, it is likely that people such as Jack would have simply been described as 'mentally handicapped' or as having 'unspecified global developmental delay', but, with progress in genetics, it has become possible to identify and name specific gene faults.

Jack's loss of his birth mother (as well as his father and other siblings), occurring via adoption, happened in the pre-reflexive part of his life when, developmentally, even without his learning disability, he would not be expected to possess language skills. Thus, his processing of his losses in music therapy needed to take place in a manner and at a level that might enable access to his preverbal unconscious experience. This was additionally important given that at the age of three Jack still did not developmentally meet milestones for speech, which was thought to be significantly affected by his learning disabilities. The referring social worker and myself felt that music therapy might be a modality for accessing Jack's early experiences, utilising both music and play rather than verbal or cognitive means. Lacking cognitive capacity for verbal reflection, Jack's psychological and emotional development could hopefully still be facilitated, despite his learning difficulties, within a playful musical modality. Additionally, in a busy family of five children, it was felt that Jack might not have as much individual attention as he needed and music therapy might provide a space that was his alone, where he could relate closely on a one-to-one basis with an understanding adult.

The idea shared by the referrer and me, that music therapy might provide a playful musical modality for Jack to express himself, certainly fit with Winnicott's (1963) thinking that play itself facilitates children's development. I hoped that by creating and evolving a playful musical relationship between us, Jack would be offered possibilities of exploring ways of relating to his early experience of loss that necessitated his adoption. Additionally, I hoped that his musical relationship with me might give me some sense of how his internal world functioned and impacted upon his here-and-now relationships.

Historically, within verbal psychoanalysis, the process of uncovering a client's unconscious inner world and sharing the sense that was made of it with the client may have been termed 'making interpretations'. Given Jack's age and learning disabilities, I would not offer him verbal interpretations of the material arising. Neither would I share such with Jack's referring social worker because although she was very aware of attachment theory she had little understanding of psychoanalytic thinking. The work of Spillius (1988), however, describes a modern form of 'sense-making' arising within the transference and countertransference, wherein the therapist might be concerned with communicating understanding to the client and others in a way that is receivable. Music therapy provided such a space in which Jack and I could experience transference and countertransference musically and playfully but so that our musical, relational experiences did not need to be turned back into words in order to be made sense of. Instead, our sense-making of what was happening could be known within our interactions, even as they were experienced within the musical play. And this could be easily discussed with both his social worker and family.

For music therapists, this sense-making process is seemingly simplified, as evidenced in this description by Wilson (2018, p. 142): 'Music . . . communicates something of the client's internal experience. The therapist's role is to enable, receive and digest these communications, and to help the client find and explore their meaning . . . through musical, verbal and thinking processes and interventions.'

Rather than making verbal interpretations, then, the music therapist enables musical play together with the client, which can allow possible meanings to emerge gradually and tentatively. Jack and I were going to be apparently simply engaged in playing improvised music together; however, within our play, relational patterns might be recognised and modulated as Jack was offered opportunities to experiment playfully with different ways of relating. For adopted children, playful relational experimentation can facilitate some reparation of relationships which have been negatively impacted by attachment styles (Gravestock, 2018). Adopted children, if given space by their adopters to move beyond descriptors of their problems, can take playful new ways of relating into family life.

Therefore, I treated all of Jack's communications in music therapy as important and significant and likely carrying potential meaning. Simpson and Miller (2004, p. 58) describe the process I advocate wherein: 'it was important to attribute intentionality whereas yet there was none, and to lend meaning to sounds which may as yet have contained no meaning . . . it seemed important to have an experience of a maternal figure who could have faith and hope.'

In music therapy with Jack, all of his sound-making was viewed as intentional and meaningful. As he engaged in a musical relationship with me, I could become for him a maternal figure who believed in the validity of his musical communications emergent in our co-created music.

Adoption theme 1: On feeling dropped and dropping things

I hypothesised that Jack had likely absorbed very primitive sensations of 'holding' from his mother prior to being removed from her care. Some of his most early experience had then been 'good enough' (in Winnicott's 1953 terms). I argue that this most early experience had probably given him an enduring capacity to be able to relate. Later sensations of an absence of maternal holding might have partially contributed to what social workers described as neglect. Once separated from his mother and others, Jack likely experienced overwhelming feelings of abandonment, which he did not yet possess mental resources to process and assimilate. Klein (1935) has described such abandonment as being related to the early infant experience of the breast; when the breast is removed, abandonment is felt. As a baby, Jack's lack of language meant he could not access linguistic descriptors of his experience, and, therefore, he experienced it as a felt bodily sensation of absence. Verrier (1993) describes this felt abandonment as an emotional wounding underlying all adoption. Developments in neuroscience have since evidenced that traumatised children carry within them an internalised embodied knowledge of early abandonment, which is stored in the amygdala (Schore et al., 1997). Adoptees who do not experience an early felt sense of holding are not enabled to integrate and manage their early mental states.

Winnicott's (1960) concept of 'holding', which is what I am referring to in the above paragraph, describes an incredibly subtle process occurring between mother and infant. He views holding as a maternal function that originates not just in the mother's physical holding of her baby but also includes her capacity to stay emotionally with the baby's raw feeling experiences. To feel psychologically held then, babies need to have their care carefully regulated by the mother, which happens literally through her physical care but also through her mental communications (Wright, 2009). If a mother cannot adapt to her baby (or, in the case of adoption, the baby loses the possibility of his mother being able to do so), then, as Winnicott (1965) says, the baby's capacity for creative action will be diminished or impaired. I imagined that Jack's early lived experiences were likely to have had this impact upon him.

For Winnicott (1960), repeated reliable experiences of a loving, mutually holding mirror gaze between mother and infant are the remedy against such negative patterns arising in a baby's internal world. He described how such gaze prevents hopelessness (or, in his terms, primal agony) from arising. The mother's face is likened to an emotional 'mirror' which the baby looks into. As the baby sees the mother's responses to him through her facial expression, he begins to experience his own feeling world. Thus, his sense of self develops as he receives a mirrored response from his mother. Such experiences had been lost to Jack with his birth mother, both during the time he was described as being neglected and later when he experienced being permanently separated from her.

Winnicott (1971, p. 103) uses the term 'falling forever' to describe how it feels to lose previously experienced maternal holding and mirroring: 'The infant may then experience libidinal mutual gazing as maternal holding and sudden aggressive looking away as being suddenly dropped, bringing about the primal agony of falling forever'. This is a relational happening, occurring in the space between mother and child. I argue then that Jack's feeling of being dropped from his birth mother's holding and 'falling forever' could be met in the 'potential spaces' of a relationship in music therapy, as I now illustrate from our first music therapy session.

Session 1: Music Therapy Example 1

Jack embarked upon a process of choosing a beater/drumstick to play a drum. He rejected and dropped many beaters, which he then refused to allow me to pick up. They had to lie there on the floor as we began playing music, reminding me visually of the 'dropping' Jack had known, now seemingly evident before my eyes in the dropped beaters. As I allowed myself to feel what Jack might have experienced in the past in this felt way in his body, I was simultaneously here-and-now able to offer a new feeling of being held in the music. I played soft, slow, sustained piano chords while allowing Jack freedom to continue to explore.

This dropping of the beaters was a significant event occurring right at the start of our music-therapy relationship. I interpreted it in my own mind as communicating Jack's internal world expectation, based on his unconscious early experience, that he might be rejected and dropped by me. He was the one, therefore, doing the dropping first, and his dropping of beaters simultaneously communicated to me the felt sense of his experience. Could he actually risk entering this relationship with a music therapist? My mental interpretations certainly reflected how his adoptive mother reported feeling as she had trouble in getting close to Jack, who she described as dropping all her love. Within music, however, a holding could be provided which Jack experienced as less invasive and therefore was able to tolerate.

Of course, this is but one interpretation of Jack's actions, and it was not possible to verbally clarify with him if he felt this interpretation was meaningful for him. However, an interpretation has value if it shifts something in the therapeutic process. I had noted Jack's affect of feeling dropped and corresponded in my countertransference feeling with a sense of not being able to hold him adequately. As Wilson (2018) suggests, it was I who needed to digest Jack's communications and work towards their meaning(s). Part of this digestion process can happen within supervision wherein the client's engagement in musical relating with me is observed and listened to by my supervisor. After I share a video of sessions in my clinical supervision alongside my own impressions from my notes, my supervisor and I enter a shared meaning-making process drawing upon the client's material, my responses and described experiences of transference and countertransference.

In my first supervision about Jack, I shared my interpretation that he feared repeated 'dropping' both in the developing relationship with me as his therapist but also with his adoptive family. On viewing moments of video from these first moments of my relating with Jack, my supervisor felt it showed very tentative relating on the part of both therapist and client. Jack was preparing to be dropped, and, in countertransference, I became afraid of dropping him. As such, it felt to her replicative of the earliest relational patterns of life between a mother and infant. Jack's expectation was of not being met in a mirrored gaze, and, in countertransference, I became fearful of not being able to provide what he needed. However, by acknowledging these states, I became able to provide musical holding, which was a safe way for Jack to know he was not now being dropped.

I was reminded about Jack's experiences of neglect and of being removed from a mother who herself likely had learning difficulties. I realised while discussing Jack's 'dropping' experience that at the moments of sensing this in the session I experienced feelings of not being 'enough' somehow for him, and the piano music that I played felt lacking somehow. I had not initially shared this feeling with my supervisor as I felt some shame, initially locating this feeling in my inadequacy as a music therapist. Supervision helped me to consider that what I perceived as arising in my own emotional landscape could be countertransference replicating feelings Jack's birth mother may herself have known.

A psychoanalytic music-therapy approach values the musical relationship between music therapist and client because of the way it might replicate the rhythms, forms and affective qualities of early mother–infant communication. Trevarthen (1999) describes musical elements such as pulse, pitch and so on that precede verbal communication in relationships between mothers and their infants. This early communication demonstrates a human capacity for what was later termed by Malloch 'communicative musicality' (in Trevarthen & Malloch, 2009) or like what Stern (1995) has also observed but which he terms 'proto-conversation'. Trevarthen, Malloch and Stern are all describing how there is at the core of relationship before language is established a musicality of proto-conversation that expresses the infant's and parent's desire to attune to one another. Similarly, in a first session of music therapy, nothing is predicted or known, and, especially in Jack's case, nothing was being brought into conscious verbal language. We were tentatively moving along together, discovering a form of proto-conversation in musical elements and finding a way to relate through communicative musicality. As music therapist, I stayed with Jack's emotional world and let him safely revisit early experience for himself while also revealing to me what being dropped had felt like.

The music that was being played in the room at the time was vital for Jack. At one level, it provided a consistent holding, with regular pacing and gentle rocking rhythm. This music could be present to his experience, a witness to it in a sense, but a witness that also participated in the safely enacted repetition of experience. On another level, the music was something that Jack was contributing to. Although he was not actually playing an instrument, his dropping of the beaters made a percussive sound, held in the overarching piano chords. Later, as Jack did begin to play a drum, he already could know that his sounds, and therefore also himself, were being musically held and thought about. While I played on the piano, Jack could act out his internal world states. We were both creating music which became a thing existent in the space between us.

Ogden (1994, p. 61) writes about the analytic third that can occur in verbal psychotherapy in the space between client and therapist. He describes how the client and the therapist each have their own separate internal worlds (by implication the 'first' and the 'second'), but that there is also a third unconscious shared world, which is an area of subjective relating that comes into being both as it is created by the therapist's and client's separate subjectivities and yet also existent between their two subjectivities. The analytic third then is an area of unconscious intersubjectivity, which is constantly being made and remade by the continuously changing interactions occurring between client and music therapist. Interplay occurs between all three partners, client, therapist and analytic third (in this case, the music), which now has its own existence. In addition, the analytic third becomes able to create the therapy dyads' subjective experience of themselves as well as being a space wherein relational intersubjectivities interact.

I suggest then that the music in Session 1, co-created between myself and Jack, served the function of the analytic third. Music exists in transient temporal form and could itself become an attentional, acoustic 'thing' between the subjective and intersubjective experiences of Jack and me. Music was also simultaneously doing something very Winnicottian for Jack by opening up a less threatening space for relational play because music had capacity to provide him with holding for whatever emerged in the playing and intersubjective relating. The music therapist Martin Lawes suggests a link between Winnicott's and Ogden's thinking:

> Winnicott (1971) proposes psychotherapy to take place in the overlap of two areas of play, those of client and therapist. Ogden brings out the unconscious subjective and intersubjective dimensions of the process, where Winnicott's concern is more with playing as this takes place in a shared space between subjective and objective reality.
>
> (Lawes, 2019, p. 12)

Lawes (2012–13, p. 12) argues that this is an important insight for music therapists, especially as music can 'sound the unconscious creative interplay of all three areas of intersubjectivity'. The music that is being played is being 'sounded' (to use Lawes' term) by both therapist and client and subsequently exists as a third thing that we call 'the music'. At the same time, the music impacts upon both client and therapist who play it. Thus, 'subjectivity is sounded musically and constellated between subjective and objective reality' (Lawes, 2012–13, p. 12). Similarly, the music therapist Sami Alanne (2010, p. 198) writes:

> Music provides possibilities for individual experiences and knowing to reconstitute and reconstruct themselves in the material . . . when music is considered in relation to time and being, it may bring experiences and meanings for an individual that arise from the past, present and future.

The music therapist Mercedes Pavlicevic (1997) has conceptualised music therapy improvisation as what she terms 'dynamic form'. It seems she is describing music similarly to how Ogden conceives of the third, or Winnicott the transitional space, as she suggests that a mutual form (or area or space) arises which consists not solely of the musical expressions made by client and therapist but which is created together and subsequently begins to live its own life.

It is significant to note that at this time, so early in music therapy, I did not choose to make loud crashing sounds that might have mirrored Jack's dropping of beaters but not held the emotional referent of his felt experience. Instead, I played soft circling repetitive chords, which in effect were an opposite juxtaposition. Music therapists in training are taught how to musically 'match' their clients' music, and we go on practising using this technique as a means of showing the client that we hear them and connect with their music. What I provided here did not, superficially, seem to match Jack's music in the manner we might usually understand it as doing. However, Wigram (2004) has described that in matching our music to our clients we are not aiming to produce music that is identical somehow to theirs but rather we are trying to attune to the emotional referent within the music, to meet its qualities, to know its affect. It is only then, I believe, that we can truly call our co-created music-making intersubjective relating. Lawes (2019, p. 11) suggests that to relate in this way requires the most authentic use of self by the music therapist:

> For the potential of music therapy to be fully realised for the client, this work is never simply about the client's process alone. Rather, music therapy involves the clients and therapists' personal processes becoming intertwined in the music, the therapist needing to be fully involved with this.

This can be problematic when client and therapist share some lived experience, as I partially addressed in Chapter 4. It is essential that the music therapist can know and hold their own experiences as they were 'in parenthesis' while being prepared to musically merge with the client.

Music's similarity to the non-verbal interactions of early life provided an audible shape to Jack's emotional experience. Music therapy allowed for the revelation of unconscious trauma relating to adoption as well as manifesting

Jack's internalised patterns of, and expectations for, relating. This process resonates closely with other adoptees I have worked with (discussed in Gravestock 2018 and 2021). Freely improvising and co-creating music together powerfully affects intra- and interpersonal responses, as music therapy exists as a temporal and affect-laden form, akin to the preverbal communications of mothers and babies (Trevarthen & Malloch, 2009). This first session with Jack had already indicated to me his loss of such early relationship. Working in improvisation viscerally opened up Jack's attachment and relational processes to me as it has similarly in the past with other clients.

Five-year-old Lily (an adopted child with Down Syndrome who had been relinquished as a newborn because of her disability, discussed in detail in my first book) enacted in a similar way. She would pick up instruments in the room and seem to take an interest in them, but at the point she appeared to be about to play, and I was prepared to accompany her, she would throw the instrument away over her shoulder. As this happened week on week, I learned how painfully Lily knew her own felt experience of being 'thrown away' and what it had been like for her to be jettisoned. Like Jack, Lily took a very long time to risk playing with me.

Music-making (and indeed Jack's lack of consciously making any music initially in this first session) within the context of a therapeutic relationship makes attachment patterns audible and visible and therefore has the capacity to regulate and shape emotional communications (Trevarthen, 1979). Holding in a Winnicottian sense can happen within the space that music *and* relationship provide for possibilities of intersubjective relating, which may also be described as the impact of Ogden's analytic third (where co-created music becomes the third, created and shared in the aural space between client and therapist). For the adopted child who has felt dropped, feeling musically held is most important from the outset of music therapy. My piano-playing, while not ostensibly matching Jack's loud, energetic dropping sounds, offered the possibility of some safety in contrasting gentle, calming chords. It was an authentic response from myself, as I experienced feelings of countertransference Jack aroused. Jack could hear that his expressions and his self were being held within this musical relating, which provided a creative modality wherein he could re-experience what had been lost to his conscious memory yet remained known in his unconscious.

In my next example from a session, a very different kind of 'third' was co-created in the intersubjective relating between Jack and myself. This time, my musical responses were much more obviously matched to his music.

Session 10: Music Therapy Example 2

Jack and I had been playing two guitars gently together for some time. Suddenly, Jack picked up the toy microphone, but, instead of singing into it, he used it to hit the guitar, again and again, and then used it to hit the floor very hard and repeatedly, before dropping it. This treatment did not break the microphone, and I felt that in this instance, the survival of both guitar and microphone as objects was important. Jack's emotion was strong and forceful, definite and purposeful, matched in his intent and action, so the instruments needed to be able to contain his expression. I immediately made a musical match with Jack, changing from the soft humming that had accompanied our guitar playing to loud vocalising (wordlessly) while beating a drum. Jack once more went and found the bag of drum beaters, but this time he chose one and joined me playing together on my drum, both of us with intensity and great volume. Then Jack moved to a teaching cupboard in the room (which had been accidentally left unlocked), took out books (which belonged to staff) and started to throw them. As each book was thrown, he laughed and seemed to enjoy something aggressive. He banged the cupboard doors, and I played loudly in big chords, strummed with bodily energy, while vocalising/singing, 'Jack is dropping things very hard today, needing to make big crashes here today.' He gleefully replied with a clear 'Yes!'

This session came some weeks later in our work. By now, Jack had become much more able to play with me in the room and to share in intersubjective relating. Interestingly, he did still at times need to revert to enacting in a very similar way to our first session. Periods of soft, reflective playing together would be interspersed with breakouts of dropping and throwing. Jack was able to be held within both kinds of music, and now I chose to match his expressions, showing him I had some understanding of what he was doing and why he might be doing it. It felt like he was beginning to experience me as an attuned music-mother (Levinge, 2015). The instruments needed to survive their treatment as they began to have a symbolic function for Jack. He needed to be able to express all aspects of himself, including the angry and destructive parts, and the instruments needed to contain his expressions without breaking. A musical object, which can be an instrument but could also be a song or a musical feature, can 'fulfil the function of tying in with precious experiences of the previous music therapy process – it is kept in mind, even if personal relationships are exposed to chaos and destructiveness' (Smetana, 2017, p.115). Musical objects in the room, and Jack's relationship with me, were certainly 'exposed to chaos and destructiveness' but were shown to be capable of containing all that he enacted.

Jack had both known and lost a seriously satisfying object relationship in his early life. Winnicott (1963) describes the stage of capacity for concern (his understanding of what Klein [1935] terms the 'depressive position'), which he links with weaning and also dropping things. To shift developmentally into what is termed the capacity for concern, an infant must have had something good at the beginning to build on. The infant needs to be old enough (around five months) to play at dropping. First experiences of dropping are unconscious and have to do with having something and then losing it. Later, dropping can be a movement towards achieving concern where two aspects of the mother can come together: the object-mother (parts of the mother that the infant thinks he created) and the environment-mother (aspects of the mother that provide the facilitating environment for the infant). This is an important developmental shift and depends on a sense of timing in relating. In Jack's at times chaotic and destructive play; this development could be creatively experienced.

Jack had lost early experiences of what Winnicott (1967) calls mirroring and Stern (1998) calls attunement. He, therefore, struggled to allow his adoptive mother to hold these functions for him now. Human experience and behaviour result from the interaction of current interpersonal relationships alternating with unconscious internal object relationships that have been formed during early development. I hoped that by having new musical experiences in the music therapy room with me, Jack might have different relational experiences which might impact on relational change beyond the music room.

Mirroring, according to Winnicott, is a stage in the development of the mother–infant relationship when the precursor of the mirror is the mother's face. The infant depends upon the mother's facial responses to him, which show his own emotional responses mirrored and which allow him to establish a sense of true self. Stern's attunement describes the processes by which a mother tracks, then reflects to her infant, her sense of having shared in her infant's feeling state. It is 'essentially non-verbal and spontaneous, and relatively outside the mother's awareness' (Wright, 2009, p. 22).

Stern's attunement differs subtly from Winnicott's mirroring as it is 'more continuous and communicative . . . and appears to attend to relational . . . needs' (Wright, 2009, p. 22). The baby's feeling states are called vitality affects by Stern (2010), by which he means a continuous background feeling tone that accompanies the baby's actions. The mother's responses offer a background of resonant feeling activity. Her attuned response is intuitive and ongoing. She does not, however, simply copy or mirror but captures, transposes and gives back a felt sense to the baby of being met and understood. Within different sessions, I felt Jack required different responses from me, some closer to Winnicottian mirroring and others closer to Stern's attunement. As a music-mother, therefore, my role was akin to that of the mother in early life and called on my authenticity in order that I could trust my intuition and subsequent musical response.

My whole approach to work with adopted children in music therapy begins from the hypothesis that the loss of an attuned relationship in early life continues to impact on the adopted child's capacity to risk, trust and relate within their new adoptive families. In Jack's case, I believed he had known a very early felt sense of maternal holding. However, his loss of a birth mum and his permanent separation from her was an early traumatic experience that remained powerful in its ongoing ability to affect current relating. This was evident in our eleventh session:

Session 11: Music Therapy Example 3

During this session, Jack delighted in throwing any instrument he could get his hands on. He engaged in a process of finding an instrument, picking it up, looking at it briefly, considering its musical usage then throwing it to the floor. This process was repeated for almost the entire session. He never played a note of music. I found the experience of watching and listening quite overwhelming, understanding it as Jack communicating over and over how dropped he had felt. I listened in a deeply embodied way, bearing witness to his experience. By this, I mean my whole self was taken up in the listening; I moved when he moved, I used my hearing with intent so as to hear on many levels, I observed Jack's physicality with my eyes and often used my body to show I was with him (perhaps offering a loud exclamation vocally or raising my eyebrows or throwing wide my arms). Jack's nameless feelings of being dropped and falling forever, which had not been attuned to in his early life, were now acted out with destructive intent in the room, which additionally served to cut him off from being able to really play in relationship with me. Later, I did play crashing glissandos and sang the word 'CRASH' and then played gently sustaining soft chords as if I were saying to him, 'Yes, I hear, I understand, and I'm holding you.' My feeling tone, expressed in the temporality of music, could hold not only Jack's behaviour as it was enacted in real time but also his early memories from the past time.

Early attunement experiences were lost to Jack when his fundamental first relationships were denied. We cannot be certain he experienced attuned mothering from his birth mother, but, if he had, then he lost what little he had known. Stern (2004) describes the embodied relational matrix in which humans remain embedded. Jack could not escape his embodied memories and needed them to be met in the body of another (Sletvold, 2014). Felt abandonment experience impacts negatively on the core of rhythmic and sympathetic impulses, which develop brain connectivity, self-regulation and attachment capacity (Schore, 2001). Jack's losses occurred at an age when he lacked resources or language for processing and assimilating his experience. Now, as a young child, his disabilities meant he was unlikely to ever fully possess language. Therefore, the creative endeavour of music therapy was best placed to work with him. As Jack's music therapist, I could attune to his feeling states and also play music myself while he threw instruments. My music could both resonate with his feeling states at times but also had the capacity to hold those feelings. My music responses in Session 11 became, in effect, a background resonant response of attunement. Music therapy, therefore, offered Jack (in the words of Sutton [2002, p. 35]) 'an experience of himself as embodied in sound and in silence'. While Jack still had times in our work together when he was unable to play and risk relationship himself, he could also still know himself as mirrored (Winnicott) and attuned to (Stern).

The music therapist Trondalen (2016) has described what she terms 'relational music therapy', which is an endeavour to understand lived experiences that are made evident when they become emergent in jointly improvised music. Her model draws upon Stern's (1995) description of intersubjective moments of meeting, which views change as happening through non-verbal processes at a micro-level. I have termed these micro-moments of attunement. I argue for my own adoption music-therapy practice that micro-moments of attunement are those that manifest in the intersubjective space of non-directed, client-led, free musical improvisations, such as I experienced with Jack. Transference and countertransference feelings experienced within improvisations help me gain a sense of adopted children's internal worlds and their unconscious early lived experience. This enables me (and, ultimately, the child and their adopter) to understand ways in which early experience influences present life and relating. A possible micro-moment of attunement is evident from Session 14.

Session 14: Music Therapy Example 4

Jack became interested in my clock, which I always have present to keep the time boundary of the session. He attempted to throw it but stopped himself, instead dropping it with deliberate intent but gently to the floor while gazing straight at me. This felt so clearly a communication of something! The back came off so I had to mend it at Jack's request. Together, we sat on the floor, looking at the clock and listening to it, our heads almost touching, our bodies in mirrored positions. I slowly evolved an improvised song based on the 'tick-tock' sounds it made, and Jack gradually began to join in singing with me, 'Tick-tock goes Joy's clock.' We sat, literally holding and watching time together and sharing vocalisations. As we reached 'time' (the end of the session), Jack signed (in Makaton) 'finish' to me, and for the first time, he wanted to tidy up my room before leaving. One interpretation might be that this was a way of pushing at the time boundary, but also it could have implied a recognition of the 'messy' feeling states from earlier sessions and possibly some ownership of these. Perhaps the beginnings of capacity for concern?

After this session, I had my second clinical supervision about Jack. My supervisor noted an increased quality of relationship between Jack and myself and a concomitant increase in his confidence within the room. She felt, as I had, that Jack made a definite, deliberate choice to drop the clock, and this playful enactment felt anticipatory of my response. It was communicative (revealed in Jack's eye gaze) and not like he was experiencing unregulated emotion and dropping things with intent to break them. Thinking about the previous, less regulated dropping Jack had consistently engaged in over 14 weeks, my supervisor felt his emotional tone now was shifting to anger, which might need acknowledging more clearly and voicing by me. I was uncertain about telling Jack that I thought he was angry although I concurred that I sensed this too. Supervision clarified some things I had felt about Jack's emotional states but I did not want to name in case this was just my own perception and not a valuable interpretation. I felt I could play now with his anger and witness it while recognising times when Jack needed a gentler holding music also.

This session illustrates how music might enable developmental reparation by providing a sense of holding for Jack's dropped self. Reparation can happen by the seemingly simplest of processes: those of listening, mirroring and becoming an attuned other (Alanne, 2010). Training in and using matching and mirroring techniques can help music therapists engage with clients at a musical level. However, genuine relatedness and empathy, which have the potential to become a musical holding and attunement, are very different to just musically copying what clients play. It was the resonant feeling state that I offered behind the singing with Jack occurring over the shared holding of the clock that became my referent, in imitation, from the inside out, of what his experience felt like. We were now engaged in a musical relationship that involved me attuning in a reciprocal shaping of Jack's emotional and embodied experience (Daniel & Trevarthen, 2017). Relationship was created in, for example, micro-moments of shared gazing, which marked out the increasing relational space between us (similar to Winnicott's 1971 'potential space', which I discuss later). Jack increasingly was becoming able to both tolerate and even desire relationship.

I constantly needed to find music that could both meet and hold Jack's experience. Sletvold (2014) calls this searching for embodied empathy (when working in verbal psychoanalysis), and which I have come to call the search for empathically embodied music contact. Physical playful initiations by Jack (surprisingly similar to those Winnicott describes in his own clinical interactions with infants) needed holding within my/our music to enable Jack to have the possibility of experiencing Stern's felt attunement. It is perhaps obvious to state that music is intrinsically part of a music-therapy setting. However, a music therapist does not play endlessly with the client, nor does the client always need to be playing. At times, I would play the piano while Jack played non-musically with instruments, enjoying them just as objects. Music existed itself as a holding presence that we could experience as separate to either of us, even as we chose (or not) to contribute to it. Music's temporality meant I could provide continual fluidity within a session, moving in an instant from mirrored crashing sounds to soft holding sounds. Playing music in therapy with an adopted child is more than just being present in the room together with them and playing together. Music has the potential to match the ebb and flow of the process of attunement (and indeed necessary mis-attunement), experienced through vitality-affect responses. I illustrate this from the last session I ever had with Jack.

Session 23: Music Therapy Example 5

After a period of very settled relational play, Jack asked for my clock and dropped it again immediately on the floor. The back fell off again, but he was immediately reassured I could mend it. It felt like something had been communicated non-verbally about our time together (which had to end prematurely due to him moving house) through singing about the clock. On a metaphorical level, our sessions, like Jack in early life, had sadly been 'dropped' through circumstances beyond our control. However, despite this replicative experience that potentially could have caused further difficulty for Jack and reinforced his earlier internal world, I felt he now had resources to survive our separation. He had a capacity to symbolise and could recognise that, like the clock, different parts existed inside of himself. He could know parts that had broken and trust that these could be integrated. His feeling state during our last session, however, was directly linked, I believed, to a resurgence of early feelings of abandonment, provoked by ending music therapy.

We returned to the instruments, and I reminded Jack verbally that this would be our last time of meeting. He suddenly seemed overjoyed to see the large djembe drum and quickly ran to find some beaters for it. I asked Jack if I should play anything, and he gave me a small drum and beater. Then he placed a small drum around each of our necks and asked if we could swap drums so we were, in effect, wearing each other's drum. Jack beat his own drum but also played mine while I was wearing it. We played together, and our pulse was steady and shared. He then moved as if to throw the beaters away but resisted this impulse and placed them gently beside the drums on the table.

Turning then to the thunder drum in the instrument box, Jack held it against his body and asked me to pull its string. My movement initiated both the rumbling sound of the drum and also its vibrations, which Jack could feel through his body. It felt as if he was internalising something of me and of our work together. Once this was repeated two or three times, Jack threw the thunder drum but then walked to it and stroked it. This led to a time of dropping and crashing with instruments which I had not experienced with Jack for some weeks. Jack was laughing, but the laugh did not feel authentic, and I asked if he was cross because this was our last session. In reply, Jack began to take instruments from the box and threw everything he could get to. He shook his head when I sang 'cross, cross, cross', but eventually, when I had to prevent him from throwing certain more vulnerable instruments, he admitted he was cross and even demonstrated a cross face.

Finally, Jack took out a turtle puppet which he had used over the weeks to represent himself. We sat on the floor, and Jack placed the puppet on my arm. Together, we regarded the thrown instruments, and I sang again, 'We are looking, looking together, at the things that got thrown.' Jack hummed the rhythm of my song and moved closer in towards me. He wanted me to hit the turtle puppet on my arm, but I declined and sang instead, 'He doesn't want to be hurt; he just wants to be safe.' Jack took the turtle and bit him again (he had done this previously in sessions). Then he took the boomwhackers (long, tuned plastic tube instruments) and began to throw them, laughing sadistically as he did so. Because the boomwhackers are tuned, the act of them being thrown produced not just a rhythmic sound but also a melody. I was able to improvise on the piano, in sustained chords again, in the key that each boomwhacker suggested as it fell to the floor. My subsequent piano music could be viewed as an expression of my mind and evidence to Jack of being held in mind. By making sounds and thereby joining my playing, Jack was able in effect to get into my mind.

Jack threw one boomwhacker into the centre of a large table in the middle of the room and wanted it back but could not reach it so he asked me to get it. I sang a previously co-created hide-and-seek song as I retrieved both the boomwhackers and beaters that had been thrown around the room ('looking, looking, looking everywhere . . . something is hiding, but it's so glad when it's found'). Jack stood on the table and began jumping while gazing straight at me. I sang, 'Jack knows his cross feelings because we finish music today, and that's OK', and he shouted and sang happily, 'Yes, yes, yes!'

This session felt like a premature ending for Jack, and there was much more work that could have been done. Unfortunately, the family was about to move to a new house, which meant that Jack would also move nursery and be placed out of the area for me. I had felt angry when initially hearing of this because I felt our work was incomplete, and I did not want to replicate Jack's early experience of being lost to his birth mother. However, I also realised that this was not the same experience, and I believed Jack had come far enough to internalise something of myself as music therapist and that he would be able to take this into future relating. This is an important part of music therapy within adoption. It is essential that children are enabled to form attachments with a music therapist and to be able to use both the therapist and the instruments as objects in their therapy. It is equally important that music therapy can translate into the child's 'real world' and begin to impact their relating outside of the therapy room. Jack's mother was reporting feeling much closer to him and that he regularly now would come to her for cuddles and for emotional care. She felt he was becoming her own child now whereas before music therapy he had felt unreachable.

Playing the small drums together when we had them around our necks felt shared and intimate. Jack's rhythms were quite literally played out and received in my body as he played the drum that was around my neck and resting on my chest. I could feel his playing resonating. He would first play a rhythm on his own drum and become aware both of what he heard and felt. Then he would play the same pattern on my drum and showed awareness that I would be feeling what he had. This felt to me evidential of him now being able to view me as similar to him yet separate from him. I had gone from being another object to be used in the room and was becoming a person in my own right. We were able to relate intersubjectively. The care he took with the beaters after this episode of shared playing showed real change and a sense that something good had been made musically between us. This experience was replicated in his asking me to play the thunder drum as he held it. Again, I felt a sense of being separate and other to Jack, and that he was beginning to enjoy experiencing being two people, playing in relationship.

The recapitulation of more destructive play as Jack threw all of the instruments at first concerned me. However, it felt as if he was laying out his whole music-therapy experience symbolically by getting out all the instruments. Indeed, we were then able to sit and take in the instruments as we shared gazing at them. I was certainly thinking of all that the instruments had contained about Jack's inner world and feeling states. He, too, was angry and upset at our premature ending and was able to express ambivalent feelings now, first enjoying relationship, then being destructive. He was reluctant to own his upset and cross feelings when I first interpreted them verbally and sang them out. Perhaps it was enough that both he and I knew the feeling referent behind the enactment. When he bit the turtle puppet, I felt he was simultaneously both attacking the physical object of the puppet and myself (as it was physically on my arm), while also again ingesting something of our work by taking the puppet into his own mouth, attempting to eat the object and to ingest something from me. The biting was gentle and playful, not aggressive. There was recognition (and probably some resentment) within this object relationship that Jack was separate from me and could not influence me to continue music therapy. Yet, also, the playful biting assured me that perhaps something had been taken in.

This felt clear again in Jack's final throwing of the boomwhackers. Although this seemed a destructive act reminiscent of the first weeks of music therapy, it became an extremely musical one. It reminded me of how, over the weeks, music had been able to hold Jack's feelings. Now Jack could allow me to play with him whilst the sustained piano chords acted as a soundtrack to his feelings. The boomwhackers dictated my chord choices, and this again became a shared improvisation experience, initiated by Jack and both responded to and held by me within my musical response. Jack's boomwhackers as an instrument of choice were important as I felt they had significance for him as psychological objects. They had resonant bodies and could resonate with their immediate surroundings, providing 'both direct acoustic and tactile-kinaesthetic feedback' (Noske, cited in Smetana, 2017, p. 115).

When Jack asked me to find the boomwhacker he could not reach, I was able to do this using a sung accompaniment. Many adopted children in music therapy with me have played hide and seek (and this will be explored further later), a game which seems to share aspects of Freud's (1920) *Fort! Da!* game. This was a game played by Freud's 18-month-old grandson involving a cotton reel. The infant would repeatedly drop the reel out of his cot whilst shouting 'Ooh'. This action forced his mother to retrieve it for him, and, when she did, he would respond with an 'Ah'. Freud interpreted these exclamations as the infant trying to state '*Fort*' meaning 'gone' and '*Da*' meaning 'there'. Freud believed this enactment gave the infant a sense of having control over an unhappy situation in which he has no control over the mother into a happy one where the mother is at the beck and call of the infant. There are elements of revenge in the game too with the infant diminishing the mother to a subservient role.

Of most significance for our work was the sense of Jack being able to understand that something that disappears can be bought back (unlike his birth mother who was forever lost to him). For example, I previously worked with Sophie, who loved to ask her adoptive mother about being 'found' by her (which felt a lot more special than just being born!). Sophie liked to suggest that it was she who had done the finding, not her adoptive mother. In music therapy, Sophie and I co-created songs about her 'finding' me as her music therapist, as she had 'found' her adoptive mother. Sophie was delighted when I could be easily 'found' in music and laughed, showing me that she felt safe in her play and not frightened. A similar 'Fort! Da!' variation game developed with Kim, who would place herself (standing) behind me while I knelt on the floor playing xylophone to accompany my singing. As I sang, 'Where is Kim?', she enjoyed teasing me before coming into my view, thus allowing herself to be 'found'. I would sing 'You found me!' and she would giggle. Sometimes in play, she would dance and twirl and even launch herself into my lap, confident that I would physically as well as emotionally be present for her and hold her. Again, the co-created sung improvisations included words about Kim 'finding' adoptive mother and mother 'finding' her, as Kim was encouraged to translate this relational experience to other contexts outside of the therapy room.

Fort! Da! has some resonances for me with Winnicott's (1941) spatula game, though Freud and Winnicott come to slightly differing conclusions. Winnicott was working with mother–infant couples at the time and observed an infant picking up a spatula from the table. He reported how the infant would play with the spatula quietly at first and interpreted this as a need to experience a moment of quiet hesitation when he has both space and presence to be in his own inner world with the object. Then he could begin to turn the object into 'something', that is, a representation of an object (an aeroplane for example), animated with great enjoyment. Eventually, the spatula would be dropped, at first maybe accidentally, but then a second game would emerge as the infant had the spatula returned only to drop it again. This dropping would be repeated, and the mother would be obliged to repeatedly return the spatula. Winnicott (1941, p. 246) states that the infant must live through 'the full course of an experience' in the presence of another who is not tempted to interfere but only functions to facilitate this development. I was holding that function as I was becoming that other now for Jack. He was no longer simply dropping objects such as the boomwhackers from a painful unconscious feeling state but was rather turning them into meaningful objects for himself with which he could act with agency and considerable enjoyment.

At the very end of this session then, although Jack had apparently regressed to the dropping enactments of our first session, there was a completely different emotional quality to what was happening. Earlier on in music therapy, Jack had appeared to lack any real volition in his dropping. It felt as though instruments almost slipped through his fingers. Now, in this deliberate throwing, there was so much more determined intent. I experienced Jack as somehow more solid within himself and able to demonstrate agency. The earlier dropping had felt as if it came from an unconscious place that was too painful to be present with. Only by having had that emotional experience witnessed and responded to was Jack now able to relate to it differently. Throwing boomwhackers was a conscious action, and Jack was deliberately, playfully looking towards me to engage with him. I would smile and playfully sigh, saying, 'Oh no, boomwhackers got thrown again', and he would laugh. Like Winnicott's infant with the spatula, he was able to repeatedly throw the boomwhackers, confident in knowing I would repeatedly retrieve them.

The anger that Jack was able to express at the end of our work felt extremely healthy too. He was not now a baby without any understanding of his situation, who lacked the means to make sense of what was happening to him. Although at first he was reluctant to own feelings that were the emotional referent behind the throwing, right at the end, he took genuine delight in owning his feelings. His final repeated 'Yes, yes, yes!' was joyous, and I felt that here was a young child who had more command of an emotional repertoire and was safe to use it. A false self did not have to be drawn upon always, and certainly within the music therapy, a true self had become available, a self that was safely expressing what Jack felt now about our relationship wherein he would be received.

This aspect from my case study, explored under the adoption theme of 'dropping', indicates that a music-therapy relationship can offer a frame and setting in the form of a place and relationship where new relational possibilities can be played with. In addition, the music and the instruments themselves can hold expressions of the adopted child's lived experiences occurring through the process of being adopted. What happens inside the music-therapy room brings about new possibilities that would not be the same outside of this space and place. Music therapy becomes a space for navigating growth. Music within the therapeutic relationship can enable intersubjective relating, and, if the idea of Ogden's analytic third is applied to co-created improvised music, it can provide safety for exploration, contact, regulation and symbolisation. Music exists in a temporal form in the intersubjective space between client and therapist. Jack's dropping shows music therapy to be durable, with the capacity to survive. Finally, in the words of Nirensztein (2003, p. 228), 'The non-verbal character of the music, the complexity of its components . . . its unavoidable physical counterpart, its capacity to address itself to various senses, makes it an ideal medium for re-creating conditions comparable to the constitutive experience of the self.' Additionally, music and significant musical objects supported Jack in developing a sense of being separate from another and being able to effectively use his relationship with me as 'music-mother'. Subsequently, I hoped he could translate new relational styles into his adoptive family.

References

Alanne, S. (2010). *Music psychotherapy with refugee survivors of torture: Interpretations of three clinical case studies.* Picaset Oy.

Gravestock, J. (2018). Attachment-based, relational, psychoanalytic music therapy: The significance of musical moments of attunement with adoptees after trauma, and how this may influence broader reparation with attachments. *Attachment: New Directions in Psychotherapy and Relational Psychoanalysis, 12*, 147–159.

Gravestock, J. (2021). *Music therapy in adoption and trauma: Therapy that makes a difference after placement.* Jessica Kingsley.

Klein, M. (1935). A contribution to the psychogenesis of manic-depressive states. *International Journal of Psychoanalysis, 16*, 145–174.

Lawes, M. (2012–13). Meaning, dreaming, relating and levels of consciousness in music psychotherapy: A psychoanalytic, developmental and transpersonal paradigm. *Journal of Music and Meaning, 11*, 85–132.

Lawes, M. (2020). On improvisation as dreaming and the therapist's authentic use of self in music therapy. *British Journal of Music Therapy, 34*(1), 6–18.

Levinge, A. (2015). *The music of being: Music therapy, Winnicott, and the school of object relations.* Jessica Kingsley.

Nirensztein, S. (2003). The knight inside the armour: Music therapy with a deprived teenager. In S. Hadley (Ed.), *Psychodynamic music therapy: Case studies* (pp. 225–240). Barcelona.

Ogden, T. H. (1994). *Subjects of analysis.* Karnac.

Pavlicevic, M. (1997). *Music therapy in context: Music, meaning and relationship.* Jessica Kingsley.

Schore, A. N. (1997). *Affect regulation and the origin of the self.* Lawrence Erlbaum.

Schore, A. N. (2001) Neurobiology, developmental psychology and psychoanalysis: Convergent findings on the subject of projective identification. In J. Edwards (Ed.), *Being alive.* Routledge.

Simpson, D., & Miller, L. (2004). *Unexpected gains: Psychotherapy with people with learning disabilities.* Karnac.

Sletvold, J. (2014). *The embodied analyst: From Freud and Reich to relationality.* Routledge.

Smetana, M. (2017). Recurring similarity: The meaning of musical objects in music therapy for adolescents with structural disorders. *Nordic Journal of Music Therapy, 26*(2), 105–123.

Spillius, E. B. (Ed.). (1988). *Melanie Klein today: Developments in theory and practice* (vol. I: Mainly theory). Routledge.

Stern, D. N. (1995). *The motherhood constellation: A unified view of parent–infant psychotherapy.* Karnac.

Stern, D. N. (1998). *The interpersonal world of the infant.* Karnac.
Stern, D. N. (2004). *The present moment in psychotherapy and everyday life.* Norton.
Stern, D. N. (2010) *Forms of vitality: Exploring dynamic experience in psychology, the arts, psychotherapy, and development.* Oxford University Press.
Sutton, J. (2002). *Music, music therapy, and trauma: International perspectives.* Jessica Kingsley.
Trevarthen, C. (1979). Communication and co-operation in early infancy: A description of primary intersubjectivity. In M. Bullowa (Ed.), *Before speech: The beginning of human communication* (pp. 530–571). Cambridge University Press.
Trevarthen, C. (1999). Musicality and the intrinsic motive pulse: Evidence from human psychobiology and infant communication. *Musicae Scientiae*, 155–215.
Trevarthen, C., & Malloch, S. (2009). *Communicative musicality: Exploring the basis of human companionship.* Oxford University Press.
Trondalen, G. (2016). *Relational music therapy: An intersubjective perspective.* Barcelona.
Verrier, N. (1993). *The primal wound.* Gateway Press.
Wigram, T. (2004). *Improvisation: Methods and techniques for music therapy clinicians, educators and students.* Jessica Kingsley.
Wilson, S. (2018). *Music–psychoanalysis–musicology.* Routledge.
Winnicott, D. W. (1941). The observation of infants in a set situation. *International Journal of Psychoanalysis, 22*(2), 229–249.
Winnicott, D. W. (1953). Transitional objects and transitional phenomena: A study of the first not-me possession. *International Journal of Psychoanalysis, 34*, 89–97.
Winnicott, D. W. (1960). The theory of the parent–infant relationship. *International Journal of Psychoanalysis, 34*, 89–97.
Winnicott, D. W. (1963). The development of the capacity for concern. In *The maturational processes and the facilitating environment: Studies in the theory of emotional development.* Hogarth Press.
Winnicott, D. W. (1965). *The maturational processes and the facilitating environment.* Hogarth Press.
Winnicott, D. W. (1971). *Playing and reality.* Tavistock.
Wright, K. (2009). *Mirroring and attunement: Self-realisation in psychoanalysis and art.* Routledge.

Chapter 6

Lullabies and their meaning for adoptees

In Chapter 5, I described how I formed some understanding of Jack's internal sense of being dropped through our musical enactments. Such enactments became, in effect, Jack's language. Understandings came not just through the sound world we created together but also through the language of movements that gave form to Jack's emotional expressions. It is impossible to play a musical instrument without using the body, and, therefore, it is important that my approach considered theories of embodiment. Internal feeling states can be expressed through the body in musical play. Consequently, it was possible for Jack to reveal and share what Stern (1985) terms 'vitality affects' in the musical, physical, playful space of our intersubjective relating. In essence, vitality affects are feelings expressed with dynamic and stimulating movements which are either unconscious or conscious. Music therapy with adoptees can enable an understanding of the prelinguistic nature of emotional experience and expression by accessing the unconscious internal world, revealed not only in the music itself but also by how that music is played from the body. By the music therapist offering experiences of holding and attunement, the negative enduring impacts of early experience for a child now placed within an adoptive family might be modified. New musical embodied therapeutic experiences can hopefully be translated beyond the music-therapy room into real-life relationships.

The psychoanalyst Valerie Sinason (1992 and 2000) pioneered using psychoanalytic thinking with adults with profound learning disabilities and impairments. She made sophisticated verbal therapy accessible to people previously thought unable to access it because they lacked cognitive and intellectual capacity. Her thinking has undergirded my own practice, and, encouraged by her work, I offer adopted children with learning disabilities the same opportunity as other adoptees to access meaningful therapy. I often receive referrals for adopted children with complex learning and physical disabilities because music therapy does not require them to possess language. The ASF recognises and funds creative-arts therapies for adopted children, thus giving value to the creative arts as therapeutic modalities. However, in reality, and in my experience, it is often difficult

DOI: 10.4324/9781003733393-6

for referrers to know what such therapy might look like and what its impact might be. Many, however, do recognise a non-verbal therapeutic modality is essential for children who have significant learning disabilities resulting in both language difficulties and difficulties with symbolisation who might consequently be considered as not able to access verbal psychotherapy.

Disabled children placed for adoption are likely to have the same internal world experiences and difficulties resulting from their early losses as non-disabled children. This material is just as likely to play out in adoptive placements if there is no opportunity for them to have a space where their communications might be understood. Additionally, their psychological and emotional needs can be complicated by their disabilities. This is especially the case if the reason that a child has been relinquished for adoption is the fact that they were born with a disability. In such instances, an adopted child's identity as a disabled child will be tied up with their identity as an adoptee because if they had not been born with a disability they would not have been relinquished. In my practice, I have encountered many disabled adopted children who somehow know deep inside themselves that they were 'given away' because of who they were, i.e., a disabled baby. I contend therefore that adopted children with learning disabilities benefit from referral for music therapy that is informed by psychoanalytic thinking about early experience and its impact and have evidenced this from previous case studies within my first book (Gravestock, 2021).

In her chapter on music therapy in *Music-Psychoanalysis-Musicology*, Darnley-Smith (2018) cites the music therapist Mary Priestley (1975), a pioneer in psychoanalytic music therapy, stating that patients who lacked a capacity for symbolising could explore new pathways in the world of the imagination as their body expressed emotion in sound. For Priestley, music is a language of the emotions, and, therefore, emotional states could be rendered symbolically in music, and, equally, the music could hold the understanding that emerged. This is precisely what Jack (like other adopted children with disabilities) was able to experience in music therapy. Embodied improvised music-making has provided Jack (and others) with a therapeutic modality that exists apart from the demands of verbal language. Music gave him an opportunity to symbolise material from his early inner emotional states that remained within his unconsciousness.

As discussed in earlier chapters, musical elements can provide the core aspects of what a baby needs in early attachment and what Jack had lacked. Co-creating music together, within a needs-led approach, meant Jack could first trust his own play then gradually let me join him. The involvement of two people actually playing music together, which is also wordless self-expression, can potentially reveal to both a level of preverbal unconscious material not previously known but which has an impact still in the here and now. This is why I believe psychoanalytically informed music therapy has special relevance for working with adopted children who possess limited verbal skills because it can provide an environment wherein music might become the first language, as it were, and thus enable the uncovering of unconscious emotional truths.

For an adopted (especially profoundly disabled) child, verbal therapy often feels dry at best, and it is impossible if the child either has no verbal language or is placed for adoption at an age where their language has not developed. It is not possible to verbally describe early experience when that experience was unconscious and occurred before language. Adopted learning-disabled children will struggle to find words for early experience if they are expected to use language to describe it. The reality of the music-therapy space is that it is not based in verbal language but is creative, imaginative and playful and offers therefore, a place for adopted learning-disabled clients to access unconscious early trauma. Winnicott felt play was valuable in understanding the impact of early life deficits. In music therapy for adopted learning-disabled children, there is value in musically playing together, considering not only what musical elements are being utilised within a session (such as tempo, melody, etc.) but also how the music is being played, the embodiment of the player and the way in which both music and relationship develop. These sorts of considerations inform my discussions with referrers. I explain that the music played within the therapeutic relationship of music therapy with adopted learning-disabled children is akin to the musical non-verbal interactions of early life (as described by Trevarthen, 1999). Music can provide an audible shape to emotional experience, which can reveal unconscious trauma and internalised patterns of relating.

When I talk here of embodied music-making, I am describing both the client's playing of music, using their body, and the music therapist's playing through their body. As discussed previously, music therapists play with our clients, so, inevitably, we use our own embodied states. Therefore, we bring our whole embodied selves to our playing. Times of active playing in a session need, for the music therapist, to be interspersed with times of engagement in deep embodied listening. This is because it is insufficient to focus upon musical elements such as melody, tone, timbre, rhythm and so on alone. Rather, music therapists are required to listen to our clients' movements, recognising rhythmic forms of posture, facial expressions, alternations of music and silence and so on. Partly, coming to make sense of the world of an adopted learning-disabled child in relationship with their music therapist is achieved through a co-created musical language. However, as Trevarthen (1999) and Stern (1985) both describe, the language of movements additionally gives form to feeling states and allows sharing of the affects of relationship. In adoption work, this enables an understanding of the prelinguistic nature of emotional experience and expression. As Jack's emotional states were witnessed by me through the embodied form they took as he was involved in making music, he could know he was heard and responded to, within this space of shared attention. Embodied musical relating gave him a vital sense of being alive in the presence of another. Jean Knox (2011) suggests that such therapeutic witnessing of embodied truth is necessary groundwork for the expression of trauma (and adoption is a very specific trauma according to the adoption community because it finally and legally separates children and parents and places children permanently in new families).

In this chapter, I describe another adoption theme arising in the work with Jack but again which has also featured on numerous occasions in other adopted children's music therapy. Looking back on my experience of adoption work, I see that almost every child I have seen for music therapy has either generated lullaby-like material themselves or has requested that I play and sing traditional lullabies that they know. When I think of how a lullaby is often shared between (often) a mother and newborn baby, it is probably one of the earliest shared embodied musical experiences. A mother might hold her baby in her arms and use her arms to provide a rocking motion or swing her hips gently to and fro in time with her singing. Alternatively, a baby in a cot might be rocked or touched gently and rhythmically in musical time. The movement is initiated by the mother but experienced by both and, as such, is a clear example of a shared musical embodied state: 'The singing joins with rocking movements, themselves characterised by rhythm and repetition, a proof of the deep link between sound and motion in the fusion of the mother and infants' bodies' (Grassi, 2021, p. 93).

Fornari (1984, p. 11) writes that lullabies are forms that can restore 'the original oneness by recovering original sounds and rhythms that, although speaking in this world, speak about another world'. Music, then, in this form, 'plays a linking function that, leading back to what was already known, allows the exploration of what is new and the symbolic recovering of what was lost in the real' (Grassi, 2021, pp. 91–2). Any song can serve as a lullaby provided it is sufficiently slow, has a steady uniform rhythm and is ideally sung in a low tone. Lullabies are quiet and gentle and used to send children to sleep. 'The baby's pleasure in listening . . . does not refer to the evident meaning of the words but to a sort of primary sound that is made up of pure rhythm and intonation' (Grassi, 2021, p. 91). Traditionally though, the lyrics of lullabies can tell either melancholic or frightening stories to children. They are 'a category of archetypal image within the realm of music and all cultures have them' (Kroeker, 2019, p. 56), and, therefore, lullabies can transmit cultural 'myths, histories and legends' (Grassi, 2021, p. 93). They can enable emotional and communication skills and the focusing of attention and develop self-regulation (Doja, 2014, p. 118). Perhaps also in the physical bond between mother and infant in the first year of life, a mother can sing of her own anxieties but held in the safety and comfort of her physical connectedness with her infant. In adoption music therapy, I argue that lullabies can sing the unsung, the unsayable, the feelings that may not yet be expressed.

In my experiences with adopted learning-disabled children in music therapy, many have found it possible to sing out (i.e., vocalise without words) rather than talk out their experiences of loss and rejection and their consequent feelings of rage and anger. Music therapist Joanne Loewy (e.g., Loewy et al., 2013), who works with premature babies in special-care baby units, has stated that lullabies embody a fear of loss, which makes sense given the precarious nature of the first years of life. This also makes sense of lullabies being utilised by adopted children to express their preverbal loss. One example that has recurred frequently in my work is the English lullaby 'Rock-a-bye Baby' (which Loewy interestingly finds featuring in her own work although she interprets it as representing the common fear of cot death). I suggest it may function as a metaphor in my work to describe the adoption loss. I will share the words of this here now: 'Rock-a-bye baby on the treetop, / When the wind blows, the cradle will rock, / When the bough breaks, the cradle will fall, / Down will come baby, cradle and all' (traditional).

The lyrics of this lullaby can evoke within an adopted child their early felt emotional and sensorial experience of being dropped (as discussed in Chapter 5). The formal structure of the song, though, can provide a frame for thinking safely about this difficult and as-yet-uncomprehended early experience. There is a risk that disabled children who are removed for adoption can feel that they somehow must be very bad inside to have to be taken away from their caregivers. They may attempt to present a false and compliant self to the music therapist in fear that their true self would be rejected, as in their inner perception of their early experience.

Returning then to my case study, Jack was gradually coming to know that he could reveal difficult emotions with me and would not be rejected as a bad self when he did so. At first, in our work, his emotional states were unregulated, obliterating my music and a sense of my present self in the process. As Jack allowed me to become more present to his emotional states, he could settle into a more coherent affect and function. This is a state that many adoptees with trauma experience will struggle to manage, but music can help to settle hyper-aroused states, as it naturally invokes embodied expression and aids self-regulation. Jack would find himself caught up in the song's rhythm and gradually move and breathe with it. I shall now go on to describe how lullaby material emerged in the work with Jack and what meaning we made of this.

Adoption Theme 2: Lullabies and reverie

Reverie (a term initially used by Bion in 1967; see Bion, 1988) might be described as a quiet state of being for an infant in which images, bodily sensations, thoughts, words, sounds or ideas can wander in and out of awareness without any particular aim or intention. In music therapy with Jack, I noticed that I would describe (in my notes) musical periods that emerged and felt at the time like we were drifting and dreaming together, perhaps then sharing a state we might call a reverie. During such times, it might again seem to an observer like not a lot is going on. This is perhaps like the good maternal care Winnicott (1960, p. 7) describes which 'when it goes well is scarcely noticed'. However, sharing such apparently simple states together with adopted children shows this to be an extremely rich and informative time, even if it exists only momentarily. The capacity for reverie is an important aspect of subjective development, yet reverie begins with the simplest experience for the infant of being held on its mother's lap (Bion, 1988).

When Jack, as a new client, was coming to his first session, I imagined him as being somehow like a new baby coming to the breast for the first feed. Winnicott (1953, p. 12) states, 'The mother places the actual breast just, there when the infant is ready to create and at the right moment.' He means the mother makes her breast available in the right way and at the right moment when her infant requires feeding. Likewise, I, therefore, needed to be attentive and aware, becoming as it were a music-mother who knew how to feed just enough to this infant at just the right time. This sits alongside Winnicott's idea of live adaptation as 'the adaptive breast is the first realisation, the infant's first creation' (cited in Wright, 2009, p. 51). Maternal adaptation to the infant's need enables the infant to believe that they had a need and they created a breast to meet it. Wright (2009, p. 52) writes that 'the adaptive mother (the mother capable of accurate identification) provides a resonant medium, and within that medium the infant discovers and becomes the self that potentially he is'. As the infant experiences the breast, he also begins to experience himself as separate to it.

This following example from the first session with Jack made me aware that he was bringing such very early experiences to our work that I simply needed to hold and experience with him, as if he were indeed just sitting in my lap, and I were lulling him.

Session 1: Music Therapy Example 1

Immediately upon entering the room, Jack picked up a toy microphone and began using it to mouth at before continuing by mimicking drinking from it. Visually this appeared to me then, in the immediate moment, very like a baby at the breast. Not much later, Jack did a similar enactment with a drumstick. This symbolic use of musical instruments so early in our work matched my sense that Jack would need to regress to early developmental positions within music therapy. Before he could truly use the instruments and enjoy their correct playing function, he needed to show me how very infantile his needs were. I have come to recognise that regression is fundamental for adopted children such as Jack as it can provide reparative experiences of the very early nurture they have been denied. While regressed, Jack required both a sense of 'holding' and 'feeding' from me in Winnicottian terms before he could begin to play with me musically.

Regressed states occurred at home too supported by the adoptive mother. She and I both viewed regressions as fundamental to Jack's reparative experience of the very early nurture he was denied. Jack would sometimes ask to be fed like a baby and want a bottle at home. This physical experience of re-feeding him gave his adoptive mum a sense that she had not missed out on sharing such early close relating with him. On a relational level, I argue that this also indicated how Jack was able to take goodness in from music therapy, internalising me and internalising good experiences to take away. These were now also translating into his home life.

My clinical supervisor, on observing video of this session, referred to the use of the microphone, noting its pink colour, and agreeing it might have symbolic function as a breast for Jack. She concurred that regression was of value for him. She also felt it was important that I had not made any attempt to directly model correct usage of the microphone to show Jack how to use it properly. My choosing not to do this meant that Jack could find for himself the symbolic function he required the microphone to have. At the time, I had felt that a part of Jack, his baby-self, simply needed to explore the world for himself while being in the presence of a safe, supporting, witnessing other. As he explored, I needed to provide a non-intrusive background of a mothering figure.

Winnicott's (1960, p. 9) statement that, 'What the infant needs at the beginning is a live adaptation to the infant's needs' had been influencing my practice then, in the moment. The adaptive mother Winnicott describes is one who mediates the world to her infant. She must first be able to identify with her infant in order to be able to resonate with his inner states/feelings, which are likely to be expressed through embodied states (or, in Stern's language of 2010, his vitality affects). She should be able to step back from her own experiencing and have the capacity to feel in touch with another experience, as should the music therapist. The live adaptation Winnicott describes amounts to the mother's ongoing process of attuned enactments. In a sense, this was what I needed to offer Jack: a background musical relational presence that could fluidly adapt and attune to his inner world and recognise how this may be expressed in his embodied states and symbolic use of instruments.

Within music therapy, the needs-led free improvisatory space that could contain Jack's feeling states as they were enacted in embodied symbolic communications, offered perhaps something akin to Winnicott's (1971) potential space. Potential space was Winnicott's term for an experience of an open, inviting, safe intersubjective field wherein an infant could be spontaneously playful while at the same time feeling connected to the mother. To experience potential space, the infant needs to have had 'experience, derived from play, which leads to trust' (Winnicott, 1971, p. 103). There are similarities, I think, between Winnicott's potential space and how I make sense of Ogden's (1994) analytic third for music therapy in adoption. Winnicott explains that potential space offers a third type of reality that contrasts with external and internal realities. This potential space then is a separate area that offers a way of being and experiencing, which is extremely variable because it is 'a product of the experiences of the individual person . . . in the environment' (Winnicott, 1971, p. 107).

The potential space within Jack's music therapy was created by various elements: the confidential safety of the same private room, the regular time of sessions, the same instruments being offered and the overall invitation to play in a relationship, providing a therapeutic environment wherein potential could exist for reparation of early experiences previously denied to Jack as an adopted child. In Winnicott's terms, 'play' is referring not only to the way that children play but also to the ways that adults might engage in creativity such as making art or participating in sports. Play to Winnicott is an integrally creative act, and, through play, he suggests self-healing can come.

I argue that the play occurring in music therapy with adoptees is like that of both children and adults, according to Winnicott's definitions. Such play is a creative act, as an adopted child leads the way in improvising and the music therapist responds. It was in response to Klein that Winnicott developed his theory of play. Klein had made a technique of play, and, as Hinshelwood (2013, p. 12). wrote, the Kleinian approach to analysing the very young child is simple: 'freedom of play could substitute for free association'. The music therapist Helen Odell-Miller (2001) suggests that free improvisation in music therapy can be seen as like the aspect of free association and free-floating attention in psychoanalytic work, thereby incorporating Klein's idea. To incorporate a Winnicottian notion of play in music therapy, however, means going beyond a mere extension of the domain of analysis.

The issue for Winnicott is not about focusing on the content of play to interpret it, but, rather, he sees the value of play being in the playing itself. Winnicott (1971, p. 54) also brings the intersubjectivity of both client and therapist into his definition as he states, 'psychotherapy is done in the overlap of the two play areas, that of the patient and the analyst'. The music therapist then needs to be able to play with the client, and, in music therapy, this means a literal musical playing-with. As I have already discussed, this has implications for the role of the music therapist within the intersubjective relating, especially if the client and music therapist have similar areas of lived experience. I argue that free improvisation offers engagement with unconscious material that originates with the client; however, it also simultaneously offers the client a new experience of relating. It is the very in-session experience, wherein transference and countertransference occur, that matters, and I shall now give illustrations from sessions with Jack where I felt lullabies and a shared sense of musical reverie were not only providing a re-experiencing of past unconscious relating but also presenting opportunities for new relational experiences.

Times in sessions where this was most obvious were those in which aspects of the maternal transference and countertransference were experienced by me as live-in-the-moment and viscerally felt in my body. This is evident in my description (below) of Jack on one occasion calling me 'Mummy'. I felt a strong transference, and this was enacted through both of our bodies in the way we played and related. Of course, the music therapist is not the client's mother and cannot literally enter that special state which Winnicott (1971) describes as being peculiar to the immediate weeks and months following birth. However, the music therapist can represent a maternal object, becoming available to the child, providing a similar function and offering some reparation thereby for the losses that accrued through adoption. In the instance below, perhaps I, as therapist, also offered something analogous to that which Jack's adoptive mother offered but which yet he had been unable to take in from her as he needed to defend against it. Music, as I described in Chapter 4, exists in a temporal form and can therefore literally move fluidly and responsively, thus resonating with a child's experience as it is happening. An example of the music representing something like the unconscious maternal object while at the same time providing new maternal experiences was evident in Session 7.

Session 7: Music Therapy Example 2

Jack asked me to play for him, and I used a lullaby structure in a steadily pulsed 6/8 timing, alternating simply between just two chords, C major and F major (each played slowly for two bars before changing to the next chord) while initially wordlessly humming along. Jack's eyes became softly focused, and I began to feel we were entering a reverie state. I felt relaxed in my playing, which I was not having to give much conscious thought to, so I could focus simply on watching Jack, taking in his whole being. Jack showed clear enjoyment of the simple musical structure. I soon noticed he was rocking very gently, almost imperceptibly, back and forth with the musical pulse. We stayed in this state quietly together for some minutes. Then I heard Jack softly say the single word 'Mummy'. I waited to be certain of what I had heard and to give space for whatever was to emerge. Jack then repeated the word a few times, and so I gently repeated his choice of word: 'Mummy'. Gradually I incorporated it musically, beginning to softly sing within the same pulse. I stretched the word to match the musical metre, singing 'mum-my' first in C, giving each syllable a half bar of music ('mum-' for Beats 1, 2, 3 and '-my' for Beats 4, 5, 6) followed by a bar of music alone, then repeating this exact pattern in F and returning to C and so on.

This music felt more relational between us (although only I played), and listening to it seemed to evoke some maternal experience for Jack. He continued to whisper 'Mummy' while sustaining lots of silent gazing/looking between us. This felt reminiscent perhaps of the early mirror-gazing whereby mother and infant first come to know one another, discussed earlier. Jack invited musical contact from me, and I felt there was potential for me easily to be experienced by him as either too interfering or too abandoning, quite easily at either extreme of the spectrum. Therefore, I had to respond delicately, moment by moment, sensitively offering that fluid and temporal sense of feeling tone. Jack rested, sat on the floor, seeming very content within the little world he and I now created. As he was enjoying the piano music and singing, I felt it could be providing him with a holding experience. Significantly, the rhythmic structure of 6/8 is commonly used in lullabies and has a rocking feel, reminiscent perhaps of the baby being held and rocked in a mother's arms. The two major keys I alternated between of C and F were uncomplicated and allowed me to not have to think at all about technicalities of playing other than using the sustain pedal. On watching video of the session later, I saw how my whole embodied response at the piano mirrored Jack's embodied state as I too was also gently rocking. (This was unconscious to me at the time.)

This episode of music, then, occurring over some minutes within Session 7, seemed to incorporate elements of what Wright (2009, p. 66) interestingly has called 'The Mother's Song'. Wright is not a music therapist, and, therefore, he is not here referring to a literal song but rather an experience. I have already described how I needed to become like the adaptive mother who can give the infant an embodied response he is seeking. This seemed to be the case in our shared rocking movements. Though I was not literally holding Jack in my arms to physically rock him, my body unconsciously shared the same state as his while the music became the 'third' in the room that fluidly existed between us and could hold us both, even as we created it (very much as Ogden [1994] argues the analytic third does). Additionally, Jack was actively seeking out a communicative facial response from me by finding my eye contact and holding my gaze. Wright argues that although both adaptation and facial mirroring are important for the infant, they do not take account of the full variety of embodied expressions through which a mother may communicate and 'sing' her baby's relational states. Additionally, then, Wright suggests that maternal attunement is also needed.

Wright describes that attuned mothers not only respond to what Stern (2010) has called categorical affects (the major emotional states their children exhibit) but also are responding constantly to those smaller changes of arousal states that I have previously described, known as vitality affects. Within these few reverie-like moments, I was needing to use my whole embodied state to read Jack's state and to sense moment to moment any changes. Wright (2009, p. 67) states that the mother 'follows him with a close yet barely conscious attention that teaches her the changing pattern of his experience', and this is how I perceived the music fluidly responding to Jack's vitality affects. The overall tempo was extremely regular, but the pulse could be shifted slightly with a hint of rubato at times that might be matched in our rocking. Jack was able to play himself, with embodied states, in the potential space that now existed between us and thereby could enter a state of reverie, wherein I could then offer him experiences of attunement, here very obviously containing a maternal quality.

Stern (2010) describes how an attuned mother is not only registering her infant's vitality affects but also engaging with responses of her own. To become a music-mother in this session, not only did I have to respond to Jack's communications but I also needed to communicate myself. It is this sharing of affects that is central within an intersubjective relationship, where room is created for both similarity and difference. Jack was slowly becoming able to tolerate me now as an other, and I did not need to exactly match and mirror him in my music or body in order for him to feel his communications were known. In Stern's terms, I could now engage in cross-modal attunement, i.e., where the matching occurs in another modality than the original one. Stern (1985, p. 161) describes this as 'the recasting, the restatement of an affective state'. For example, the baby might utter a sound, but the mother responds with a gesture. The shape of the gesture will encapsulate something of the shape of the sound.

I had initiated the lullaby musical form based on what I felt was 'implicit relational knowing' of Jack's emotional state. (Implicit relational knowing is a term used by Lyons-Ruth [1998] to describe a non-verbal and unconscious relational 'knowing' about how to be with another and will be discussed further in later chapters.) I sensed Jack was searching for a form to be made of his experience, and the lullaby structure provided this. This knowing seemed to match with Jack's feeling state, which was then evidenced with his utterance of 'Mummy' as I began to play, and the interaction that then emerged, incorporating reverie, holding, facial mirroring and cross-modal attunement. Another way of describing my response might be that I was responding in the transference to Jack and identifying with something maternal I represented to him, and therefore I played out in my countertransference what he wanted from me.

This complex shared embodied experience, enacted within the music, can be seen as a non-verbal analogy to real life. Winnicott, towards the end of his life, increasingly valued an approach that moved away from interpretations and rather privileged the analyst becoming a responsive other in relationship: 'Psychotherapy is not making clever and apt interpretations; by and large it is a long-term giving back to the patient what the patient brings. It is a complex derivative of the face that reflects what is there to be seen' (Winnicott, 1971, p. 117).

Perhaps embodied music-making is such a 'complex derivative'. In the music that I played, I was able to become for Jack a 'music-mother' who sang both to and with him, using the lullaby form, and in so doing gave back to him the experience he had felt in transference with me. I did not offer any verbal interpretation of this musical relational experience back to Jack but let it exist as it was. Later, in supervision, I thought about some interpretation as described above, and yet in the music-therapy room, the responsive music-making between us had been enough. It offered Jack a reparative experience.

In supervision, my supervisor and I discussed how working with relational embodied musical states had potential to evoke Jack's early experience (which remained stored in his unconscious but embodied memory). His associated emotional states seemed to be activated and shared in what could be understood either as implicit relational knowing or transference. His early experience could thus be revisited safely with me while also being transformed into something new in the moment. It was my hope that Jack would be able to take these new experiences of relational intersubjectivity out from the music-therapy room and into his adoptive family life. My supervisor discussed Jack's use of the word 'Mummy', coupled with the sense of reverie we subsequently experienced. I realised I had not felt surprised somehow when the word 'Mummy' emerged, and we seemed to drift quite easily into the reverie state, aided by the music. I had almost felt as if it were not I that played but rather that something was being played through me. Maybe this is what Ogden (1994) is describing when he talks of the analytic third becoming something separate and existent in its own right.

Later, I came across the idea of states of dreaming within music therapy discussed by Lawes (2019). I think in reverie with Jack we were perhaps attaining to something like that which Lawes (2019, p. 13) describes from his own experience:

> I needed to allow myself not to fully understand what I was playing and why. I had to trust that I was operating at some deep level of emergent knowing very different to that of everyday clinical reasoning where I might be able to justify or explain the particular music I was playing as if I had worked it out in advance. I had to believe in unconscious 'thinking in music' and its primacy in music therapy. While I created the music I played, in a sense it created me.

I argue that Lawes began by trusting his own implicit relational knowing, as I had, and then played from an unconscious place. When he did, he stated this: 'The music is as if created by an ineffable dreamer within . . . a deeply unconscious aspect of the individual as subject "who" is never experienced or known directly' (Lawes, 2019, p. 13).

Lawes interestingly then goes on to draw, as I have myself, on Ogden's (2000) thoughts on the idea of dreaming: 'It could be said that we are most fully ourselves in the dreaming of the dreams that dream us' (Lawes, 2019, p. 13). In this statement, Lawes is referring to playing music as being equivalent to entering this 'dreaming' process and that the music therapist/dreamer can confidently relax into playing in the third space, allowing themselves to dream their own music while waiting for other music ('the dreams that dream us') to arise. In this instance, as I was engaging my most complete, authentic, musical self in this music-creating with Jack, then reverie (not unlike a shared dream) could arise between us. I was unafraid of the simplicity of the music, and, therefore, my hands could play themselves as it were. Out of this simple lullaby form emerged a complex musical intersubjectivity.

My supervisor felt it was clear that Jack was now becoming able to use both music and relationship. As I had been prepared and able to relinquish any certainty of knowing what exactly was going on in the session, I became able to respond with fluidity; Jack had been able to find for himself an experience that contained something symbolic of the maternal. I wondered if what was being evoked in his bodily memories were those most early positive recollections of his birth mum. It was possible that he had, in his earliest days, known himself as being held and rocked by her. If so, there was the possibility that a very early felt sense of cross-modal attunement existed for him, which was evoked as we rocked and played and sang. If so, then perhaps Jack had internalised something good from his birth mother, which he was now experiencing, as a dream of a memory, in present time in the music with me.

This would be optimistic information about Jack re-experiencing attuned states within his adoptive family, as they were already there, deep in his lived experience, to be called upon. My supervisor suggested that I continued to meet Jack's requests for playing piano as this instrument seemed well able to contain what was happening relationally. Almost every session now, Jack directed me to the piano and not to other instruments. I felt I was able to draw strongly on my adult identity and maternal aspects of myself while using the piano. While seated and playing, I could move and rock and accompany myself singing as well as reflect verbally on Jack's verbal responses while remaining grounded. Interestingly, the piano can sometimes prove to be a physical block between a client and therapist in music therapy, and this is where I feel the music, with its capacity to become Ogden's third, could exist in the aural and temporal space between us. We did not need to be physically very close or touching because we each heard the music in our individual ears and felt it resonating in our bodies. Music could touch, hold and join us in experience.

I have previously described (Gravestock, 2021) my music-therapy approach in post-adoption support work as 'needs-led': that is, without any goals or aims imposed. Instead, the client has a relational experience within the music-therapy room that cannot be prescribed as an aim. Neither can the capacity for entering authentic dreaming states described above be taught as a technique to enable intersubjective experience. Music therapy with adopted children, from a psychoanalytic perspective, depends upon the therapist being able to engage in the present moment with free improvisation and to trust what emerges. Often, referrers to music therapy want to see what techniques I might draw upon and how my work is evidenced. I have successfully argued with adoption workers who refer to music therapy that it is a state of musical 'being' that is offered, which equates in some way to early states of being that have been lost to the adopted child. As this being state is made available, together, we learn more about the child's early experience and what might be required to create new relational experience. As the post-adoption social workers I work with are trained in thinking that recognises the significance of early life experience, they have received this approach with understanding and have come to value it. I articulated this when I was asked to write the British Association for Music Therapy (BAMT) national literature on music therapy on adoption. (This information is available to any professional or parent who contacts BAMT for information on what music therapy offers in adoption support work.)

This needs-led focus is why I generally do not use pre-composed songs (unless, of course, these are introduced by the client; as discussed in my first book). Rather, I offer a space of free improvisation, which can become a potential space wherein intersubjective relating might be given opportunity to occur. Pavlicevic (1997) argues that our improvised music-making might not often be or sound nice (indeed to an observer, it may sound discordant or nonsensical), but it is music that can meet whatever our client is both doing and being, in the moment. As such, it can become like an adaptive mother (Winnicott) or attuned mother (Stern). Offering a needs-led free improvisatory space meant I could simultaneously be fluidly adapting to the more obvious material Jack was bringing while also attuning to his feeling states as they arose, emerged and changed. He and I together then co-constructed (or, in Lawes' terms, 'dreamed') a completely new world that we could enter. The experience is indeed similar to how a new nursing couple starts getting to know one another. I had anticipated that our very first session might evoke early infantile experience for Jack, which was evidenced with his symbolic creation of a 'breast' out of a microphone, preparing us both to share, by Session 7, reverie or dream wherein he could experience a symbolic sense of something maternal. Further experiences became evident in our very next session.

Session 8: Music Therapy Example 3

Jack entered the room and came to stand at the keyboard while facing me. As he was opposite to me, he had access to all the keyboard (but upside down), and so we were immediately physically mirrored in our position. He began by soundlessly stroking the instrument's keys. As I stated earlier, it is impossible to play any musical instrument without bodily involvement; therefore, playing is always automatically an embodied experience. I was also increasingly aware of Jack identifying me with the keyboard by always requesting that I play it, so it had become in effect a part of me, and it felt as though Jack were gently stroking a part of me. While mirroring Jack's embodied position, I also began to mirror his gesture, similarly stroking the keys. Gradually I increased my pressure and began to put weight into my touch and play the keys, albeit very softly. Jack immediately looked up at me and whispered 'Mummy' again. Something in this shared musically mirrored and embodied state once more resonated something of the maternal for him. He asked me then for a 'mummy song', which I took to mean something like the singing we had shared together last time.

Therefore, I set up again a repetitive chord sequence, this time using three chords of C, F and G major, also in a slow 6/8 time. This pattern of the tonic, subdominant and dominant chords (Chord 1, Chord 4 and Chord 5) played in succession and repeated became an ostinato. (This is a musical form which many adopted children have either requested from me or discovered for themselves and which I shall explain later.) Over this repeated pattern, Jack immediately began to sing repeatedly the word 'Mummy'. I sang back this time, 'Jack is here today in music with Joy.' Once more, the repeating chord structures, held within a steady repeating rhythm, could offer Jack a sense of regularity and certainty both musically and relationally. Many small but extremely significant interactions between a mother and her infant are repetitive (feeding, for example, has a regular repetitive rhythm). Jack gazed intently at me throughout, which felt replicative again of the gaze between mother and infant. His body rocked rhythmically with my playing, and I found myself once more manifesting similar slow rocking in my own body, unconsciously, in reaction. We were 'resonating' together as I/the music again became a symbolic maternal object Jack could now use.

Very suddenly, Jack became tearful, now crying 'Mummy'. I played and vocalised, adapting the music to his feeling tone and then also experiencing a (possibly countertransferential) need within myself to move physically closer in towards him as a supportive presence. At this moment, I felt a strong countertransference of not being able to be a 'good mum'. I doubted that the simplicity of this music was adequate or that it could hold adequately and so had moved my body to get nearer to Jack. I worried that the staff in the nursery might hear his crying and wonder why I was not stopping it. I then immediately wondered if my experience resonated with Jack's birth mum's feelings of being learning-disabled and not always able to get it 'right' for him. Although she may have provided some initial attunement for him, this had not been consistent, to the point that she was deemed unable to adequately care for him. Was I simultaneously also in countertransference, becoming like Jack's adopted mum and fearful that what I could provide would not be able to be received?

When I shared these feelings a few days later in supervision, my supervisor felt Jack's sudden change of emotion and real distress came from a deeply felt early experience. Jack was an extremely independent little boy and would not usually take physical comfort. However, she felt he did gain something emotionally from my closer physically embodied repositioning. As in Session 7, she felt the type of music I was playing was exactly that which was being called for. This music, albeit a simple and repeated ostinato form, was once more existent in the space between us and was adequately holding Jack psychologically. The offering of regular pulse, combined with repeating chords, meant I was able to continue to attune to Jack's vitality affects, in a reverie state.

It felt like a different sense of the maternal had been evoked in this session. Jack was crying the word 'Mummy' this time, and his feeling state was dramatically different. I sensed this could now be more about the loss of the attachment he had so briefly enjoyed, possibly, in those early moments of attunement with his birth mum. When Jack became upset, he would quite quickly become distressed and would seem alone. He would be unable to show any care for himself, and his eyes and nose would both run, with him making no attempt to dry them. He would stand, arms by his side, looking completely dejected. Perhaps this was why I felt so strongly the need to get nearer and offer physical comfort. However, these were also important feelings to allow space for. This time I had sung 'Jack is here in music today with Joy', though, as I believed the music, as a temporal form, was again both evoking a past sensation while also holding us in the here and now. To remember the past was painful, and I did not want Jack to be flooded entirely by unconscious sensations. My words, therefore, provided an orientation to the new experience he was simultaneously having in the here and now. There was a constant, fluid, ongoing conversation between conscious and unconscious aspects of Jack within the music and relationship.

Winnicott (1971) does not use the specific term 'reverie' himself but defines a similar special state of receptivity to the infant, located within the mother in the earliest days of life, that he calls primary maternal preoccupation. He proposes this to be an intense temporary state existent between mother and infant which will (indeed must) naturally pass as the infant develops. Winnicott goes so far as to call it a state of illness because for the infant to develop, the state must end and the mother recover from it. She is described as ill because the state is overwhelming and necessarily excludes all other things which she would normally be focused upon. The father is described as holding the mother during this phase to enable her to hold their infant. (At times, I felt that my supervisor became like the father holding my work with care and thought so that I was enabled to hold Jack in varying states of reverie.) As the infant feels held, he can relish the mother's presence if she can manage to be with him in a non-invasive way so that his own personality can emerge. Examples of this felt present in a slightly different way in Session 6 (for which Jack's adoptive mother was present).

In my work, I tend to always begin with individual music therapy for a child (as usually, it is the child who is referred). Often the work opens to include adoptive parents and/or siblings, where there is value in doing so (and recognising the potential enormous difficulty for a child having to share their therapist). I wanted Jack to be able to experience some of the maternal feelings he got from me, but now with his mum. She had reported at the point of referral that he was hard to get close to, and so I hoped that a positive experience within music therapy of possibly some degree of attunement might enable them both to carry this into their daily lives together. In my next example from Session 6, I felt this was achieved.

Session 6: Musical Example 4

Jack once again requested that I play piano while this time he enjoyed cuddling up with his mum. Playing music for them as they sat together immediately felt like I was gently putting a soothing blanket around a nursing couple. Jack was rocked gently on his mum's lap and lay in her arms, gazing up at her, very like a nursing baby. I instigated the 6/8 rhythm again in time with their shared rocking motion, using the same chords to form an ostinato. I experienced a profound sense of reverie in the room. As I was sensing this, Jack fell asleep, and, as he did so, his mum took the opportunity to quietly speak about strong maternal feelings that he aroused in her as if he had become her flesh-and-blood child. I continued to play as we talked, feeling that now, in this moment, I/the music could become like the father holding the mother, in Winnicott's terms. Jack's mum spoke openly about her feelings, which I supported her to continue to share by playing with my hands while simultaneously listening with my ears. Her whispered tone added to the dreamlike quality, and I felt the need to keep playing to sustain this.

In this session, Jack's mother was now able to provide maternal holding for Jack in a very literal sense. I attuned musically, in a different mode. While Jack's mother literally held him, the music I played held the whole space that we were all contained within. Also, the music could react spontaneously to their vitality affects, which they shared now as a couple in these attuned moments which they and I and the music together created. As I played, the music that emerged could hold Jack and mum together in their reverie but could also hold mum and me as we spoke. I suspect that mum was able to voice things with me in the music that she had not done before elsewhere, as music provided a background soundtrack as it were that made her verbalisations feel less exposed. Music, which appeared like an easy light background to our conversation, was so much more than this, however, as it needed to be the right music at the right time and in the right way. In addition, the feeling tone of the music and the therapist's presence needed to be at the same time both unobtrusive and supportive.

Music here had such a broad function once again. Its continuous yet fluidly responsive presence could offer holding for all these vitality affects and responses to be enacted and experienced. My role was to remain authentic in my music-making within the experience and open to whatever emerged, responding to it within the shaping of needs-led improvisation. Then I felt I was hopefully offering a sense of what Stern (1994) terms 'continuous background feeling tone', by which he means a process that can capture the emergence and continuous shifting of affects over time.

Again, in this session, ostinato was the musical form that I felt was best able to provide both holding and also space for the shifting tones of attuned relating happening now between Jack and his mum. I mentioned earlier that it is a form much used in this work and one which some children, without being aware of the form, have nonetheless naturally fallen into playing themselves or requesting from me. Simply put, a rhythmic ostinato is a short, constantly repeated rhythmic pattern. In this case, the rhythm was the main feature of the music. I did not use a melody at this stage over the chords but just allowed the rocking back and forth between C major and F major to provide a chordal and rhythmic form. As I used only two chords in this session (as in Session 7), the repetition was easily predictable to Jack and now to his mum. Two bars of C major were immediately followed by two bars of F major, and the whole pattern was repeated over, and over, and over.

Repetition and predictability are elements of what a baby needs from the mother, and which Jack had lacked, but here those elements could be provided in a literal way. I was not providing something *like* repetition and predictability; I was *actually* providing them! Over this ground then of regularity, Jack and his mum could improvise relationally. Ostinato provides something calming, beautiful and almost hypnotic – the ideal background then for reverie or dreaming. In Session 8, I used three chords and formed the pattern tonic, subdominant, dominant (or Chord 1, Chord 4, Chord 5), then repeat. This pattern is used in numerous pop songs because of its repetitive function. Things that repeat frequently are easy to learn and remember, and pop songs need to be able to do this if they are going to be picked up by their audience and become popular. Chord 5 also contains the dominant 7th note of Chord 1 and therefore is requesting completion by returning to Chord 1 again where the anticipation set up by the dominant 7th is resolved by a return to the tonic.

Early on in my practice, I was surprised when a 14-year-old adopted boy, 'Tom' (who was a self-taught musician of reasonable competence), began to find his own functional ostinato by bringing his favoured pop songs to our sessions. Initially, I felt these songs were a defence against playing freely improvised music, which might have been too anxiety-provoking for Tom to consider engaging in at that stage of our work. However, it soon became apparent that it was not necessarily the songs themselves that were important or not but rather their chordal structure or, indeed, ostinato. As Tom played songs by his favourite bands himself on the keyboard, it became apparent to me that he entered a different emotional state. The use of Chords 1, 4, 5, also shaped by a repeating rhythm, led to Tom being able to access some emotional regularity for himself as he played. At this time, a diagnosis of ADHD was being considered for Tom alongside an attachment disorder diagnosis he had already accrued. However, as we found he was able to access emotional regulation in music therapy, and I was able to share this function with his adoptive parents, they began to search out music with this repetitive rhythmical chord pattern that they could play around the home. This offered a background soundtrack to daily life and an undergirding of interactions with musical stability. Eventually, as Tom became more able to regulate his own emotional states, his behaviour also accordingly changed; the previous attachment disorder diagnosis was revoked, and no ADHD diagnosis given.

Within music therapy, we could feel the fear and dysregulation that Tom as a baby would have felt, but now the emotional experience could be held within the music, and especially within this ostinato pattern. Wright (2009, p. 68) states that 'the need to find forms that hold and reflect the self is an existential one . . . and the search for such forms is rooted in early relationship', and Tom had found a musical form that could achieve this for him.

Obviously, having experienced this work with an older child like Tom (who did not have any learning disability) could help me when I was working with a much younger non-verbal child like Jack. Although he could not offer me confirmation of my hypotheses or interpretations about possible unconscious memories, I could trust (from what I had learned with Tom and others) that there would be meaning in the emotional states of reverie and dreaming that the music evoked. Also, Jack became a much more settled child and was able to relate much more intimately with his adoptive mum. This, in turn, improved the situation at home as she felt she now had some response back from Jack and therefore was more able to continue making overtures to him. I never set this out as an aim of work, but it happened relationally.

Alanne (2010, p. 198) suggests that 'the meaning of being in music has a similar meaning to when a mother is holding and attuning to her baby because the presence of a small baby activates auto-affects of caring, loving, joy, etc. in the mother'. In other words, as the baby relates and seeks relationship with the mother, this engenders a response from the mother. Often, as Alanne states, these are positive responses, but for the adopted child this may well not have been the case. Here-and-now though, in the music-therapy relationship, an adopted child can know that they can activate positive responses. Jack and his mum probably had their first experiences of being attuned to one another within the music therapy. Via this, they had shared a meaningful experience that itself had activated pleasant feelings for them both. Having had the experience within the music and being held by it and by a therapeutic relationship with myself, they were now feeling more equipped to risk 'playing' together outside of the therapy space.

Within this chapter, I have described how music therapy offers something valuable for adopted children because the playing of music together is a shared embodied experience. As such, it can replicate and resonate with the early embodied shared experience that exists between a mother and infant. Shared embodied music can give a music therapist a felt sense of what a child's early relational experience might have been like. I am then sometimes able to share thoughts about how that early experience may still be in evidence and enacted in the difficulties that result in adoptive families being referred for some help. The language of music is also a language of bodily movement and can provide a means for communication that is especially helpful for children with learning disabilities as it does not rely on them possessing any verbal ability. Working with older verbal children has made it evident to me that adoptees do have an unconscious and embodied memory of their experiences, especially of familial trauma, which may have led to them being adopted. Some children with learning disabilities may also know deep within this embodied memory that their disability is the very reason they were relinquished. Music therapy can offer some purchase for such children on symbolic experience which can help me, and others working in the team around the child, to engage in meaning-making with the adopted child and family.

The music-therapy relationship offers an experience that is akin to the non-verbal interactions occurring in early life that can lead to attuned relating. In therapy, when a music therapist can offer live adaptation and attunement, children can allow themselves to safely play with feelings within the potential space that Winnicott describes. The free play of free improvisation in music therapy can in part equate to free association in verbal psychoanalysis (as Odell-Miller [2001] argued), but I suggest that something more is available too because the musical play has meaning in and of itself.

I have described how musical forms such as ostinato and musical structures such as lullabies can evoke states like Bion's reverie and Ogden's dreaming. Within my therapeutic experiencing of such states, I have worked with an understanding of maternal transference and countertransference that additionally has enhanced my understanding of a child's early experience. Finally, this enables me to, in the language of Winnicott, 'give back' to the adopted child what they have brought, largely unconsciously, to music therapy. They have come with their unconscious, embodied memories which together we have been able to access through a musical relationship. Then, as in the case of Tom, I can literally give back these memories to the child, or, as in the case of Jack, give them back to his adopted mum (who was able to then continue enabling a still-very-little, adopted, learning-disabled boy to make sense of his world). Children's difficulties, which have been enacted within their new adopted family life, often prompt a referral to music therapy. Within my approach to music therapy, early traumatic memories can be given back in a more processed state in the hope that understanding can be integrated into family life, thus reducing the need for enactment and enabling the adoption to be sustained long-term.

References

Alanne, S. (2010). *Music psychotherapy with refugee survivors of torture: Interpretations of three clinical case studies.* Picaset Oy.

Bion, W. R. (1988). Notes on memory and desire. In E. B. Spillius (Ed.), *Melanie Klein today* (vol. II: *Mainly practice*, pp. 17–21). Routledge. (Original work published 1967.)

Darnley-Smith, R. (2018). Jung and the transcendent function in music therapy. In S. Wilson (Ed.), *Music – psychoanalysis – musicology* (pp. 136–151). Routledge.

Doja, A. (2014). Socializing enchantment: A socio-anthropological approach to infant-directed singing, music education and cultural socialization. *International Review of the Aesthetics and Sociology of Music*, *45*(1), 118–120.

Fornari, F. (1984). *Psicoanalisi della musica* [*Psychoanalysis of music*]. Longanesi.
Grassi, L. (2021). *The sound of the unconscious: Psychoanalysis as music*. Routledge.
Gravestock, J. (2021). *Music therapy in adoption and trauma: Therapy that makes a difference after placement*. Jessica Kingsley.
Hinshelwood, R. D. (2013). *Research on the couch: Single-case studies, subjectivity, and psychoanalytic knowledge*. Routledge.
Knox, J. (2011). *Self-agency in psychotherapy: Attachment, autonomy and intimacy*. Norton.
Kroeker, J. (2019). *Jungian music psychotherapy: When psyche sings*. Routledge.
Lawes, M. (2019). On improvisation as dreaming and the therapist's authentic use of self in music therapy. *British Journal of Music Therapy, 34*(1), 6–18.
Loewy, J., Stewart, K., Dassler, A. M., Telsey, A., & Homel, P. (2013). The effects of music therapy on vital signs, feeding, and sleep in premature infants. *Pediatrics, 131*(5), 902–918.
Lyons-Ruth, K. (1998). Implicit relational knowing: Its role in development and psychoanalytic treatment. *Infant Mental Health Journal, 19*(3), 282–289.
Odell-Miller, H. (2001). Music therapy and its relationship to psychoanalysis. In Y. Searle & I. Streng (Eds.), *Where analysis meets the arts: The integration of the arts therapies with psychoanalytic theory*. Routledge.
Ogden, T. H. (1994). *Subjects of analysis*. Karnac.
Ogden, T. H. (2000). Foreword. In J. S. Grotstein (Ed.), *Who is the dreamer who dreams the dream? A study of psychic presences* (pp. vii–xv). Analytic Press.
Pavlicevic, M. (1997). *Music therapy in context: Music, meaning and relationship*. Jessica Kingsley.
Priestley, M. (1975). *Music therapy in action*. MMB Music.
Sinason, V. (1992). *Mental handicap and the human condition: New approaches from the Tavistock*. Free Association Books.
Sinason, V. (2000). Learning disability as a trauma and the impact of trauma on people with a learning disability. *British Journal of Psychiatry, 176*, 32–36.
Stern, D. N. (1985). *The interpersonal world of the infant*. Basic Books.
Stern, D. N. (1994). One way to build a clinically relevant baby. *Infant Mental Health Journal, 15*(1), 9–25.
Stern, D. N. (2010). *Forms of vitality: Exploring dynamic experience in psychology, the arts, psychotherapy, and development*. Oxford University Press.
Trevarthen, C. (1999). Musicality and the intrinsic motive pulse: Evidence from human psychobiology and infant communication. *Musicae Scientiae*, 155–215.
Wilson, S. (2018). *Music–psychoanalysis–musicology*. Routledge.
Winnicott, D. W. (1953). Transitional objects and transitional phenomena: A study of the first not-me possession. *International Journal of Psychoanalysis, 34*, 89–97.
Winnicott, D. W. (1960). The theory of the parent–infant relationship. *International Journal of Psychoanalysis, 34*, 89–97.
Winnicott, D. W. (1971). *Playing and reality*. Tavistock.
Wright, K. (2009). *Mirroring and attunement: Self-realisation in psychoanalysis and art*. Routledge.

Chapter 7

'Hide and seek' and the baby with the broken head

Adoption themes 3 and 4

In this chapter, I describe two adoption themes. The first is a theme that, without exception, every single adopted child I have seen for music therapy has chosen to explore. I shall describe psychoanalytic interpretations of the game of hide and seek and how I have come to understand it manifesting within music therapy. I shall cite examples from my practice and the in-depth case study of Jack and meanings suggested in this work.

The second is a theme that specifically every adopted child with a learning disability has explored in varying ways. Each child has, in some manner, indicated symbolically that they are aware of their learning disability and, in some cases, are also aware that it is their disability that led to them being relinquished for adoption. For these children, their identity as a disabled child is inseparable from their adoption narrative. I will root the theoretical ideas in therapeutic work and experience, again discussing case examples from practice, before citing detailed session material from work with Jack.

Unrepresented early experiences enacted with metaphor and stories

So far, this book has explained how I have come to understand that adopted children can reveal themselves (including their past experiences and ensuing internal working model) in music therapy. This usually happens when children utilise musical metaphors and/or symbolic play. I provide resources in addition to music for working symbolically and incorporate a small range of toys in my work. (In order to engage with using other equipment such as toys or other materials, it is advisable that music therapists seek out further training to enable work with symbolic play.) In addition to my range of instruments, I tend to also use a small range of puppets that a child can use to explore something symbolically in a safely externalised way. There is also a baby doll available that might be used as a symbol to represent a child's sense of their own inner baby self. There are fleece blankets available for children to curl

DOI: 10.4324/9781003733393-7

themselves up in or ask to be wrapped up in by their adopter (when they feel able to request maternal nurture and holding). The music-therapy space then offers experiences of playing and singing music, which can be enhanced with a selection of small toys, puppets, the doll and blankets, whereby early experience might come alive in the room and be shared. Music is always though the prime means of communication and other materials are employed within the container of musical play.

Hide and seek

I previously introduced Freud's (1920) description of the *Fort! Da!* game and its similarities with hide and seek. Freud thought this game gave the infant a sense of control because the mother was always at the beck and call of the infant. Freud also writes that elements of revenge exist in the game, too, with the infant diminishing the mother to a subservient role. For most adopted children I have met in practice, including Jack, the main function for this game in music therapy has appeared to have been for the child to begin to recognise something that disappears can be bought back. This is often a new experience for an adopted child who has forever lost their birth family.

Later I shall also draw upon Sinason's (1992) work again with people described as having learning disabilities. She has written about hide and seek being used by her clients, which she sees as an essential precursor to other forms of playful interaction: 'The prerequisite for play is being able to hide and find, being able to bear absence because you know presence will come and because presence means someone you are attached to will not be abusive' (Sinason, 1992, p. 186).

This chimes with Winnicott's (1965, p. 187) statement that 'it is a joy to be hidden but disaster not to be found'. Being hidden needs the corollary of being found because both are about playing with states of absence and presence. An adopted child with some sense of being attached can enter a passive state of hiding, waiting for their seeker to actively search for and find them. Also, if an adopted child can bear the absence of another during the waiting period, they are likely to have some internal sense that the other will return. I have, like Sinason, come to positively view times when this game is initiated because adopted children often engage in it at a point when they are beginning to risk playing in other, relational ways. This demonstrates the capacity of the holding presence music therapy provides when a child's emergence of a capacity and willingness to play becomes possible. Adopted children can learn to trust in a presence that might come and go during the course of their music therapy but which is never abandoning.

For such children, the playing of hide and seek can enable them to access previous earlier parts of themselves, the parts that had known loss and abandonment. This is how unrepresented earlier experiences can be made manifest in the music-therapy room. Therapist and client are playing in the here and now, as I have previously described, and yet are simultaneously playing with earlier versions of the client's self, which was both hidden and found within the adoption process. The experience of being removed from the original mother happened when no one was there to witness and make meaning of such experience for the baby. Therefore, the adopted child carries an internal presentation that has been felt but not yet represented. This is why children who were unable to have thoughts about what was happening to them need to find acts to express their felt experience. Affects can be transformed in both music and play. Then, what one of my Ph.D. supervisors termed 'the un-past' (Williams, 2021) can be turned into a historical past and meaning made.

'Lily'

In my previous book, I described working with 'Lily', who had profound disabilities and who was relinquished to adoption because of those disabilities. Lily evolved many games within our sessions that were her variations on hide and seek. I had to first learn how to play from her and then follow. Freud (1920) might feel that this was because Lily was asserting control of me, but it is what I willingly chose to engage within a needs-led approach. People with learning disabilities have such little opportunity to demonstrate personal agency or volition because they are constantly cared for by others. Music therapy gave Lily a space to be the leader and to teach me. I was made to be subservient at these times, however, and she likewise definitely enjoyed feeling she could control me, an available object. At first, when I am used in this way in music therapy, I offer a waiting presence, simply being there for the child. This is the foundation from which I might become a good object. The music also can then become something a child can use in the work, but it is imperative that the relational is established first.

Lily would bring boomwhackers (long plastic tuned tubes, each tuned to a different note of a C major scale) to me one at a time, requesting that I held them upright in front of my face. The more boomwhackers I held, the more my face was obscured from her view. From this evolved a game of peek-a-boo, which itself is a sort of hide and seek children use from just a few weeks of age into toddlerhood. Babies up to about six months old can look shocked and startled by peek-a-boo, as they think that not being able to see the person playing with them means they have disappeared. Once an infant can understand that the person playing the game is simply hiding, they are then able to enjoy the anticipation of them coming back. The game then is perfect for showing when children have reached a stage of object permanence.

This play by Lily did not exist in a vacuum, however. I needed to think about its meaning for her and take the play she was creating, shape it musically and give it back to her in a digested form, or, in other words, give her back parts of herself. Singing was the main medium of communication during these repeated enactments of being hidden and being found. As Lily was playing with the boomwhackers and hiding me, I would sing 'hid-ing, hid-ing, where has Joy gone?', with each syllable having its own note (as indicated in the breaks between my sung words, above) and simply repeating an interval of a fourth (F, C, F, C, F, C, F, C). The regularity of the way I set the tempo of this little phrase, coupled with the repetition of words and notes, offered Lily a safe background to explore from, or in Winnicott's (1971) terms, a potential space to play within. Each time I ended my phrase, Lily would smile and wait with anticipation for the next repetition. By occasionally adding either temporal or melodic suspensions, her anticipation was heightened and the whole experience became great fun for her.

Initially, I could not know what Lily was working out in the play, but gradually, over time, I changed my words and sang about her finding me not just in the play but also as her music therapist, who she could now have a relationship with. In early sessions, our work had been just about finding each other. Now, having established relationship, Lily could know I was there to be found by her, and she could experience me as an available object. Then I could be repeatedly lost and found again over months of music therapy. Also, though, I was finding aspects of her experience that had not yet been known. This was not a once-and-for-all experience because at times Lily needed to lose aspects of the experience again. At times, when experience was too much, the music could make it tolerable, and Lily could play out what she needed me to find with and for her. In later sessions, I sang how she had also found her adoptive mother, and her mother had found her, and they were not going to be separated.

Lily was always delighted when I could be easily found in our music and would laugh, showing me that she felt safe in her play and not frightened that I had vanished. Once Lily found me, I would let the boomwhackers fall to the floor and pick up the C and F toned ones and use them to sing 'Found again, together again.' After some weeks of this game, Lily would play with me, sharing the boomwhackers and singing 'Found you, found you!' The game, rooted within music, had been a device she could use in order to come not only to playing music herself but also, most importantly, knowing the experience for herself.

'Ewan'

A similar game of hiding and being sought out developed with 'Ewan', aged five, who also had learning disabilities and was adopted. Ewan would place himself (standing) behind me while I knelt on the floor where my keyboard was also placed. As I sang, 'Where is Ewan?' he would enjoy teasing me before coming into my view, thus allowing himself to be found. I would sing, 'You found me!' repeatedly, and he would giggle. Sometimes, in play, he would dance and twirl, and I would play waltzes on the keyboard that could express something of what his body was doing. On occasions, he would physically launch himself into my lap, confident now that I would literally physically be present for him but also recognising the musical holding between us. Again, over time I developed sung improvisations to include words about him finding his adoptive mother and mother finding him, aiming to playfully encourage him to translate this embodied experience to other contexts.

'Michael'

Two-year-old 'Michael' had recently been adopted. Prior to his adoption placement, he had experienced significant physical abuse at the hands of his birth parents. He also had a diagnosis of foetal alcohol syndrome. His adopters were struggling to form any kind of attachment to him because, they told me, he was 'too frightened of people'. They reported that after any times of perceived closeness, Michael had afterwards always demonstrated angry, violent behaviour. They were despondent about Michael having been placed with them, though, at the time of placement, they had been pleased to have such a young child. Despite attachment training received in the adoption process, they could not really believe a young child with a moderate learning disability could be so affected by early experience.

Michael came to music therapy mostly accompanied by his adoptive dad. He seemed extremely shy and nervous and did not really use his dad as a safe object but rather ran away from both Dad and me. The music therapy room had two keyboards, and Michael would always go behind one, taking a dragon puppet, covering himself with a blanket, and telling us he was hiding. Michael did not demonstrate the emotional robustness that Lily or Ewan had, and I felt his play needed setting into a musical background that could provide gentle, tender holding. I played soft repeating chords on my keyboard as Michael's dad and I had a conversation. We knew Michael was listening, and so we playfully wondered aloud together about where Michael might be and stated our wish to find him. In the initial stages of music therapy, this was all that happened between any of us, and it continued like this for some weeks.

Gradually, I introduced some gentle wordless humming, and, to my surprise, one week I heard Michael humming also. When I stopped humming, so did he. A wordless musical connection was made. In the following weeks, Michael's hand, with the dragon puppet on it, began to creep out from around the bottom of the keyboard. I sang about this appearance, and immediately the dragon roared at me and retreated. This happened repeatedly. Eventually, I became able to sing about the dragon and sang that although he seemed scary, Dad and I would not be frightened. Gradually the song evolved, and I sang about a dragon who was so frightened himself that the only way he could cope with being with people was to make them feel as scared as he was. Some weeks after this, Michael arrived and immediately said, 'Dragon song!' which I played and sang. However, on this occasion, the dragon gradually bought Michael out into the room. Michael showed the dragon, now as just a puppet, to Dad and me and let us touch it carefully.

I deduced that Michael's dragon play communicated how hidden he needed to be to feel safe. His dad witnessed this in our session and began to buy into the idea that what was happening was not 'just play', but that the play had some meaning for Michael. Early in the work, this enabled both adoptive parents to go more slowly at home with him and to relinquish some of their own expectations for affection from a child (which they had desperately wanted but now recognised their desperation might be pushing away).

Meanwhile, I was wondering if the dragon might symbolise a frightening as well as frightened part of Michael. Initially, when Michael was attempting to frighten us, I started thinking about Michael as a child who had known physical abuse. Was he frightened by rage and anger, which he had only known as expressed in violent outbursts at home in his birth family? Could he safely own his rage without feeling that he was becoming like his birth family who had hurt him? How might I help him express anger safely? This thinking had underlaid my dragon song and seemed to resonate with Michael. As gradually we had been allowed to get to know the dragon, we discovered that, despite appearances, he was friendly! I discussed my interpretations of Michael's play in liaison with adoptive parents, and they began to trust that he may well have embodied his early experiences and have difficulty trying to make meaning of them.

I argue that play like this is more than play therapy with music alongside it because the music is integral to the playing process. I had first identified a dynamic that I intuited would provide holding for Michael's baby self and so filled the room with soft sustained major chords. I also utilised ostinato deliberately (as described previously), hoping that the repetition and rhythm might be musical elements also contributory to a holding space. It is interesting that what I felt was our first intersubjective relating happened through wordless humming. As I hummed, I received a response, and Michael was experiencing something similar. This felt important before moving on to create songs with words. I could not be certain at that stage what verbal capacity Michael had, nor did I know how he was able to receive spoken language. The humming felt as if we entered a very infantile place for Michael, and it contributed to the overall music. Thus, I argue again that music had become the third (Ogden, 1994) wherein we could dream together. Out of this state, which felt replicative of very early states between mother and infant, play could gradually emerge. In Winnicott's (1971) terms, the potential space had been created, and only then was Michael able to play.

Gradually, over a series of sessions, I learned that Michael's comprehension of verbal language was good, though his verbal skills for speech were delayed. He could, though, receive my verbal interpretations of his play with the dragon, all of which were couched in song. Throughout, the song used the same ostinato, and I kept the melody very simple, with not much variation in pitch, rising from the first (tonic) note to the fourth (subdominant).

Everything musical was kept small and quiet, using musical elements that had a sustaining quality. I hoped this musical holding might gradually enable Michael to feel safe enough to reveal himself, as he felt heard, witnessed and understood. The result of this period of music therapy was that his adoptive parents gained much more insight into his inner world and became more able to think about his behaviour as a response to early trauma. This, in turn, engendered more loving and caring feelings within Michael's adopters for a little boy who had experienced much hurt as an infant that he could not describe. They were enabled to go at his pace and recognise their own expectations might have to wait a while longer to be satisfied. When Michael ended music therapy, he was more settled and able to give and receive physical affection in his adoption placement. I recorded the dragon song for the family to take away, and they used it to remind themselves at difficult moments about what might be happening for Michael, but also for him to self-soothe with. The placement continued, and the risk of breakdown was managed.

Learning from case-study material

Many adopted children struggle if they cannot visibly see their music therapist and will therefore have difficulties with longer gaps than those between weekly sessions, such as holidays. Games like hide and seek, where they can feel in control of enactments of the coming and going, can be a way of attempting to exert some control and be able to manage feelings. Even waiting from one week to the next to see their therapist can be difficult for a child who has not previously had an experience of being held in mind and cannot believe, therefore, that they will be held in mind by their music therapist. Some adoptees will need to retain a tangible reminder (such as a photograph of their music therapist) to enable them to manage. Musical recordings that a family can take home can also provide a way for the child to feel connected with the music therapist. Yet, just as an adopted child needs to know that they can see and be seen by their music therapist, there also needs to be space for them not to be seen or to look and then look away. Wilkinson (2010) identifies that people who have experienced attachment difficulties need to be able to re-experience the maternal gaze but not so much that the experience feels overwhelming. They need to look and be looked at but also must be able to look away from. Sufficient shared relating is required for a child to feel held and thought about, but not so much that they are overwhelmed. Michael's parents had a very real experience of learning this from his music therapy and adjusted their expectations of and behaviour towards Michael accordingly.

I have learned, therefore, to follow the pacing of children like Lily, Ewan and Michael, and it often takes weeks, even months, before I even think about beginning to verbalise any interpretations I might have about their playful musical enactments. Rather than having the experience of visually gazing at one another (although visual gazing can happen sometimes simultaneously), we are audibly gazing. Any musical over-anticipation within this sensitive process of replicating the lost early gaze would lead to a child feeling less in control at a point in the therapy when they needed to know both their autonomy and independence. Coming gradually to know that it was safe to be found musically by myself and relating this musical experience to having been found by their adopters can aid a growing recognition of a child's need of others. This, I argue, needs to be a very steady journey indeed for children who have necessarily and protectively created a defence of pseudo independence.

Schore (1994) demonstrated how gaze plays a crucial part in the development of a sense of self and of other underpinning all relating developing from early relational lived experience. I argue that the playful, musical interactions I have described above, led by the adopted child, contain transformational power, but this transformation happens predominantly through audible means rather than through the visual in music therapy. A 'musical gaze' from myself can be embedded in even the most fleeting of affective interactions and in silences (which are still a part of music, as without silence, there would be no music). In Lily's, Ewan's and Michael's cases, musically experiencing repetition and anticipation, interspersed with silence, enabled them to gradually tolerate mutual audible gazing, to 'look/look away' (in Wilkinson's 2010 terms), or to engage in what I tend myself to call now 'sound-gazing'.

I want to return now to Winnicott's (1965, p. 187) statement that 'it is a joy to be hidden but disaster not to be found'. Winnicott (1965, p. 179) was reflecting on 'the right not to communicate'. He described how the infants' need to communicate is countered by the equally pressing need to defend against communication with the secret self. This has felt even more pertinent for adoptees in music therapy, especially those who have also experienced enormously invasive experiences such as physical and sexual abuse. Such children come to adoptive placements needing to be delicately held, and often in my practice I have seen placements floundering because adopters have expected too much too soon from their children. I have learned to stay with certain enactments that need to be repeated for a long time. This means tolerating perhaps my own boredom (such as when playing the same simple ostinato pattern week after week or engaging in the simplest of actions . . . such as humming to a child who remains hidden behind a keyboard).

Sufficient time and space then must be allowed for a child to fully experience the joy of being hidden. Only then is it possible to risk being found. Only then might I begin to make some sense with the child, and possibly parents also, about what might be going on. Great care, therefore, is needed when making any interpretations of what children are doing in music therapy. Hopefully, over time, adopted children can allow themselves to be truly found, i.e., known and understood exactly as they are by their adopters. There were many instances of hiding and being sought out that occurred in the work with my case-study client, Jack, using similar sorts of play to Lily, Ewan and Michael, which I shall now describe:

Session 3: Music Therapy Example 1

Jack had arrived for this session already clearly letting his mum and myself know what he wanted to do. He used a lot of generalised gestures and some very simplified Makaton to instruct both of us to do as he directed. Mum was sent to sit on a chair in the corner and watch him while I was told to play keyboard. Jack initially also sat at the keyboard next to me but then dived beneath it. I played dramatic music on the keyboard with tremolando octaves in the bass and minor chords in the treble as he hid himself away, abruptly stopping my music as he 'disappeared'. A short anticipatory silence held his hiding. Then, as he peered out from under the keyboard with a huge smile on his face, I changed to big, joyous, sustained major chords. There was no need verbally for any words within this musical interaction and the ensuing play, which was repeated over and over. I made a sad face while Jack was hiding, as did Mum, and we beamed when he was found again. The change of tonality from minor to major matched my facial expressions and showed Jack our delight when he was found.

Hide and seek was used again later in this session, this time utilising the thunder drum. Jack placed his entire face and head into the thunder drum then also covered his mum's face with one hand. He shook the thunder drum with his head inside it, and I sang the words of a simple improvised song: 'Inside, outside, shake it all about until we can see if Jack comes out.' Again, I accompanied from the keyboard with octave tremolando to match the timbre and dynamic of the thunder drum. Jack pulled his head out, laughing as he did so, and simultaneously uncovered his mum's face as I played strong sustained major chords. Jack and Mum were then able to enjoy finding one another as I played some celebratory reunion music.

Jack then began a succession of similar games but now engaged in playing directly with Mum while I offered a soundtrack to their interactions. The music amplified the played-out enactments and helped to make sense of them. I used fewer words because the music seemed to be sufficient, but whenever Jack and Mum were reunited after periods of him hiding himself, I sang 'Found you!' and used the same celebratory music.

I was most struck (when later watching the video of this session) by Jack's enactment with the thunder drum. As his whole face and head were inside the drum and then suddenly were pulled out in a rush, I could not help but think of him being born. My sung words reflecting on what had been 'inside' now becoming 'outside' incorporated this sense, though at the time I had not thought of it concretely as an interpretation of what might be going on. Perhaps something of the play had, though, unconsciously communicated a felt experience to me, and I was certainly playing music that built up and up in anticipation of the climactic moment of 'birth'. Interestingly, Jack covered and uncovered his adopted mum's eyes at the same time as he emerged, and this felt like it made her part of the birthing experience. I was struck by the fact that she had not been able to share that most significant moment of him coming into the world, and it was some months later before they were able to see one another in adoption introductions.

Otherwise, initially, the game at the start felt like a little child playing peek-a-boo, and Jack's pleasure in hiding under the keyboard was obvious. When I gave space to this aspect of his play, the silence seemed to sound around us while he remained under the piano. He enjoyed the musical feel of exploration that I was offering. Neither I nor his mum needed to show that we were happy when he allowed himself to be found; the music did this. Music also showed the joy of the 'finding' indicated in the change of modality from minor to major. As Jack oscillated between states of hiding and states of revealing his presence to us, the music was able to express this too, and we needed no words. I did not choose to offer any verbal interpretation whatsoever because this felt redundant. We had the experience, and it existed in the temporal space of the music, and that was sufficient.

Session 4: Musical Therapy Example 2

Jack and his mum entered the room together, and he immediately picked up the guitar and passed it to me. He indicated that I had to accompany him and his mum as they moved around the room. I began a simple strummed pattern, oscillating between two chords. Jack sat his mum down on 'her' chair again and chose to get a pair of plastic drum brushes out. These were as long as his face, and he explored one of them sensorially in detail, stretching out their bristles and enjoying their tactile nature. He asked his mum to similarly enjoy discovering the second brush, which she did, and it was as if they came together in enjoying this simple sensorial exploration. I continually played on the guitar, utilising music that matched them in a similarly sensorial way; long stretched-out arpeggios as the brushes were stretched, and spiccato 'pinging' of the strings against the fingerboard to match the brushes flicking back into place.

Then Jack began hiding his face with a drum brush, first with the bristles held thick together in front of his face then fanned out (which meant his whole face was covered). He asked Mum to copy what he had done and then parted the bristles on his brush so he could see through them to her and thus allow himself to be discovered. This was very much a game of peek-a-boo, with elements of both 'hiding from' and 'being found'. Once again, I accompanied the play musically in a cross-modal form, while singing about Mum and Jack finding each other. This was all the interpretation I offered, although later, Jack's mum spontaneously commented to me, 'It was like playing peek-a-boo with my girls when they were small.' She had picked up the meaning of what was happening. Again, I had the sense that Jack and his mum were making reparation for the time that had been lost to them, and, within this regression, they were able to share some of Jack's baby self.

Session 13: Music Therapy Example 3

In this session, Jack for the first time became aware that there was a door leading out of our room (in addition to the main entrance door). He had never been curious about it before. I knew it led into a store cupboard. Jack could not contain his curiosity and eventually opened it. He sat in the doorway hiding from me, but then and again, he would lean out to grin at me. This new game was another elaboration on hide and seek. I sat on the floor also, remaining in the main music-therapy room, on the other side of the door to Jack. I picked up a recorder that happened to be the first instrument to hand. It proved to be appropriate as I could use it to play sounds that mirrored Jack's play. While Jack was hidden, I played a long slow trill on a low C sharp/D semitone. This set up a sense of anticipation as the trill needed to resolve, so when Jack appeared and I could find him, I again made a happy face and resolved on to the D, followed by playing a rapidly ascending chromatic scale up to top D, ending abruptly without sustaining the last note. Jack laughed, and I had the sense that he could now feel the experience first of hiding and then of being found by me (as he allowed himself to be found, though not by me pushing for this). This musical interaction glimmered with his joyous feelings. When he laughed, it was impossible not to join him, so the whole experience was shared and part of our relating.

As I used the recorder in this session, I recognised this was the first time I had used a blown melodic instrument with Jack. I enjoyed it as I could use my face to match the sounds I was making, for example, raising my eyebrows with the ascending scale. Both sound and movement happened within and from my face. Again, the attunement was cross-modal and led by Jack's actions but shaped by my musical receiving of what he communicated. Jack seemed to relish the anticipation of the trill, followed by its resolution, and, on repetition of this play, he started to mimic movements I had done such as tilting my head gradually back as I played the ascending scale. We then shared both a musical and embodied experience.

Session 14: Music Therapy Example 4

In this session, Jack changed the drum brushes to hand chimes as objects used for the face-finding game with his mum in Music Therapy Example 2. Mum was not present; it was just him and me. He chose to pick up two hand-chime bars, the notes D and A respectively (an interval of a fifth apart). I was told to sit again at the keyboard while Jack stood in front of me. The finding game then proceeded, whereby Jack held up the two hand-chime bars together in front of my face. He then gradually moved them aside so I could be found by him.

With the game played out in this way, Jack was completely in control of the finding, which he enjoyed and repeated for much of the session. I was able to continue to play the keyboard, locating my hands on the keys, while also engaging facially with him. I played open fifths between D and A in both hands, and, at the point of being found, I played D major chords. The interval of a fifth, without any sense of major or minor modality, was chosen partially to match the tonality of Jack's hand-chime bars but also to match the open anticipatory finding process. I did not want to colour the play emotionally with any key at this point, but I moved into D major (simply by adding the third note of a chord, an F sharp) at the point of Jack being found. After this enactment in play, Jack took the chime bars from me and danced while holding them, one in each hand, and vocalising wordlessly in a happy tone. It seemed that once he had found me Jack was able to go on and enter some shared music-making.

Session 22: Music Therapy Example 5

This was our penultimate session, and Jack used it to repeat every form of hiding and seeking we had engaged in during our work together. After playing for some while, he 'discovered' my video camera in the room (by this, I mean that he had allowed himself to find it, as it had been there every week in the same place, but he had not taken any interest in it). At the end of the session, Jack looked into the video viewfinder and was able to see an image of himself. This intrigued him. He then wanted to see me on the camera so I showed him how he could do so, and then I walked into a space where I knew the viewfinder would pick me up. Jack spent the last moments of this session asking me to walk in and out of view and told me to say 'Boo' when I was in view. In a sense, he was asking me to hide and present myself to him while he remained in charge of the camera and, therefore, ultimately managing whether I would be found or not. I picked up the recorder again and used it to reflect my embodied actions, using ascending scales to indicate me coming to view and descending scales when I moved out of view.

The video recorder in situ in my room has been significant within the music therapy of many adopted children I have worked with. Some children never show any interest in it whatsoever, but when others do, it seems to be used to connect also with their adoptive experience. The video is very specifically an instrument for seeing and being seen with. Jack returned the following week to viewing his own image in the viewfinder and enjoyed videoing me in return. I felt this, too, was an exploration of seeing and being seen by, which continued in Session 23.

Session 23: Music Therapy Example 6

This was our final session. On arrival, Jack stated 'picture' and pointed to my photograph on my name badge. He went to my video camera and said he would take a picture with it. I altered the tripod to his height. Jack wanted both to see himself in the video and also hide from it. He requested (using

Makaton) that I play 'hiding music' on the keyboard as he looked at his own face in the viewfinder. I offered music of the sort we had used before, containing elements of expectation and anticipation. Jack then wanted to see me, so I turned the viewfinder round. He moved it from floor to ceiling, taking in the whole room, before signing in Makaton 'going away' before picking up the entire tripod/camera and walking further into the room.

The musical game of hide and seek was emphasised visually in this session by Jack's camera usage. When he signed he was going away, I felt he was aware of our ending music therapy today and alerting me to his knowledge of this. He came back into the main instrument area and seated himself at the keyboard. I suggested that maybe we could have some goodbye music. Jack sat next to me but on a separate chair as I began slowly and steadily to improvise and started singing about saying goodbye. He improvised vocally but wordlessly softly above me in the upper register. He was in the same key and matched my tempo. We were now co-creating the music we played together. He then laid his head on the loudspeaker of the keyboard and listened carefully before pointing at it, verbally saying 'Joy'. I sang 'Goodbye, Jack' three times, finally adding 'I have heard you play.' He smiled, stopped and then very clearly enunciated 'We're done.'

It was clear in the session that Jack knew our sessions were ending. The ending had come suddenly and unexpectedly. Jack had managed to internalise what this meant and was able to show me this symbolically in numerous ways. I often felt during the session that Jack wanted to be the one in control of the ending of our work together and that he would rather end things prematurely himself than have to deal with me initiating the final goodbye. His closing words had an angry tone, covering or defending, I suspected some sadness underneath.

Later, in supervision, I described how Jack's sense of me being existent somehow in the keyboard was curious to me. The sound was clearly emerging from the speaker, which he had equated with me. I wondered if the music therapist comes to exist for some children within the musical objects/instruments that are played and within the music itself also. I argue then that an adopted child might absorb something of the music therapist from their shared musical experiences. Jack's head on the speaker reminded me of a child laying in his mother's lap and hearing her internal bodily sounds against their ear as reassurance. It felt like this was what he might have taken from the keyboard, through the speaker, which he identified with me. My supervisor discussed the various ways that hide and seek had been played out with Jack, which had then been followed by musically held games with the video camera, of looking for and finding both himself and myself. She felt that both he and I were in a relationship where we now wanted to be found by each other, and all enactments of this game had offered a way of repeatedly addressing his earliest needs. The musical soundtrack had been essential for him to explore his early lived experience as he gradually had come to rely on my matching and mirroring soundtrack to his play. Thus, he had finally also become able to play musically with me despite an unexpected premature ending to the music therapy.

The baby with the broken head

Valerie Sinason is a psychotherapist who, perhaps more than any other, has helped me to understand something of the interior world of adoptees who have additional trauma because they have learning disabilities. 'All human beings have an inner world as well as an outer one, an unconscious as well as a conscious, and therefore those with a handicap need just as much attention to these aspects of life as others' (Sinason, 1992, p. 74).

It used to be thought that the preverbal baby lacked emotional intelligence, but we now understand that babies can know their early experience through embodying it. Adult adoptees who experienced the preverbal trauma of being removed from their birth mother as tiny babies often have an enduring sensation of tremendous loss and separation. Such prelinguistic experience may be expressed behaviourally because the experience came before language. The beginnings of living functioning lie much deeper and beyond language. Music, which is similarly wordless, can connect with inner sensations, thus evoking prelinguistic stirring and expression of feeling that is incapable of being put into words. Therefore, as I have argued earlier, the experience of two human-embodied people playing music together can potentially reveal to both a level of preverbal unconscious material. This is especially significant when working with children who have limited verbal skill because of a significant learning disability. This is why many referrals to me for music therapy are for adopted profoundly disabled children who would not be able to access verbal psychotherapy.

I have argued that the impact of the trauma of the loss of the mother as the first attachment figure causes an infant to erect defences. This is no less the case for children with even the most profound disabilities. Jack, as the other children I have discussed, had absorbed overwhelming sensations of abandonment while not possessing resources to process and assimilate them. Developments in neuroscience evidence that traumatised children carry within them an internalised embodied knowledge of their early abandonment which is stored in the amygdala. So, I argue that Jack carried in his deepest cell memory what had happened to him. His feelings, though unavailable to conscious recall, governed his relational repertoire. Wilkinson (2010) describes this beautifully as old material being manifest in the present, being alive still in a child's internal world. Accessing this internal world, and modifying its impacts, are core aspects of the music-therapy approach that I have evolved within adoption.

Lily

Many children in music therapy have chosen to use the baby doll that I mentioned previously. The doll can represent many parts of experience that are wordless yet known and has been a way that adopted children have shown me how they have felt about their baby selves. This experience has been especially profound for me as I have experienced it in the music therapy of children with learning disabilities. Early on in her music therapy, Lily began using the doll, which she invested with symbolic significance. At times, the doll apparently represented aspects of Lily's self, and she called it 'Gigi' (her pronunciation of her own name), yet at other times it was an object into which she projected her feelings about the world, revealing further aspects of her inner world functioning. At other times, the doll represented other non-disabled babies Lily had encountered and was also used to represent her adopted (younger, male, Down Syndrome) sibling.

Varying symbolic representations of these types could coexist in a single musical episode. For example, over many months, the doll's head was bashed repeatedly off the guitar strings (as it lay on the floor), resulting in sounds I responded to musically and vocally. This play felt distressing to observe and was difficult to remain with over such a long time. However, I could musically hold and contain the sounds that emerged from the play. I would accompany the bashing with huge crashing dissonant piano chords and would also vocalise wordlessly and loudly, as Lily herself was doing. Lily could communicate her distress about being a child with disability and being different from others while simultaneously giving me a symbolic message about her 'damage' and 'difference' being located in her head in the context of her learning disability (Cottis, 2009). For a long time, it was necessary for me to hear her pain and to witness what it truly felt like. Initially matching and mirroring her distress vocally, I would then dial down my vocalisations to offer her a holding musical environment and to lead her into a more emotionally regulated state.

This was perhaps akin to Lily communicating what Bion (1988) terms 'beta communications', and which I had to hold and transform into 'alpha' to be able to give her a transformed experience. Bion argues that it takes the connection of mother and baby with a good enough relationship for thinking to occur. If the mother does not receive the feelings of the child and transform them into something manageable, the child will be left with unconscious dread. Lily had been able to express how damaged she felt by repeating this play. The damaged doll who had its head bashed then later had to be repeatedly thrown away and rejected. This was a devastating enactment of Lily being given up to adoption for the very reason that she was born with a disability. Lily would laugh sadistically as the doll was thrown, giving me an impression of how she believed her parents had callously abandoned her. Once more it was music that could hold her enactments and return her to a state of emotional equilibrium before leaving the session.

Après-coup

This play with the doll seems to hold the quality of the *après-coup* or afterwardsness (first known as Freud's *Nachträglichkeit*, 1954, and later translated by Lacan as *après-coup* and by Laplanche as afterwardsness). Phillips (1994, p. 33) puts what is a complex term into simple language – 'memory is reprinted, so to speak, with later experience' – drawing on Freud's (1991) explanation of occurrences in analysis where 'the effects of the scene were deferred but . . . had the same effect as though it were a recent experience' (Phillips, 1994, pp. 276–7). In my work, there is often a sense of an experience occurring 'here and now' in the music-therapy room that is bringing back something that makes sense of earlier experience. With Lily's broken-head early experience, as enacted with the doll, I picked up her affect and understood her play as being rooted in early memory. As she had new experiences of being held and cared for (both in music therapy and significantly in her adoptive family), she could test me to see if I could bear the repetition of her trauma. *Après-coup* is the idea that meaning comes after an event. The first experience for Lily would have been her relinquishment by her birth mother. The second experiencing helps the first to be known. I think Lily had a second experience with her adopted mother, but Lily was only able to reject her care. In music therapy, Lily had a third experiencing, which could give meaning to earlier experiences in both her birth and adoptive families. The adopted child has their first early experience and meets this for a second time with their adopter, but this is experienced as traumatic. In the third experiencing, in the space of the therapeutic relationship, the experience can be thought about and thereby gain meaning.

Towards the end of our work together, Lily's use of the doll changed dramatically. She became able to provide soothing nurture for herself, using her own voice, by singing ostensibly to the doll but also to her internal baby self. After some *years* of music therapy, she could tenderly, softly care for her 'baby'. 'Gigi doll' was then sometimes wrapped in a blanket, which Lily extended around her own body while listening to me play lullabies. 'Rock-a-bye Baby' was a favourite tune that spoke of her lived experience but provided a frame for thinking about it safely. Lily was often hospitalised because of her disability and health problems, and in music therapy 'Gigi' had to have the same procedures as Lily. I was able to work with Lily during her hospital admissions and sang about procedures with guitar accompaniment as they happened to her, which helped her to tolerate them. Both adoptive mother and I viewed Lily's painful play enactments as fundamental to her sharing her lived embodied experience of being denied holding and nurture. On a relational level, Lily's later ability to show the doll care indicated that she was able to take goodness in from music therapy, internalising myself as a maternal object and internalising good reparative experiences to take away into her life. From my experiences with other clients, I was not surprised then when Jack began to play with the baby doll in a similar way as the following examples show.

Session 3: Music Therapy Example 1

Jack became distressed during our session for no apparent identifiable reason, and I was relieved I had his mum in the room on this occasion. I needed her presence because Jack was desperately trying to communicate verbally with me, and I was rarely able to understand his verbal utterances. Mum could help, being obviously more familiar with his speech; however, his words were difficult even for her to understand as they did not seem to relate to any specific context. Jack was telling us a story about a 'bouncy castle' and that he had fallen and hurt his head. There was such urgency in his little voice, and it felt that this message needed to be thought about symbolically. Mum continued to receive his communication beautifully while I played piano gently in the background, intending to soothe and regulate his distress and make speaking easier. I vocalised some words, reflecting that we heard what Jack was saying and checking out we understood correctly. Four identifiable words were 'castle', 'hurt', 'head', 'bang'.

Later, I found myself thinking about this symbolic communication. I imagined where a sensation of being 'bounced' might come from, relating this to him being born and 'bouncing' into the world but then subsequently being 'bounced' out of his birth family. Both his learning disability and that of his birth mum were in my mind when he talked about a 'hurt head'. As stated earlier, many adopted people with learning difficulties I have worked with have used very similar terms to describe their sense of being damaged somehow and showing awareness that their damage is located in their head, with regard to having a learning disability. Jack was desperate to communicate and to feel heard. I wondered if he wanted his mum to know his awareness of his damage/learning disability. Children in special schools will often look at other children around them and recognise that they are all different from their own relatives, and different from each other, and different from non-disabled children. In time, such recognition of difference can dawn on a child as being the reason they themselves are in special education and are therefore like those others. I wondered if Jack was communicating a sense of both his birth, his adoption and his learning disability (and, in fact, how his learning disability, like that of his birth parent(s), was inextricably bound up in his adoption). I considered how I might explain this idea to Jack's mum and hoped to be able to meet Jack musically if this material arose again.

I was also struck by the castle image Jack verbalised. Many adopted children in music therapy have described their birth homes as being 'castles' they have come from. In part, this can match a fantasy that their birth parents might be kings and queens and they could really be princes and princesses. Tom, who was referred to in an earlier chapter, used a song that incorporated ostinato and these lyrics: 'One minute I held the key, / Next the walls were closed on me, / And I discovered my castle stands, / Upon pillars of salt, pillars of sand.' Tom later explained how he felt banished from his birth parents' home. Interestingly, a line further on in the song states, 'Now the old king is dead, / long live the king!' In a sense, all adopted children leave what could be described as the kingdom of their birth and are relocated in a new kingdom. The line about the old king dying and the new one living seems redolent of the adopted child's dying to their birth family and having a new position in their adoptive family. Jack may have felt internally that he had been bounced out of his birth kingdom, away from his castle, and this being so because he had a learning disability.

Session 11

Jack suddenly, during a period of crashing loudly on every musical instrument, caught sight of the doll. He walked over to it, picked it up, looked in its eyes, then turned it away from himself, saying, 'No good, bad head.'

Although the doll is always available as a part of my equipment in the music-therapy room, it is interesting when children seem to discover it for themselves. Often this is at a point in therapy where they feel held enough to symbolically use the doll. I was not surprised, given my previous experience with Lily and others, that Jack immediately decided the doll had a bad head. Upon making this pronouncement, he looked away, feigning disinterest in it. I simply stated, 'Oh dear, the doll has a bad head.' In my mind, I was imagining Jack being known to have a bad head with regards to his learning disability by professionals who then removed him. I wondered if he experienced this as feeling his parents were disinterested in him because he had a learning disability.

Session 13

Jack struggled with strong feelings during this session and had hit out at a couple of instruments. He had even half-heartedly used a boomwhacker to gently hit me with but had been easily dissuaded from doing so. It is important that children can have somewhere to place their anger in music therapy while being clear that it is not OK to take this out on another person. This is partially what the instruments can offer. After the attempted hitting, Jack became more tender towards me, and I played some music to enable him to self-regulate. He came close to my keyboard and reached out, not to hit this time but instead to touch my hair. He sat facing me and stated simply, 'Hair'. I reached out in response and touched his head stating, 'Hair' back to him. Immediately following this, Jack moved away and, as he did so, pretended to bump his head. I sympathetically said, 'Oh dear', to which Jack's response was 'Bad head Jack' as he slapped his own head. For the remainder of the session, he continued to gesture to his head, without verbalising actual words again but rubbing his head occasionally while mouthing the word 'bad'. Finally, at the end of the session, he picked up the doll and dropped it behind him, as if rejecting it. Again, he stated, 'Bad head.'

Over some weeks of therapy, I had sensed I had become an available object for Jack to use. Now he could use other aspects of music therapy made available to him and was, therefore, able to use the doll as a transitional object. Adopted children who have experienced trauma need a transitional object to represent their experience. In a process of figurability, something that has no form is given form. Jack's experience did not exist for him before as it was unrepresented, but now it could be created in our playing.

I was encouraged that now Jack was clearly expressing anger and frustration safely, for the most part. He did not have to worry about my response, having experienced now that both I and the instruments were strong enough to take his emotional expressions, including anger. A lot of work must happen to get to the point where this sort of music therapy is possible. In later chapters, I shall explore states of being the music therapist needs to adopt, and especially states of quiet, authentic, 'being with' our clients. Having the power to make something else make a sound was proving to be a way of helping Jack express his feelings about his inability to be understood through language. I wondered if he saw me as being like the instruments and in a sense being just another object in the room. I only had to verbally tell him once not to hit me, and he stopped. His move (in the session above) to become tender towards me was perhaps a means of recognising a slight possible rupture in relationship and seeking to repair this. Jack's touching of my hair felt like more of a recognition of me as a person, like him, but someone who was also unlike him regarding me having any (as far as he knew) learning disability. So, soon after this, he referred again to his own head being somehow hurt and this becoming then not only hurt but bad.

Conclusion

I root these ideas very firmly in the writing of Sinason (1992) who works with adults described as having significant and severe learning disabilities, using a psychoanalytic approach. She states that the position of (in her deliberately chosen language) 'mental handicap' (or learning disability) in psychoanalytic history is painful and about exclusion. Assessing which kinds of patients were suitable for treatment, Freud (1954, p. 254, cited in Sinason, 1992, p. 60) considered that 'a certain measure of natural intelligence and ethical development are to be required'. Later, Sinason goes on to cite Chidester and Menninger (1936, p. 616, cited in Sinason, 1992, p. 60), who write: 'Mental handicap has long been looked upon as an organic condition, therapeutically hopeless, and probably for this reason, few psychoanalysts have attempted to apply their methods to the study of retarded children.'

Jung (1963, cited in Sinason, 1992, p. 6), however, argued that 'although patients may appear dull, apathetic or totally imbecilic, there is more going on in their minds, and more that is meaningful than there seems to be'. In 1978, Symington (1981, cited in Sinason, 1992, p. 6) started to develop his argument that 'handicapped patients had conscious and unconscious processes at work that could be enriching or debilitating'. Working psychoanalytically with mentally handicapped people, Sinason (1992, p. 214) argues, offers possibilities for thinking the unthinkable thought: 'It is that they have emotional intelligence: somewhere they know and understand what is happening within and around them.' She recognises, however the significance of the differences of learning disability and that it is essential to explore the extent of what this means for each individual client: 'Some things are organic, and nothing can be done about them. Yet in order to accept what cannot be changed it matters being able to explore the extent of knowing' (Sinason, 1992, p. 97).

This then leads Sinason (1992, p. 6) to conclude, 'no handicap in itself meant that a patient could not make use of therapy'. Indeed, she recognised that for years preceding the 1990s, music therapists had already been working with people with learning disabilities and were applying psychoanalytic thinking in their work. However, verbal analysts were still tending to agree that a minimum degree of cognitive intelligence was necessary for psychotherapy to happen. I would argue that music therapy provides a modality for adopted clients with significant learning disabilities because a different sort of intelligence, emotional intelligence, is privileged, and verbal language is not required.

Writing about learning-disabled adults who experience the death of their parent-carers and usually a subsequent move to institutional care, Sinason says this produces a double loss: loss first of family and then loss of home (if learning-disabled adults need to go into public care). Similarly, I argue that adoption produces at least a double loss for the removed, disabled child. They lose their parents and other family members (siblings, grandparents and so on) and also lose access to their social and cultural heritage. Even if the child's disability is not entirely the reason they are being placed for adoption, they may still hold an internal sense that something about their self-perceived badness is the reason they are given up. Sinason's work, therefore, has encouraged me to know that children experiencing such loss and subsequent difficulties attaching and attuning to their adoptive parents can make use of music therapy.

Sinason (1992, p. 271) powerfully addresses the issue of a client with a learning disability attacking their therapist and the impact such an attack might have on a therapist: 'Struggling with feelings of guilt at being normal is a very big burden for those who work with the handicapped, as well as a wish to deny that handicapped people have any envy or hatred for their carers.'

Jack's one attack on me, albeit half-heartedly, alerted me to my power in the room and his lack of it. This immediately bought to mind our differences, he as a learning-disabled child and I as a cognitively competent professional. Jack had turned immediately from hitting me to slapping his own head, symbolically showing me in varying ways his sense of his learning disability. Sinason (1992, pp. 113–14) explains such attacks on others and self as follows:

> Attacks on the head were the commonest form of violence against the self, posing questions of whether the organic damage left a feeling of physical discomfort within the brain as well as raising psychodynamic questions as to the nature of the attack.

The German music therapist Niedecken, writing in 2003, discusses the exclusion of learning-disabled people from psychoanalysis, arguing that additional secondary handicap (a term coined by Sinason to describe the particular use a person makes of their handicap) is developed right from birth during early interactions of caregiver and infant. A learning-disabled child must not only manage their original handicap (such as cognitive impairment) but also develop a secondary handicap as a defence to manage the original handicap and the responses of others to it. For example, a child may find they get laughed at in the playground because of their handicap, and they may then become deliberately comedic in response. However, this way of defending from bullying may be taken out into other areas of life where 'playing the fool' becomes a secondary handicap. Therefore, a psychoanalytic therapeutic approach focusing on the particular early life experience of learning-disabled people is required.

Cottis, in 2009, drew together twelve leading professionals working in this specialist field who were clear about drawing on the work of psychoanalysts such as Bion, Winnicott, Sinason and Alvarez. The back cover of their book states that the authors answer the question of whether psychotherapy for people with learning disabilities is worth it. It is incredible to think that a little over 20 years ago this was still a debatable issue. In 2019, Corbett edited a text focusing on the theory, practice and influence of Sinason. It describes how contemporary disability therapists have discovered, used and adapted Sinason's core concepts, illustrating how crucial her work has been. Yet, still working psychoanalytically with learning-disabled people is seen as somewhat specialist, and clients themselves are still othered. However, as Sinason (1992, p.77) recognises, 'What most share is a belief that there is meaning in the actions and feelings of people with severe disabilities and that if the therapist is able to lend himself adequately to the task, change will happen.'

All the writers above acknowledge the value of the creative-arts therapies for people who may not be able to use verbal language. Sinason (1992, p. 170) writes about one of her own clients:

> Some retarded individuals can become transformed in their love of music . . . he started singing a beautiful lullaby . . . when he finished he said to me gently 'It is my language and it is what you sing when someone goes to God.'

Deeply moved by this client's use of music, she suggests it is possible to use the same approach to trauma with people with learning disabilities as with any other human being, drawing on Goldschmidt's trauma work: 'The patient must re-experience the traumatic situation bit by bit but in the presence of an object which assumes the function of a shield against stimuli' (Goldschmidt, 1986, cited in Sinason, 1992, p. 132). This concurs with the findings of my case study of Jack. When the capacity for transitional phenomena was there, he used it. However, Jack's nursery staff found it incredulous that I was working with him because of his adoption experiences. They considered him to be too young and too learning-disabled to know anything about his early losses. Sinason argues that such responses are defensive reactions from colleagues who are unable to bear the possibility of knowing that a child such as Jack might indeed carry such painful embodied early memories. I was needed by him as a music therapist who could become both receiver and transmitter of his psychological communications. This was the heart of our work together.

The mother of an adopted 19-year-old with profound multiple learning and physical disabilities once stated to me, 'You and the music have become her interpretation to the world.' Only when we can achieve this for an adopted client with a learning disability are we able to do what Winnicott says is necessary, i.e., give the patient's experience back to themselves. Sinason, drawing on Mannoni, describes how a psychoanalytic approach may enable this to happen with learning-disabled people: 'We have given back to himself the child walled in . . . non-communication so that in his turn he may belong to the world' (Mannoni, 1973, cited in Sinason, 1992, p. 133). This has been my approach within music-therapy work: to allow clients to first enjoy being hidden before enabling them to move to being equally able to enjoy being found. Within this process, I hoped Jack has been able to first experience himself as being fully human and then to communicate his early life experiences in ways that can be held and thought about safely. Finally, it is my hope that music therapists can be enabled by this work to continue to develop relationships in the here and now with their adoptee clients, wherein adoptees' whole selves complete with all their varied emotional states, might be known, understood and loved.

References

Bion, W. R. (1988). Notes on memory and desire. In E. B. Spillius (Ed.), *Melanie Klein today* (Vol. II: *Mainly practice*, pp. 17–21). Routledge. (Original work published 1967.)

Chidester, L., & Menninger, K. (1936). The application of psychoanalytic methods to the study of mental retardation. *American Journal of Orthopsychiatry, 6*, 616–625.

Cottis, T. (Ed.). (2009). *Intellectual disability, trauma and psychotherapy.* Routledge.

Freud, S. (1920). Beyond the pleasure principle. In *The standard edition of the complete psychological works of Sigmund Freud* (24 vols., 1953–74, vol. 18, pp. 1–64; Ed. J. Strachey). Hogarth Press.

Freud, S. (1954). *The origins of psychoanalysis: Letters to Wilhelm Fliess, drafts and notes, 1887–1902* (E. Mosbacher & J. Strachey, Trans.; M. Bonaparte, A. Freud, & E. Kris, Eds.). Basic Books.

Freud, S. (1991). *Case histories II.* Penguin.

Goldschmidt, O. (1986). A contribution to the subject of psychic trauma based on a course of psychoanalytic short therapy. *International Review of Psychoanalysis, 13*, 181.

Jung, C. G. (1963). *Memories, dreams, reflections.* Fontana.

Mannoni, M. (1973). *The child, his illness, and the others.* Penguin.
Niedecken, D. (2003). *Nameless: Understanding learning disability.* Brunner-Routledge.
Ogden, T. H. (1994). *Subjects of analysis.* Karnac.
Phillips, A. (1994). *On flirtation.* Harvard University Press.
Schore, A. N. (1994) *Affect regulation and the origin of the self: The neurobiology of emotional development.* Erlbaum.
Schore, A. N. (2001). Neurobiology, developmental psychology and psychoanalysis: Convergent findings on the subject of projective identification. In J. Edwards (Ed.), *Being alive* (pp. 57–74). Routledge.
Sinason, V. (1992). *Mental handicap and the human condition: New approaches from the Tavistock.* Free Association Books.
Symington, N. (1981). The psychotherapy of a subnormal patient. *British Journal of Medical Psychology, 54,* 187–199.
Wilkinson, M. (2010). *Changing minds in therapy: Emotion, attachment, trauma and neurobiology.* Norton.
Winnicott, D. W. (1965). *The maturational processes and the facilitating environment.* Hogarth Press.
Winnicott, D. W. (1971). *Playing and reality.* Tavistock.

Chapter 8

Making sense from case studies

Building 'ground up' theory for adoption-specific music therapy

Within this penultimate chapter, I shall describe elements of what I consider is 'going on' in music therapy, both musically and relationally, that enables adopted children such as Jack to share their early unconscious experience. My central idea about adoption music therapy is that it is the musical revealing, sharing and meaning-making of material from early lived experience that enhances understanding of the relational difficulties adopted children are struggling with. Understanding subsequently enables a new and hopefully reparative attachment relationship to be formed by an adopted child with their music therapist. This new therapeutic musical attachment brings with it opportunities for exploring different ways of relating, which can impact positively upon the child's relationships beyond the music-therapy room and especially within their adopted family. It is, therefore, the combination of musical and relational explorations in music therapy that is seen as contributing towards strengthening adoption placement relating.

I have earlier described 'micro-moments of attunement' occurring in music-therapy sessions, which I understand as being significant moments within a musical relationship that are akin to Daniel Stern's (1985) notion of early affect attunement. These attuned moments have relevance because they can offer reparative experiences of being held, attached and attuned to, which often have been previously denied to the adopted child. It is these moments that also carry potential for change, which is the hope of adoption-specific music-therapy practice.

To illustrate how this works out in therapeutic practice, I shall now draw upon the case study of Jack (presented in Chapters 5, 6 and 7). The themes in work with Jack were unsurprising to me as they have been evident from my earliest practice as a music therapist in adoption and therefore already felt familiar to me. In this chapter, I situate Jack's case study in the context of my wider music-therapy practice, thereby adding to sense-making about work with him as a single case study that might inform other work. In this way, I illustrate how therapeutic practice has been the route to meaning-making with adopted children and their families.

DOI: 10.4324/9781003733393-8

My thinking as an insider-researcher (see Costly, 2010) has been rooted from the start in understanding that there is something specific about the nature of adoption that is traumatic. In fact, some adult adoptees within the adoption community use the term 'adoption-specific trauma' to describe adoption as an act constituting trauma. I have previously described the adoption community as:

> The shared networks of individual lives that are connected by the experience of adoption, in some way. Membership of this community is gained by being either an adoptee or an adoptive parent/grandparent/relative, but with the lived experience of adoptees being privileged.
>
> (Gravestock, 2021, p. 15)

Aspects of musical relational experiences in therapeutic work draw inevitably upon my own lived experience also. Both my lived experience and my searching for theory have enabled my own sense-making of what constitutes adoption trauma. In this chapter, these elements combine, contributing to my argument for music therapy to be a modality of choice for working within adoption support. I believe that there is nothing 'old-school' about music therapists using case studies in our witing, in our speaking at conferences and in our research. It is through a close examination of our work and reflecting upon it that client needs can be understood and therapies conceived that are of more benefit to specific communities.

During the process of researching my own practice, it became apparent from my case studies that before a music therapy can happen at all with adoptees (before we can play together), a therapeutic 'presence' first needs to be offered. What I define simply as presence provides an essential basis for any relational engagement that arises within music therapy. I shall describe in this chapter how the presence that is offered by a music therapist (and in the instance of myself one who inevitably brings her own lived and embodied experience into a musical intersubjective relating) invites adoptees to share something about their adoption-specific trauma. I am therefore producing insider-research and work, given my situatedness and context (Costley, 2010) with my research client and other clients in the adoption community.

I have described my music-therapy approach being formed directly out of experiences in the music-therapy room and how this is needs-led by clients. Working in non-directed free improvisation means that all occurrences and soundings in music therapy are welcomed, thought about and eventually played with. An adopted child can potentially play in many ways but only when they sense the music therapist is present to them, accepting, holding and thinking about their communications. Awareness of the significance of how I offer a music-therapy presence accelerated during my research, and I shall argue for what such presence might look and feel like in music therapy.

In her foreword to my first book, Helen Odell-Miller writes, 'Making music in the music therapy room can resemble and recreate the motherese or protoconversation, which may have been lost through separating the child from birth parents. Each case is unique, and there is no direct model or solution' (Gravestock, 2021, p. 9).

These two sentences sum up my practice in their recognition first that an adopted child can have a second chance at experiencing 'motherese' (the non-verbal language existent between mother and infant prior to the emergence of language, first described by Newport et al., 1977). The music therapist does not literally become another mother for the adopted child but evokes something representational that can be worked with therapeutically. The term 'music-mother' was apparently coined by Levinge (2015, p. 98). However, interestingly, I had also been using this exact phrase to describe my own work prior to reading her work. I think the fact that two music therapists arrived at this same descriptive phrase encapsulates how close the metaphor is to our work. Being a music-mother is not gender-specific and is linked to certain aspects of early experience the mother provides, especially holding. These could all be provided by a non-female music therapist. In becoming a music-mother, the music therapist's self, the music and the relationship all become part of the holding maternal function.

Second, each child I work with is not slotted into a model. Rather, by individually engaging in needs-led improvisation, an alive responsive new musical relationship with elements that resemble motherese can emerge in every therapy. Each adopted child I work with helps me develop my approach, which is constantly evolving. Odell-Miller recognises this individualised nature of my work, describing how this is underpinned by presence, writing, 'literally reaching a pure form of attention to others is repeatedly demonstrated through interactive music-making' (cited in Gravestock, 2021, p. 11). She affirms that a musical and relational *presence* can lead to 'increased loving relationships within the family, or within children and young people themselves, through the music therapy process' (cited in Gravestock, 2021, p. 11).

Prior to embarking on sense-making about my case study of Jack that is the central focus of this book, I shall first account for the 'being presence' that undergirds all my work. I shall describe processes of becoming present to what was alive and happening in the music therapy. This is complex due to the momentary, fleeting nature of music. Music itself exists as a temporal form and therefore is difficult to pin down in verbal description. Tempo is a fundamental part of any therapeutic musical framework and involves movement from one moment to the next. Levinge (2015, p. 125) writes that 'tempo can create a holding framework in which the moment-to-moment musical connections can evolve'. By consistently offering a form of attention/presence in time (that Odell-Miller identifies in my work), throughout interlinked temporal moments, a musical space for representation was created for Jack (and other adoptees) to 'be' in and use.

Presence precedes play

Part I: Winnicott – playing in the presence of

Winnicott (1965, p. 30) writes:

> Although many types of experience go to the establishment of the capacity to be alone, there is one that is basic, and without a sufficiency of it the capacity to be alone does not come about; *this experience is that of being alone, as an infant and small child, in the presence of mother*. Thus, the basis of the capacity to be alone is a paradox; it is the experience of being alone while someone else is present.
>
> (Italics in original)

As previously discussed, all adopted children have, however early their separation from their birth mother, lost out to at least some degree on the experience Winnicott describes above. Winnicott recognises that we first learn to be alone while being with the mother/another, and first experiences of play occur in the presence of the mother. To enable the opening of a potential space to play in (Winnicott, 1941), the mother needs first to find ways to become present to her infant in a manner that means he feels held and understood but not impinged upon.

Winnicott's description of the literal mother and infant becomes a metaphor I employ for the maternal presence utilised in music therapy. 'Presence' begins with a free-floating attention that the music therapist needs to pay to the client. This includes listening and silence, which needs to be offered to the client in a way that does not lead them to experience it as empty and barren. If a music therapist can offer from the first a presence that incorporates authentic, embodied, resonant, intersubjective attunement to the client's material, demonstrating empathy and musical responsivity, then the client has ground or space to form a relationship. The music therapist can then invoke notions of maternal holding and repair that come before language. I shall now describe how I first offered presence for Jack as a prerequisite for developing the potential space in which he became able to play and relate.

A shared music-therapy experience is created in time by the interlinking of musical moments. Shared 'being' states precede any 'doing' as Levinge (2015, p. 125) writes: 'First sharing a musical presence can provide a sense of ongoing-ness . . . an ongoing musical-ness.' As musical moments layer up over time, the client begins to feel met and gradually comes to experience the therapist's presence as reliable. This echoes the relationship of the mother–infant dyad in time, which Winnicott thinks undergirds the forming of potential space for playing in. By offering space with presence to Jack, he could first discover his own experience then go on to have new intersubjective experiences in relating musically with me. Together, these experiences had potential both for the reliving but also the reparation of early adoption-specific trauma, as Jack was held by a symbolic music-mother.

Winnicott's core conviction is that what matters in both a mother–infant or therapist–client situation is not what the mother or therapist does but rather that the infant/client is given an opportunity to live through the 'full course of an experience' (Winnicott, 1941, p. 246). This occurs in music therapy when a client can be in the presence of a witnessing other who can bear, hold and think about their experience. It requires that the mother/therapist 'watch, but don't interfere' (Slochower, 2018, p. 100), but I argue it is so much more than this implies. It requires much patient waiting on the music therapist's part to allow the client to reveal themselves. To understand this more, I shall now explore Heidegger's concepts of 'waiting' and 'releasement', which are both philosophical notions that make sense to me in an explanation of music-therapy presence. Wilberg writes that an embodied psychology of listening 'unites Heidegger's philosophical understanding of listening with the psychological understanding of thinking developed by the independent school of psychoanalysts in Britain' (Wilberg, 2002, p. 10). I discuss how I also have come to view aspects of Heideggerian philosophy as helpful in making sense of my practice as a music therapist.

Part II: Heidegger – waiting presence

Heidegger's (1966, p. 68) statement that 'In waiting, we leave open what we are waiting for' chimes with what I recognise myself doing when providing musical relational presence. Presence incorporates waiting, holding an open, expectant, responsive position, for whatever is going to emerge but without forcing it to do so. Heideggerian waiting is without particular expectation, and this resonates for me with Bion's (1967, p. 260) injunction to the therapist to come to the client aiming for 'a steady exclusion of memory or desire'. Waiting, without memory or desire, creates a potential space that is neither inactive nor vacuous; rather, it is open and inviting. Brodie (2020, p. 56) writes how space must always be kept 'potential' if it is to be 'tolerated, used and lived in'. He argues this can only be achieved

> if it is *filled with something* . . . if it is not allowed to be experienced as a void . . . it is an area of experiencing that has to exist but cannot be allowed to exist, a space that can exist only if it is filled, 'potential space'.
>
> (Brodie, 2020, p. 56; italics mine)

In music therapy, this means ensuring the space is filled with an expectant presence. Therefore, when an adopted child enters my music-therapy room, I aim to offer something akin to the maternal presence Winnicott describes. My whole self is tuning into the adoptee while not interfering in their space. As the adoptee explores, I am waiting and expectant and ready to respond musically or listen. They are not simply expected to turn up and play in a vacuum, but, rather, they play into a space that can receive them, acknowledge them and respond to them.

Potential space becomes available when a continuous holding, supportive presence is made available to the client via music that feels profoundly alive, relationally responsive and requires the music therapist to be emotionally and bodily engaged. I sense Levinge might also subtly be drawing upon Heidegger as she writes in similar language to his, 'we can provide that which is waiting to be found' (Levinge, 2010, p. 125). The music therapist's presence tunes into the adoptee's musical sounds (or, if the client is silent, just to their embodied state), becoming ready to respond and enter music-making from a not-knowing stance. This is the beginning of meeting the adoptee moment to moment and waiting while providing a witnessing, receptive presence. As free improvisation then emerges between client and music therapist, a musical relationship is begun.

This process is evident in my case study of Jack. I was constantly thinking about and interpreting material emergent in his sessions in my own mind at the same time as entering into musical, relational, embodied, intersubjective experiences with him. However, I described in earlier chapters how in music therapy, interpretations are not made verbally explicit because the musical elements themselves as they occur and are experienced in time have intrinsic therapeutic potential. Lawes (2021, p. 6) writes about managing his desire to interpret at times but recognising that 'it was not necessary to interpret imagery in a psychodynamic way for the process to be worked through . . . my focus was more on helping F explore the meaning of her experience in her own way'. Music can offer the client meaningful, uninterrupted Winnicottian full experiences that do not require verbal unpacking.

It is essential that music therapists connect with their own sense of self (including resonating lived experiences arising in the music) to acknowledge and contain their self-experience. Only then is it possible to offer an entire, authentic, being presence to clients. Jack, like other adoptees, required my presence to consistently offer a holding that was alert and engaged, while being neither too interfering nor abandoning, for him to enjoy 'going on being'. I shall now consider how Heidegger's notion of 'releasement' might also be applied to my description of musical therapeutic presence.

Part III: Heidegger – releasement as attitude underlying presence

The music therapist Sami Alanne (2010) also draws on Heidegger's notion of releasement to describe the philosophical underpinnings of his work. Releasement is defined as a form of contemplation and wondering, without calculation, analysis and interpretation. Alanne describes releasement as a useful attitude and approach for music therapy, arguing that it means trusting our capacity to be with, witness and bear our clients' suffering while we patiently wait. I argue that releasement might be an attitude underlying therapeutic presence, describing more what is not done in music therapy rather than any technique used for doing music therapy. Or, as Zinker and Nevis (1994, p. 385) write, releasement offers a way of 'being with, without doing to', which Yontef (2002, p. 15) writes requires 'authenticity, transparency and humility'. This echoes my earlier statement that the music therapist's self-experience is unavoidably foregrounded if we are truly offering our presence to clients. Presence that contains an attitude of releasement lies

> at the heart of the concept of co-creation in relationship making possible this sense of mutual influence, of both persons changing in response to the other . . . remaining fully present is probably the most challenging skill for both therapist and researcher alike.
>
> (Finlay & Evans, 2004, p. 115)

Work with Jack revealed to me how consciously adopting a Heideggerian attitude of releasement, coupled with a waiting presence, allowed him to simply be and exist in an engaged, Winnicottian holding. In other, simpler, words, working with Jack and others has taught me the therapeutic value of first simply being with another.

From being, to going on being: Authentic music-therapy relationship built upon presence

At the beginning of this chapter, I state that working with adoptees means working with adoption-specific trauma. Even children like Jack, who was removed early as a tiny baby from his birth mother for adoption, will experience a fundamental break in relational being. Winnicott (1960) describes how additionally a false self can be born because of early interference in the going-on-being state between mother and baby. This false self is manifest in compliance to others and other inauthentic ways of being. Music therapists need then to ensure that presence and potential space are offered where the client's capacity to be a true self can be re-experienced. I argue that this happens within music therapy because both music and relationship exist in temporal form, occurring in the 'now'. I concur with Levinge (2015) that a sense of ongoing-ness or an ongoing musical-ness comes to exist, offering reparation for early ruptures in going-on-being. The total musical relational experience means an adopted child can be met anew, in a temporal presence, providing opportunities for new musical going-on-being states to occur.

Winnicott describes the alternative to being as reacting, where reacting interrupts continuity of being. By reacting, Winnicott means that an infant's states of being can be impinged upon in ways that negate them. I argue this is the case when children removed for adoption have their first attachment relationship severed brutally, even if this transition is exceptionally well managed. The birth mother ordinarily provides the holding environment, which would hopefully reduce the number of impingements her infant has to react to. However, at the point of removal from her, the child loses this first facilitating environment. Subsequently, they then must somehow make sense of their new adoption placement, which may or may not be able to provide the sort of holding required.

Part I: Holding preceding playing

Holding environments (discussed in previous chapters) are where an emotional holding is connected with a physical holding. Even in physical holding, the mother has to respond sensitively and continuously to her infant's needs, as Brodie writes here:

> How does the baby want to be held? What feels good to the baby and what does not? What degree of firmness is too much or too little? It is the mother trying to discover *who this baby is* (as opposed to all the other babies in the world) and to respond accordingly. It refers to the way the arms of the mother probe the infant, seeking to discover who it is, so that they can respond to its idiosyncratic needs.
>
> (Brodie, 2020, p. 20)

When I, therefore, attempt to provide a therapeutic musical holding, I am also trying to discover who my client's baby self was and how that sense of self gets enacted in the world. I often have the words 'being' and 'reacting' in my mind. I ask myself questions like Brodie's above: Am I able, musically, to 'be present', and thereby provide a context wherein an adopted child might experience a state of going-on-being (Winnicott) and of ongoing-musical-ness (Levinge)? Can I allow free play to emerge, or do I respond quickly, reacting prematurely to their playing with musical copying that is not matched with their emotional referent? How do I avoid playing too little (which might leave the child feeling musically abandoned) or too much (which might mean they feel I am interfering and overwhelming)? Only if the right sort of musical holding is offered can the adopted child begin to reveal and discover unconscious parts of themselves.

Compliance, and other manifestations of the false self that Winnicott describes, must be considered in music therapy with adoptees. There is a danger (especially when we are newly qualified) for music therapists to view any engagement in musical play as a positive sign in their client of a healthy, creative, true self. One clear example of apparently engaged musical play, which is not creative and relational, is of children with autistic savant musical ability. Such children (without any formal musical training) may be able to play highly complex pieces of music from memory, having heard them just once. There is sometimes a degree of innate technical skill and facility.

However, the played music itself acts as a form of defence against connection and relationship. It is often almost impossible to be allowed to join with such music, as it lacks nuance and any sense of emotional relatedness.

Not dissimilarly, I have experienced adopted children who have come to sessions and played perfectly beautifully. This can be seductive to the inexperienced music therapist. Such children might also ask me to tell them which instrument I want them to play and how to play it. This is compliance. The issue for music therapy in adoption is not that the adopted child makes music; the issue is in the child first accessing an authentic self who can truly play in music. Bringing authentic self-states into the music makes it possible to risk experiencing real relational connectedness. Only then can an adoptee truly be said to have been able to play in a Winnicottian way.

As I am writing this chapter, an adoptee I have worked with over some years has recently discovered his deep anger (around physical abuse he experienced as a tiny baby). In so doing, he has become destructive in the music-therapy room and is swearing and shouting. Another professional stated this was 'behaviour' that was 'unlike the good little boy' she has known to date. This adoptee at referral was described to me as 'the perfect child . . . easy . . . compliant . . . kind'. How much had he needed to project this false self into the world, to keep his adoptive placement safe from breakdown if he became naughty or difficult. And how difficult it is for professionals to acknowledge the awfulness of what adoptees may have experienced even as tiny babies and to recognise the dreadful rage that results from such abuse and trauma. I am helping the team around this adoptee to understand and even value his surfacing anger.

Part II: Playing

What then is the value of these opportunities and experiences of authentic playing for adopted clients? Should music therapy not be looking to 'do something' with the experience? Can it be enough that musical play is just allowed to 'be'? I argue there is immense value in experiencing shared playful going-on-being states because early adoption-specific trauma might be revealed, emerging simply as it is, as music provides perceptual conditions for this.

Within the music-therapy relationship with Jack, I provided attentive presence, holding and a protected potential space wherein his emotional expression could be facilitated (similar to an approach which Slochower (2018) argues for in her work with clients with attachment difficulties). Significantly though, this is a musical holding and space, vital for adopted children like Jack who have additional learning disabilities. Jack had little verbal capacity, and many other adoptees I have worked with have had none whatsoever. A musical holding and space provide a modality for expression that does not require words or language because 'music is the carrier of the emotion' (Cooke, 1959, p. 199). Through shared musical relating, early experiences of need and lack can be known together by therapist and client. The client's baby self is enabled to be creatively, playfully present. As music therapy moves on from this basis of presence and holding, a potential space for playing becomes available. Within this, clients might be enabled to have Winnicott's full course of an experience repeated many times, and, in the process, both therapist and client also learn more about the client's early experience and its continuing impact here and now.

Play is key in Winnicott's writing and for music therapy. One form of music-therapy play is termed 'free clinical improvisation' (or, more lately by Sutton, 2021, simply as 'music therapy improvisation'). In essence, this basically means engaging in music that is composed in the moment and improvised. Improvisations have previously been termed clinical because they differ from improvisation in other musical contexts. In clinical improvisation, the music therapist strives to attune to the client's emotional/psychological states, responding and resonating with the client's sounding of themselves (which may include the client's music, gesture, embodied presence). Jack's case study describes many extremely playful experiences, and I've described how his felt resonance with me echoed perhaps early, positive experiences with his birth mother. This may have been at the root of his capacity to use music therapy so well, so playfully. Perhaps he could re-experience embodied memories of holding that later had been overwritten in the process of being removed from her.

The playfulness required for such work is summed up in Slochower's (2018, p. 105) statement, 'The patient both is and isn't a baby; the analyst is and isn't the mother.' The relationship itself must be entered into with playful imagination. As I willingly took on the role of music-mother to Jack, he brought and played with parts of his baby self in music therapy. From the earliest moments of life, there is 'a pool of music and sound in which a baby is bathed' (Imberty, 2002, cited in Barale & Minazzi, 2008, p. 948). Anzieu (1976, cited in Nagel, 2013, p. 21) describes this as a sound envelope that then 'evolves into language and affects that define relational exchanges with others'. I argue that the music of music therapy can offer something of the early unworded experience, which is inseparably both musical and relational.

Malone (drawing on Ogden's description of reverie, as a personal experience of the analyst but one that is infused with the experience of the patient) writes, 'the analyst must allow himself to be in a state of not always fully knowing what is going on and remaining open' (2018, p. 15). Taking this idea into music therapy terms, Seligman writes that a music therapist who is playing music with their client has an experience of being 'involved while paying attention' (Seligman, 2014, p. 649). As I played music together with Jack, I was simultaneously taking in his early experience. His initially merged states with me (such as crying 'Mummy' to me at the piano), once known, gradually separated out to the point that we became two individuals who could now play music together. Music has a capacity to create states of both merging and separateness as two people can play on two separate instruments but be held (or even meshed) together in the music itself. Music enabled Jack and me to enter the shared dreaming state that Lawes writes about. Within musical reverie or dreaming that arose as Jack played in the presence of a music-mother, he could re-experience, and I could make sense of his early experiences.

Slochower (2018, p. 103) describes the necessity of this process for clients who have experienced trauma to bring 'very early, unmetabolized experiences into the therapeutic situation'. I argue that shared musical play in a potential space enabled Jack to know and recall early attuned states of being met and attuned to with his birth mother and then express his sadness for the loss of her. Loss constituted an enormous impingement to Jack's going-on-being, and music therapy could provide 'an antidote to the experience of ongoing impingements (trauma) that had characterised the patient's infancy' (Slochower, 2018, p. 104). Lawes (2021, p. 6) writes about the value of playing for its own sake, drawing on Winnicott's understanding of play, arguing,

> change can take place without it being necessary to interpret or even understand unconscious content. It is the activity of playing itself that counts, the therapist needing to help the client play who is unable to do so. Simply playing together may be what matters most, not symbolic meaning.

This concurs with my argument that nothing needs to be done regarding interpretation. Rather, musical play, by offering a whole experience to an adopted child itself directly addresses unconscious material.

Part III: Listening

I conclude this section by returning to Wilberg (2002), who, although not himself a music therapist, has much to say about the value of a playful musical therapeutic relationship. In his philosophy of listening, Wilberg argues that therapists should focus more on what is going on in the between spaces of therapeutic relationships. In musical language, he describes how 'tones of being – shared wavelengths of attunement – connect us to our own being and at the same time link and join being with another' (Wilberg, 2002, p. 27). He does not separate listening and being states because he writes:

> To listen with our whole being is also to communicate our whole being – and must be if we are to attune to another individual. In doing so, we also convey the essential tone of our own being – which becomes a carrier wave on which messages are not only transmitted but also received wordlessly by the listener.
>
> (Wilberg, 2002, p. 16)

The above paragraph could describe what happened musically between Jack and I, and how we both were simultaneously transmitting and receiving. Interestingly, Wilberg turns to a musical analogy to make his arguments about shared being states:

> In music, a single note or chord might tremble with a certain incompleteness and, in this sense, quest a response from an answering chord or note. There are no verbal questions and answers in a piece of music, and yet we hear in its tones a constant questing and response. The same is true of the music of feeling. It is through tones of feeling that we quest an answering response, not in words.
>
> (Wilberg, 2002, p. 26)

I argue then that music therapy can provide exactly what Wilberg argues for, that is, a wordless, playful way of being present together, through which feeling states can be experienced, communicated, shared and known. Listening is described in all schools of counselling and psychotherapy as a prerequisite therapeutic skill. However, for the music therapist in adoption, it is essential because offering a receptive deep listening state to an adoptee's sounds provides 'a most primordial way of being with and bearing with another human' (Wilberg, 2002, p. 26). In the next section, I shall discuss how, having established listening, presence and holding, music therapy as an embodied non-verbal modality can offer opportunities for the adopted child to encounter micro-moments of attunement.

Music therapy as embodied playing and listening

Music is not a tangible, visible object, and it is therefore incredibly difficult to describe in words that do justice to both the way it is created in part in the mind but experienced (played, heard and felt) in the body. There is a need then for some sort of analysis of ideas about mind and body and how I understand these in interplay in music therapy. Merleau-Ponty (1968) argues we perceive and know the world subjectively through the body. Poetically, Heidegger describes embodied knowing, claiming it is we that hear (that is, our entire embodied self) and not just the ear as the organ of hearing. Both philosophers invite therefore consideration of how entire beings hear. A philosophical appreciation of embodied states seems essential for undergirding writing about music therapy because in any act of playing music the body is implicitly involved. Listening also is inevitably embodied as we hear both through the physical mechanism of the ear but also through resonances felt deep within the body at multiple levels. Embodiment allows empathic moments of playing music with another to become a 'form of openness to a relational embodied intersubjectivity' (Finlay & Evans, 2004, p. 118).

The music therapist Gro Trondalen (2016, p. 5) writes that in any relational music therapy the body is 'the primary source of knowledge'. To engage with sense-making about her work, she has, like me, developed a multi-theory approach. This necessitated philosophical exploration on her part too, and she uses Merleau-Ponty's description of 'the living body' (Trondalen, 2016, p. 77) alongside Knoblau's concept of 'resonant minding' (Trondalen, 2016, p. 78) as theories enabling her descriptions of musical intersubjectivity. She describes Stern's thinking on intersubjectivity resonating 'intuitively with my own personal experience of relationships inside a music therapy setting and in life in general' (Trondalen, 2016, p. 36). However, she also needed to turn to theories beyond those commonly drawn upon by music therapists, as I found I also needed to do. As she notes (Trondalen, 2016, p. 77):

> In an improvisation the client quite often moves rhythmically to the music and uses her or his body intentionally to express inner states or feelings through music. The performance by the client's subjective body very often seems to promote vitality and the feeling of being alive.

I would add that in addition to intentional movement, quite often, I experience both myself and the client moving unconsciously and seemingly without intent, but in a shared embodiment. For example, I described myself physically rocking when playing lullabies with Jack. Embodied manifestations arising directly from shared moments of empathic music-making might be important to any music therapy, but I argue these have particular relevance for adoption work.

The early adoption-specific trauma of separation from his birth mother that Jack had known was remembered through physical, regulatory systems within his body, which held affective memory through non-verbal somatic processes (Van der Kolk, 1994). In less literal biological terms, I argue that Jack's adoption trauma was unconscious but was remembered and held within his body and could therefore be communicated through embodied states in music therapy. As my embodiment resonated with Jack's during shared improvisations, his early experience could be manifest and known by me as it was felt in my embodied states. Such early material as Jack's (as he was only weeks old when removed from his birth mother) could never have been verbally processed by him (not least because it is unlikely he will ever develop significant verbal ability). However, in an embodied musical relating, his unconscious affective memory could be manifest, seen, witnessed, held and ultimately integrated.

I shall continue now to describe how Daniel Stern's work on vitality forms (which Trondalen sensed resonating so intuitively with her music-therapy practice) can offer explanations that indicate the value of shared, embodied music-making experiences in adoption music therapy.

Embodied music therapy: Stern and vitality forms

Earlier chapters have discussed Stern's (2010a) concept of forms of vitality, which I have argued has significance for thinking about embodied music-making. His vitality forms are comprised of five elements:

1 Movement
2 Force
3 Space
4 Intention
5 Time

Stern asserts that of all these elements, movement is of prime importance for human beings, as movement is life. Interestingly, Stern connects movement directly with music, which he describes as 'sound in motion' (Stern, 2010a, p. 89). This has obvious relevance to music therapy, especially given my earlier discussion of music's temporality and how music and movement and relationship all occur in time. Stern (2010a, p. 89) writes:

> Things move, and then out of that movement, you can get approach and withdrawal, and out of approach and withdrawal, you can get different emotions. From there you can get concepts consisting of all different things, bodily concepts, or psychosomatic concepts. And then you can get language that is built upon what the body already knows.

This short paragraph above by Stern offers rich gleanings in relation to developing an understanding of my case study of Jack. His process in the work seemed to follow Stern's trajectory. He would often arrive in the music-therapy room, and, without my needing to do anything, something would happen immediately in the space between us. This was not always music initially, but, as I waited, simply taking in his sounding presence as it were, his whole embodied self was welcomed into the potential space available. In fact, many adoptees I have worked with have come to music therapy in silence, either choosing not to play or being unable to play due to their emotional, physical or learning difficulties. In silence, however, the body still speaks, and a body-music can emerge. This could be something as simple as hearing the rhythm of a client's breathing or the tapping of their hand upon a chair. By responding to the client's embodied communications, I can begin the relational process of 'approach and withdrawal' that Stern writes about. With Jack, for example, as he began moving about in the room, making vocal sounds and eventually playing instruments, his self was manifest. I could begin to play with these embodied expressions, and, in a language that his body already knew, Jack could respond. Thus, even behaviour like him dropping and fiddling with my clock could communicate early states that were both evoked in and held by the music created between us. Stern (2010a, p. 90) goes on to link movement to time, writing: 'If you move, you create time – time being what we add to the experience of something moving in space . . . with space, there's movement . . . with music, there is movement in space. There is a temporal structure that gets laid out.'

I have argued that music is unique because of its temporal structure and therefore has a special use in adoption work because of these musical temporal structures it provides. Jack was always very interested in time and how his experiences existed in time (e.g., his focus on my clock and singing about time). Stern (2010a, p. 90) describes how time is linked to subjective experience: 'There is a lot of movement in the mind which is strictly subjective . . . and so it is with music . . . When you hear a musical tone, it invariably takes some kind of trip in space.' Jack could make musical tones himself and know he existed in time and could reach me through the sounding space between us, ultimately resonating too within my body. Simultaneously, I could present my subjective self in the room, and he could encounter me. Musical play makes this a less threatening experience for an adopted child who may not tolerate physical relating such as accepting hugs from their adopter(s). It is not necessary to be physically close to someone to hold them musically, as music exists in the spaces between two bodies and resonates physically within both. Stern (2010a, p. 91) continues:

> There is some kind of special movement of mental event that is going on when you hear music as well as the temporal structuring because time gets structured so that it becomes a real thing for us . . . There is an intention behind it all. The intention in music as it moves along is very hard to say exactly . . . we're finding the same kind of natural gestalt which I'm calling a form of vitality.

I am reassured to learn that Stern, too, finds this musical experience difficult to translate into words. However, I wonder if he is referring to very core elements of music here, which are temporal structures, such as pulse and rhythm. Earlier, I cited Levinge (2010, p. 125) writing, 'tempo can create a holding framework in which the moment-to-moment musical connections can evolve'. Music has a particular beat or time signature that is both a structured patterning of time but also can be felt as a form of vitality. We describe music as having a pulse which is the closest language I can find to describe the way in which Jack and I were relating rhythmically together: it is as if we had a shared pulse. This very idea evokes an early state of in-utero being when mother and foetus share a pulse through the umbilical cord that connects them.

Levinge does not mention Stern at all in her writing (her text solely explores Winnicott), yet I think his concept of vitality forms is extremely helpful in making additional sense of what might be happening in music therapy. Stern argues the value of vitality forms is that they are not tied to a context. He writes (Stern 2010a, p. 91), 'They float freely, they are totally multi-modal, they are totally interdisciplinary from the point of view of sensation, cognition, emotion etc . . . there is a certain something that music touches all the time.' Again, descriptive language is hard to find for something so ephemeral, but Stern recognises the power of music as a 'certain something', reaching a person at every level.

As I read about vitality forms, I think of how as Jack played and I responded it became possible for us to evoke early experience together, share it and make sense of it. As Stern (2010a, p. 92) writes:

> Vitality is one of the most essential things there is in our psychological experience certainly of other people, and of what they do, and of what they perform. And that will include music . . . Vitality is really the stuff that music creates and plays with, and it's what we, in communicating with one another, create and play with.

This makes me hopeful about what music, and therefore music therapy specifically, has to offer to the adoption community. Stern so strongly argues that vitality forms convey an embodied experience of the other, and music is one way he identifies this happening. I am encouraged that he links vitality, music, creativity and play, which are all evidenced in my case study of Jack and my work with all adoptees. By co-creating music with me, Jack could communicate experiences that could be played with, both musically and symbolically. Music could touch Jack and other adoptees all the time in a way I do not think another modality could have done.

Having discussed the nature of vitality forms, and specifically how Stern argues that these relate to music, I will now explore how sharing vitality forms in a music-therapy relationship can lead to an adoptee experiencing what Stern calls intersubjective attunement. For adopted children who missed out on early experiences of attunement with their first attachment figure, music therapy is well placed to offer a re-experiencing of this basic shared understanding of what it is to fundamentally be with another. I have earlier addressed the little-explored part that the music therapist will inevitably play in intersubjectivity. I argued this is especially significant because the music therapist plays with their client and therefore is engaged in embodied relating whether this is explicitly acknowledged or not. In a musical intersubjective relationship, a shared reciprocal experience is had wherein the experience of each individual has an impact on the other individual.

Intersubjective attunement and vitality forms

The term 'intersubjectivity' predates Stern. As early as 1964, Merleau-Ponty (1968, p. 138) described intersubjectivity as 'a reciprocal insertion and intertwining of others in ourselves and of us in them'. Music therapy has looked to

Stern for some time, especially incorporating his thinking on intersubjectivity. 'Forms of vitality' was a theory Stern was still working with at the time of his death and which is now becoming more used by music therapists. Pavlicevic (1990) has defined the concept of 'dynamic form' which Stern later related to 'vitality forms'. She argued that dynamic form existed musically from her own experiences of free improvisation in music therapy. However, she did not apply Stern's newer specific notion of vitality affects as described above.

Part I: Matching

When music therapists seek to respond musically to a child, we do not copy them but rather we *match* them, and it is this matching that captures the shape of the child's experience. Wigram (2004, p. 84) has defined matching in music therapy as 'Improvising music that is compatible, matches, or fits in with the client's style of playing while maintaining the same tempo, dynamic, texture, quality and complexity of other musical elements.'

While very close similarity of musical form can exist between music therapist and client, there is also always at least some degree of difference. I argue that the reason an adopted child can feel matched, and experience themselves as being known, is because music enables vitality forms to be communicated, picked up and shared.

For example, at times I played with Jack on matching instruments (such as two drums). However, the drums were separate instruments, and as we played them at times, the musical dynamic of each of our playing differed, or the emphasis on the placement of the beat might not have been exactly the same. It is possible to play similarly to while incorporating variations (e.g., in musical textures or elements such as melody, timbre, tone and colour). Co-created music provides space wherein both differences and similarities might be known. Jack's experience could be known via forms of vitality being musically, implicitly shared. Wright (2009, p. 8) writes that 'In music, a specific emotional contour can generate unlimited musical depictions, all loosely linked through formal similarity.' As music therapist, I would hear Jack's soundings, both musical and emotional, and respond in a manner that linked my playing with his, matching him as Wigram describes. I would continue listening as I played, taking in 'the various layers of musical, emotional, cognitive, physical and analytical and deep unconscious contents as they occur simultaneously' (Kroeker, 2019, p. 107).

This may have given Jack the experience of beginning to feel that he could know another person and predict their response (this is the implicit relational knowing, by Lyons-Ruth [1998] that I mentioned earlier). Implicit relational knowing occurs when spontaneous moments of authentic meeting exist in the therapeutic relationship. Such moments can 'effect psychotherapeutic change without the need for transference interpretation' (Lawes, 2021, p. 6). This, in turn, seems like Winnicott's understanding of play as being important in and of itself, without interpretation. However, Jack's early experience was also made known to me through projective identification in our transference (for example, in my responses when he called me 'Mummy'). Stern (2004, cited in Lawes, 2021, p. 12) differentiates 'the non-conscious dimensions of intersubjectivity associated with implicit relational knowing, from the dimensions of intersubjectivity which are psychodynamically repressed and thus unconscious'. I understand implicit relational knowing occurring when I would have a sense of how to do something with Jack that was distinct from conscious knowledge: 'The implicit relational knowing of patient and therapist intersect to create an intersubjective field that includes reasonably accurate sensing of each person's ways of being with others, sensings we call "the real relationship"' (Lyons-Ruth, 1998, p. 282).

Or, as Lawes (2021, p. 7) again puts it, 'the work . . . may also involve working collaboratively with unconscious creativity which never becomes fully conscious when playing together in music'. I concur that both implicit relational knowing and transference were in operation in music with Jack.

An intersubjective music therapy then must involve joint but not identical musical experiences. Sharing a sense of felt similarity is important because of the way in which this enables, through forms of vitality, the creation of shared, embodied musical states. A degree of difference is also essential. Within the intersubjective relationship, possibilities arise for shared experiences of attunement, central to my work. I shall now describe how I see music therapy providing such for adopted children.

Part II: Musical attunement using vitality forms

Jack had lost out on early attuned experiences, first by losing any initial good experience he may have known with his birth mother, and, second, by not apparently experiencing attuned states with his adoptive mother (according to her descriptions). Stern (2010c, p. 94) writes, 'this kind of intersubjective matching which we call affect attunement is at the base of so much relationship'. Music therapy offered Jack an experience of intersubjective relating where, via an ever-shifting contour of forms of vitality, he might also experience affect attunement, especially via musical matching. For example, if Jack played loudly at a fast tempo, I might match by playing at the same tempo but quietly, matching him not identically but cross-modally, to match the emotional referent implicit in the music, utilising other forms of vitality. I was thus presenting myself as an 'other' whom he could encounter and relate to and with.

Music's language has many descriptors for forms of vitality. 'So, we have crescendos, decrescendos, staccato, legato, forte, piano, fortissimo – we have sforzando – to really attack the note. All of these are forms of vitality, the dynamic forms' (Stern, 2010c, p. 94). These adverbs do not tell us *what* note to play but do tell us *how* the note should be played. Music then can provide various forms of vitality; for example, the note G could be played for three seconds, commencing with an initial sforzando (sudden loudness) fading to pianissimo (very quiet). The note G itself is the same throughout that time but is played with different qualities over time. Or a 6/8 rhythm could be played either as an invigorating waltz or a slow, stilling lullaby. The *rhythm* is the same, but a slower or faster *tempo* changes its *quality*. Music has the potential to be played with vastly varying forms of vitality over time, responding in a moment, thereby providing the immediacy required for attunement with another.

When Stern described affect attunement occurring between a mother and infant, he noticed that the mother might exaggerate certain aspects of her way of being in a selective imitation of her baby. In this way, via forms of vitality, she is, 'shaping from inside how she wants him to feel about what it is that he does. So this becomes an absolutely vital technique in having emotional and other communication with other people' (Stern, 2010c, p. 94).

Jack, having possibly lost this early experience with his birth mother, might have needed to erect defences in his adoptive placement. He may have been fearful that if he allowed himself to feel something again, he would also be at risk of losing it again. Music therapy could provide shaping of his experience, which allowed his communications to be manifest in a non-verbal symbolic form, held by myself, and gradually attuned states could emerge between us, which were safer for him to feel.

Stern describes how an infant knows that his mother understands what his experience was like. He writes that if the mother were to simply imitate the infant then the infant would receive the imitation but not know that his mother knew what it *felt* like to do as he had done. For the child to know their communications have been felt, the mother has to do something different, and this is what Stern calls cross-modal attunement. The mother needs to take the same thing which the child did, 'the formal parts of it, the parts that do the form of vitality, and she will keep those and imitate them but put them into a different modality' (Stern, 2010c, p. 94). In Jack's music therapy, rather than literally copying, for example, his dropping of instruments, I instead provided a musical matching of the dropping. One example I gave was of playing a glissando down the piano, ending on an emphatic final low note. The glissando matched the vitality form captured in Jack's dropping of beaters, but as it resolved into a sustained held low note, it could simultaneously provide some holding of his experience.

I argue then that in music therapy, an adopted child can understand their experience is known because the 'music-mother', via cross-modal attunement portrayed through vitality forms, illustrates from her musical experience that she knows what it was for the child to have their experience. More than this, I also suggest that by moving from one vitality form to another (in this instance through a glissando to a sustain) the experience might also be held through time.

Part III: Embodied 'movement signatures'

Stern writes that cross-modal attunements leading to intersubjective contact and relating are 'probably the single most necessary aspect of any successful therapy' (Stern, 2010c, p. 98). Music therapy provides such necessary experience, working as it does through the body, which earlier in this chapter I described as embodied playing and listening. Stern argues that when we begin to identify with another in an embodied sense, we might also start to assume their movement signatures. This certainly became the case in my work with Jack when moments occurred that I could describe in the following way Stern (2010c, p. 98) writes about: 'You have to, somehow, with mirror neurones, go into their system so that you capture their signature of vitality forms'. Stern draws on neurobiology in this reference to mirror neurons, and, certainly, the neurobiology of musical effects in the body can be argued for. However, I would argue that assuming movement signatures and vitality forms with my clients has been more about resonating with an unconscious state and allowing potential space for this to be manifest in embodied playing together. Erskine (2015) is a verbal psychotherapist who moves away from the idea of neurobiology and the notion that mirrored neurons undergird attunement. He writes that:

> Attunement involves using both conscious and out-of-awareness synchronising of therapist and client process so that the therapist's interventions fit the ongoing, moment-to-moment needs and processes of the client. It is more than simply feeling what the client feels: it includes recognizing the client's experience and moving – cognitively, affectively, and physically – so as to complement that experience in a contact-enhancing way.
>
> (Erskine, 2015, p. 28)

This fits more with my sense that in a psychoanalytically informed music therapy I can think of attunement arising out of early unconscious material in an implicit felt sense. As these 'movement signatures' which Stern describes occur with my own clients, I begin to feel something being made manifest in my own body, which has first been expressed musically by a client. However, prior to any of this, perhaps more sophisticated musical relating, Stern (2010c, p. 100) insists that holding is of vital importance: 'You've got to have some degree of using holding techniques which you know of in order to really soft-pedal the level of arousal and the range of dynamic forms that can be put into play.' I argue, therefore, that the states of being and holding I described earlier are essential precursors for the potential space of play to be created wherein embodied play and listening occur so movement signatures, resulting from attuned states, can be jointly experienced.

Trondalen (2016, p. 53) has described similar experience of how attunement might occur musically:

> The process of attunement is an implicit (non-verbal) one based on micro-shifts with the essential elements of timing, intensity, and form. Affect attunement emerges when the individual matches the persons movements and mental states in such a way that . . . these inner feeling states can be shared.

She clearly acknowledges Stern's theorising in the way she describes matching both movements and mental states, and that the two are combined intrinsically in embodied states. She also defines timing, intensity and form, as does Stern, but I suggest that here she is thinking simultaneously much more specifically about musical elements. She refers, as I argued earlier, to how music can utilise in particular pulse, rhythm, timbre and structured patterns such as time signatures to match and amplify communications.

Part IV: Authentic musical intersubjectivity

The music therapist Martin Lawes (2021, p. 5) writes that

> one of the most important and well-established ways to understand and work with intersubjectivity in music therapy involves theories of transference and countertransference. Here the focus is on the unconscious dynamics of the relationship between client(s) and therapist, both within and around the music. Such intersubjective content is understood most fundamentally in terms of the mother–infant relationship.

I have described how music therapy with Jack was drawing on Stern's understanding of that mother–infant relationship. Unconscious aspects of it, described as transference and countertransference, were enacted in the co-created music arising between us. The work with Jack demonstrates how the free improvisation approach I advocate for in music therapy has the capacity to spontaneously respond in each moment (and through one moment to another, and another) to the client's temporal experience, while simultaneously offering holding within the very music that is being co-created.

Erskine (2015, p. 29) writes:

> Attunement is a kinaesthetic and emotional sensing of the other – knowing their rhythm, affect, and experience by metaphorically being in their skin, and going beyond empathy to create a two-person experience of unbroken feeling connectedness by providing a reciprocal affect and/or resonating response.

Although not describing music therapy here, I think Erskine values here some of the most significant musical elements (e.g., rhythm) which I draw upon. Rhythm, reciprocity and resonance are all key elements I have discussed earlier. Interestingly, rhythm has the most significance to Erskine (2015, p. 38) because 'rhythm is one of the primary ways in which people, out of awareness, assess the quality of their contact with each other. When two people are rhythmically attuned, their transactions mesh together easily'. He focuses on the shared experience of cross-modal attunement occurring out of awareness (unconsciously), arguing then that transactions mesh together. This leads me to think of music forming a kind of 'mesh' that can knit two experiences into one felt intersubjectivity. Erskine concludes with the most musical metaphor for attunement I have yet discovered 'Hearing all the *nuances of the client's melody and rhythm* and responding from and with the *harmony of one's whole therapeutic orchestra*, verbally and non-verbally, is what attunement is all about' (Erskine, 2015, p. 41; italics mine).

Stern (2010b) suggests extreme sensitivity is required by the music therapist to create such a shared experience with their client. The music therapist must not 'create big arousal jags' (Stern, 2010c, p. 100) because, if they do, 'you throw the person out – they are no longer there' (Stern, 2010c, p.100). What is required is a 'progressive temporal violation' (Stern, 2010c, p.101) of the relational and musical dynamics. This is the process I described above of shaping a note or rhythm during time while also changing it. To create what Stern (2010c, p. 101) calls violations 'requires that exquisite sensibility as to where each of you is in the process in order to shape the vitality forms and their timing that they will work in establishing the relationship'. I am interested that Stern (2010c, p. 101) acknowledges that 'there is no technique that tells you what to do . . . you have to find something authentic within yourself as a response'. This resonates with my own approach to music therapy in adoption support, which combines various flexible elements rather than being a set method. Above all, it requires an authentic responsive music therapist.

This pertains to my earlier discussion of intersubjective relating, regarding the therapist's need to bring her authentic self to musical relating, acknowledging the impact of her needs, feelings and lived experience upon the therapeutic relationship. As I create musical states wherein clients such as Jack become vulnerable, I have a responsibility to be constantly aware of how I participate and use myself in the relationship. As a music therapist who is a member of the adoption community and working within it, I need to constantly expose to the light any sense that I might repeat my own trauma or become dysfunctional in what I consider to be countertransference. My own experience can then be brought into the room in a way that helps me to think more about my client. As one of my Ph.D. supervisors puts it, my own trauma should be processed enough so I do not find I am acting out. Then I can know it and put it in parenthesis in order to truly be with the client's trauma. To come to the client without memory or desire (Bion,

1967), it is imperative that I have first known and explored all my own memories and desires, as much as is possible.

I conclude this section then by clarifying my main argument for adoption music therapy: music therapy has the potential and capacity to offer adoptees opportunities to experience relationship in a moving-along process involving the regulation of emotion and affects at a non-verbal level, one in which micro processes play a crucial role. Wright (2009, p. 49) argues that creative therapies can provide artistic means of reparation because 'artistic activity is one such way of making good the original deficit' and 'artistic activity is a means of fashioning mirroring and containing forms, and thus a way of realizing and restoring the self'. A music-therapy relationship reliant upon non-verbal dialogue is well placed to work with non-verbal clients whose experience of adoption trauma was preverbal. Music therapy is a 'communicative structure that gives preverbal language dialogic meaning' (Trondalen, 2016, p. 15). Music therapy's capacity to evoke and share shapes of human feeling privileges the significance of non-verbal communication, with music a modality for re-experiencing. Intrinsic elements that comprise music give form and meaning to an adopted child's preverbal experience, and it is this that makes music therapy so relevant a therapeutic modality for adoption.

As child and music therapist become able to play together, this has significance for relational change in the child's familial context. As Trondalen (2016, p. 42) writes:

> There is a reconstruction of aspects connected to how it is to be with another. Such a view implies an expansion of the therapeutic setting, as *the client is carrying this new reconstruction as a lived experience when encountering other people* . . . Hence, an expansion of the intersubjective field is a *potent experience of change.*
>
> (italics mine)

Trondalen's idea that it is possible for clients somehow to have a second chance, developmentally, of experiencing secure emotional attachments is the hope I also work with. In my own approach, I have needed to draw upon psychoanalytic and developmental and latterly philosophical theories in order to make sense of what De Young (2003) describes as the thickly populated encounters that I encounter in music therapy and adoption. Psychoanalytic thinking enables me to conceive of the adopted child's early life experience and the ongoing significance of this, and intersubjective, and other developmental thinking enables me to conceive of how such early experience impacts current relationships. Essentially, 'the "here and now" contains something of the "there and then" where subjectivities of one person elicit those of another' (Finlay & Evans, 2004, p. 118).

Constructing an adoption-specific music-therapy space

My therapeutic practice, my previous book and my research argue for this approach that I now call 'adoption-specific music therapy'. As stated at the start of this chapter, central to the approach is a philosophy that adoption is a specific trauma with a specific quality rooted in early loss for the child. Adoption trauma is remembered in embodied ways, however old a child was when removed from their birth family and placed for adoption. I argue it is essential that music therapists working with adoptees first understand the nature of how this discrete phenomenon may manifest in the work. If music therapy is to be seen as relevant and desirable in post-adoption support services, it must take account of adoption-specific trauma and listen to the lived experience of adoptees.

Interestingly, during my research (and indeed as long as I have been working in adoption), I struggled to find much in the literature that defines loss of the birth mother, through adoption, as a distinct trauma in itself. Rarely is adoption constructed as trauma in professional literature because an adoption placement is inevitably positively framed. Adoption is construed by some professionals as a happy ending for children who have been seen to suffer significantly within their birth family in order to necessitate their removal in such absolute terms. Other lived experience gets lost in our desire to read adoption as a 'happy ever after' narrative. Professionals can collude in this silencing of the huge negative experiences and impact of adoption. Music therapists, involved when professionals are establishing new placements and families, can advocate for the voices of lived experiences within the adoption community to be heard and properly valued. This is not an easy task when other professionals may be less willing to hear about difficulties that can emerge and, perhaps most significantly, the extent of the trauma and loss that always emerges. This is why, along with the adoption community, I continue to argue for free lifelong access to therapy to be available for all adoptees.

Generally, therapeutic adoption work has tended to sit alongside work with fostered children and those in kinship care. This generalist siting of all types of care beyond that of the immediate birth family does not recognise adoption as a discrete experience qualitatively different to others (adoption being the only process whereby all ties are legally severed with a birth family and subsequently legally made with a new family). Additional experiences of other trauma that occurred within the birth family (such as neglect or emotional, physical and sexual abuse) may contribute to removal for adoption. However, common to every adoption experience is the *permanent* separation of mother and child, which in earlier chapters I referred to adoptees describing as an internal 'hole' (discussed in Verrier, 1993). This lived experience of early loss, internalised by the child, is manifest in definitive and distinctive ways that must be understood by music therapists working with adoptees.

Concluding thoughts on a synthesis of philosophy and practice for adoption-specific music therapy

This chapter has described the underpinnings of my philosophical approach to my music therapy practice and research, incorporating other theoretical understandings I have drawn upon to make meaning, with my clients, from their experience. Fundamentally, my approach acknowledges that it is the music therapist's use of her own states of being that enables clients to reveal aspects of themselves through needs-led work, at the heart of which is freely improvised music. First engaging in a non-directed improvisatory musical relationship with a client, I am later aided by supervision and continued theoretical exploration to engage in sense-making of what happened in the musical relating. 'Techniques' are not applied; rather, a relationship evolves and can be thought about.

Rather than techniques, the music therapist needs to become able to offer a sense of presence to the client. Presence undergirds states of being that arise between therapist and client and precedes and underpins any 'doing' that might go on in music therapy. By adopting Heidegger's attitudes of waiting and releasement, adoptees are offered something that is rarely found elsewhere in life. Such being is not vague and is informed by a music therapist's tradition, training and creativity. This means, of course, that the music therapist might draw upon techniques (such as Wigram's matching and mirroring) but can also choose whether to use them or not. What is most important is the receiving and holding of the client's communications as they are experienced moment to moment in relationship. Opportunities then arise for clients to experience 'going-on-being states', in Winnicottian terms. This requires that the music therapist has an ability to become authentically present in offering both self and music for the client. Following on from Trondalen, I concur that 'the client and therapist offer their being, doing, and symbolizing in a joint yet not identical field of musical exploration' (Trondalen, 2016, p. 78).

Music therapy can then go on to contain perceived high points that include micro-moments of attunement. These attuned moments seem very significant musically and relationally, but I suggest that also the more gradual, regular working-through of material is of equal importance. What a relief it is then to read of Winnicott's valuing of the ordinary devoted mother! Some musical play can even feel boring (as actually many parents describe repetitive play with babies and toddlers), yet it is still working with music our client may be calling forth from their deepest levels. I argue that it is this that provides a musical sense of 'going-on-being', in Winnicott's terms.

Gendlin (1996, p. 297) writes that 'the essence of work with another person is to be present as a living being', and Jaenicke writes that 'developmentally traumatic affect states can be understood only in terms of the relational systems in which they took form' (2008, p. 103). If then music therapy wants to offer what the adoption community is seeking, I conclude that it needs to offer both the specific presence and being states described in this chapter, alongside therapeutic reparative experiences of going-on-being, intersubjectivity and attunement described here and in previous chapters. I close with a quote by Erskine (2015, p. xxvii) which sums this up:

> Therapeutic presence is provided through the psychotherapist's sustained attuned responses to both the verbal and nonverbal expressions of the client. It occurs when the behaviour and communication of the psychotherapist at all times respect and enhance the integrity of the client. My premise is that healing of emotional and relational wounds occurs through a contactful therapeutic relationship.

My research shows that a holding, embodied, attuned, intersubjective relational music therapy offers these possibilities for adopted children, echoing the writing of Lawes (2021, p. 12):

> The value of music as a psychotherapeutic modality at this level lies in the way it may be able to be used to gain access to otherwise hidden and inaccessible areas of experience and trauma before and beyond the reach of words.

This was the case for Jack, as an adopted child with significant learning disabilities, who lacked language and experienced trauma that came even before language might have existed. It is similarly the case for other adoptees I have worked with, especially those with additional disabilities. Where words fail these children, music speaks and can represent their early unconscious experience.

References

Alanne, S. (2010). *Music psychotherapy with refugee survivors of torture: Interpretations of three clinical case studies.* Picaset Oy.

Anzieu, D. (1976). L'enveloppe sonore du soi. *Nouvelle Revue de Psychanalyse, 13*, 161–177.

Barale, F., & Minazzi, V. (2008). Off the beaten track: Freud, sound and music. Statement of a problem and some historico-critical notes. *International Journal of Psychoanalysis, 89*(5), 937–957.

Bion, W. R. (1988). Notes on memory and desire. In E. B. Spillius (Ed.), *Melanie Klein today* (vol. II: *Mainly practice*, pp. 17–21). Routledge. (Original work published 1967.)

Brodie, B. R. (2020). *Object relations and intersubjective theories in the practice of psychotherapy.* Routledge.

Cooke, D. (1959). *The language of music*. Oxford University Press.

Costley, C. (2010). *Doing work-based research: Approaches to enquiry for insider-researchers.* Sage.

De Young, P. (2003). *Relational psychotherapy: A primer*. Brunner-Routledge.
Erskine, R. (2015). *Relational patterns, therapeutic presence: Concepts and practice of integrative psychotherapy*. Karnac.
Finlay, L., & Evans, K. (2004). *Relational-centred research for psychotherapists: Exploring meanings and experience*. Wiley-Blackwell.
Gendlin, E. T. (1996). *Focusing-oriented psychotherapy: A manual of the experiential method*. Guilford Press.
Gravestock, J. (2021). *Music therapy in adoption and trauma: Therapy that makes a difference after placement*. Jessica Kingsley.
Heidegger, M. (2000). Conversation on a country path about thinking. In *Discourse on thinking* (J. M. Anderson & E. Hans Freund, Trans., pp. 58–90). Harper & Row. (Original published in 1956.)
Jaenicke, C. (2008). *The risk of relatedness: Intersubjectivity theory in clinical practice*. Jason Aronson.
Kroeker, J. (2019). *Jungian music psychotherapy: When psyche sings*. Routledge.
Lawes, M. (2021). Trend of differentiation and integration in UK music therapy and the spectrum of music-centredness. *British Journal of Music Therapy, 35*(1), 4–15.
Levinge, A. (2015). *The music of being: Music therapy, Winnicott, and the school of object relations*. Jessica Kingsley.
Lyons-Ruth, K. (1998). Implicit relational knowing: Its role in development and psychoanalytic treatment. *Infant Mental Health Journal, 19*(3), 282–289.
Malone, J. C. (2018) Relational psychoanalysis: Not a theory but a framework. In M. Charles (Ed), *Introduction to contemporary psychoanalysis: Defining terms and building bridges* (pp. 208–226). Routledge.
Merleau-Ponty, M. (1968). *The visible and the invisible* (A. Lingis, Trans.). Northwestern University Press. (Original work published 1964.)
Nagel, J. J. (2013). *Melodies of the mind: Connections between psychoanalysis and music*. Routledge.
Newport, E. L., Gleitman, H., & Gleitman, L. R. (1977). Mother, I'd rather do it myself: Some effects and non-effects of maternal speech style. In C. E. Snow & C. A. Ferguson (Eds.), *Talking to children: Language input and acquisition* (pp. 141–177). Cambridge University Press.
Pavlicevic, M. (1990). Dynamic interplay in clinical improvisation. *Journal of British Music Therapy, 4*(2), 7.
Seligman, S. (2014). Paying attention and feeling puzzled: The analytic mindset as an agent of therapeutic change. *Psychoanalytic Dialogues, 9*(2), 129–159.
Slochower, J. (2018). D. W. Winnicott: Holding, playing and moving towards mutuality. In M. Charles (Ed.), *Introduction to contemporary psychoanalysis: Defining terms and building bridges* (pp. 97–119). Routledge.
Stern, D. N. (1985). *The interpersonal world of the infant*. Basic Books.
Stern, D. N. (2004). *The present moment in psychotherapy and everyday life*. Norton.
Stern, D. N. (2010a). *Exploring dynamic experience in psychology and the arts*. Oxford University Press.
Stern, D. N. (2010b). The issue of vitality. *Nordic Journal of Music Therapy, 19*(2), 88–102.
Stern, D. N. (2010c). *Forms of vitality: Exploring dynamic experience in psychology, the arts, psychotherapy, and development*. Oxford University Press.
Trondalen, G. (2016). *Relational music therapy: An intersubjective perspective*. Barcelona.

Van der Kolk, B. A. (1994). The body keeps the score: Memory and the evolving psychobiology of posttraumatic stress. *Harvard Review of Psychiatry, 1*(5), 253–265.

Verrier, N. (1993). *The primal wound.* Gateway Press.

Wigram, T. (2004). *Improvisation: Methods and techniques for music therapy clinicians, educators and students.* Jessica Kingsley.

Wilberg, P. (2002) *Being and listening. counselling, psychoanalysis, and the ontology of listening*. New Yoga Publications.

Winnicott, D. W. (1941). The observation of infants in a set situation. *International Journal of Psychoanalysis, 22*(2), 229–249.

Winnicott, D. W. (1960). The theory of the parent-infant relationship. *International Journal of Psychoanalysis, 34*, 89–97.

Winnicott, D. W. (1965). The capacity to be alone. In *The maturational processes and the facilitating environment: Studies in the theory of emotional development* (pp. 1–276). Hogarth Press. (Original work published 1958.)

Wright, K. (2009). *Mirroring and attunement: Self-realisation in psychoanalysis and art*. Routledge.

Yontef, G. (2002). The relational attitude in Gestalt theory and practice. *International Gestalt Journal, 25*(1), 15–35.

Zinker, J., & Nevis, S. (1994). The aesthetics of Gestalt couples therapy. In G. Wheeler & S. Backman (Eds.), *On intimate ground: A Gestalt approach to working with couples* (pp. 356–399). Gestalt Institute of Cleveland Press.

Chapter 9

Conclusions, key findings from therapeutic work and research and a message for future adoption-specific music therapy

'Latoya'

It is Latoya's second music-therapy session, and she forms a connection with the large gong by walking up to it and gently wrapping her arms almost right around it. It is a wide gong and bigger than her, and I am struck by how, as she embraces it, in turn, it almost seems to be holding her. She finds the soft gong beater and gently touches it to the gong, producing a soft rippling sound. This sustained vibration, repeated over and over, creates a real atmosphere as gentle layers and waves of sound build in a growing crescendo until the room feels filled with the vibrations she is creating. I accompany her on the piano with a consistent and enduring piano bass octave, which rocks along in time with her gong play. We share a rhythm, and there is an emerging thickness to the quality of sound or perhaps a feeling tone which I think is mysterious, as if a musical mist was surrounding us. Suddenly Latoya jumps backwards, exclaiming 'Did you see that?' She rushes to the opposite side of the gong to hide. Her mum and I confer and say we haven't seen anything. She shrugs her shoulders and says, 'Maybe it was a ghost then that only I could see?'

This musical play with Latoya was repeated over many weeks. Each time she would build a musically dense atmosphere, out of which experiences did seem to emerge, almost like shadows coming in and out of a mist. Latoya continued to reference these experiences as 'ghosts' in our room. Her adopted mum and I said we were listening to the ghosts that she told us she could also see. On one occasion, I found myself moving to the xylophone to play, as Latoya was verbally offering a narrative about ghosts, which I could create melodic support for. Quickly, she found my melodic line and joined it. She began to wordlessly half speak and half sing in a quasi-rap style. I moved to the piano, grounding her songs once more with sustaining bass octaves. Latoya's lyrics then changed to a narrative about a 'ghost baby', that, in her song, she said she could hear crying in the room. The baby was never given a name other than 'ghost baby', but Latoya seemed sad as she sang with great intent.

DOI: 10.4324/9781003733393-9

This sad feeling tone needed acknowledgement and holding. After some weeks of witnessing the sadness and giving space for its expression, I instinctively felt my own music-making at the piano changing. I began playing in 6/8 time, the classic rhythm of a lullaby. This music provided sound-holding for both Latoya and her adoptive mum. I rocked gently between octaves and noted that Latoya's body began to rock in time, as though the piano's melodic line was expressing her sadness, while the rhythm was simultaneously holding her embodied expression of it. As she rocked, I wondered about her internal baby and how Latoya as a baby might have longed for her birth mother. Perhaps her inner 'ghost baby' was musically held here and now in a recapitulation of an early experience? Could the 'ghost baby' be comforted in this lullaby rhythm? Latoya's embodied rocking enabled her to also hold and soothe parts of her younger self, embracing the abandoned little baby she had been. She longed to feel secure belonging to her adopted mother, but her internal ghost baby painfully reminded her that children can lose mothers, so it was terrifying to risk trusting and loving.

We never spoke about this playing, and I did not think a verbal interpretation was required when the music and playful symbolism seemed to be doing its work. In later sessions, Latoya asked her adopted mum to wrap her in a blanket and hold her like a baby. Throughout this regression in their joint enactment, I sustained the 6/8 lullaby, and, in its repetition and rocking, I was reminded of the rhythms a baby needs to feed at the breast and which Latoya had lost out on with her birth mother as she had come to her adoptive family aged just six months. New relating could now emerge between Latoya and her adoptive mum, and experiences from Latoya's early life that had previously been lost to them could be safely and imaginatively recreated in the music.

As I did in Chapter 1, I have chosen to begin the final chapter of this book with the narrative of a case study. Hopefully, the reader will now be informed by the chapters preceding it and will be able to make sense with me of the way I chose to work with Latoya and my thinking behind the work. This example consolidates many of the ideas that have been discussed in this book.

Ghosts have been a feature of many adopted children's musical playing (see Chapter 1), and I have concluded that when children speak or sing about them, they are engaging with something of their early life. This remains present for an adopted child but in a 'ghostly' form. The adopted child has unconscious memory of their preverbal and pre-adoption experiences but has no way of speaking about this precisely because the memory is unconscious. Psychoanalytically informed music therapy (in this case, the gong's layered sound, held within the sustaining sounds of both piano and xylophone, together creating a sound environment that expressed resonance, sustainment and decay), provides a space for the unconscious to be expressed. Latoya had feelings that were attached to her early lived experience, and these feelings were evoked within the music we played together. As she expressed her sadness while playing music in her chosen way, simultaneously, the musical relationship that was co-created between us could contain her feelings.

Lullabies, previously discussed, are illustrated in work with Latoya. I eventually found myself playing in a lullaby form, with a rhythmic structure created initially by me, but Latoya took this structure into her own body. She then rocked herself in the same rhythm. She became rhythm as she embodied the sound I had created. I was not required to physically hold her because she could use the blanket to wrap around herself and begin to self-soothe while knowing and feeling herself held in my rocking rhythms as well as being held in my mind. She did not have to find words to express her losses that came about through being adopted. Nor did I have to put the musical experience back into language. It was enough that it had existed, or, as Winnicott would say, it was enough that we had this shared experience. Finally, in this lullaby rhythm, we both experienced something that I think is akin to the rhythms emergent in breastfeeding between mother and infant. Gradually a rhythmic relationship is built between a mother and infant who are beginning to breastfeed, and I argue that similarities are found in the musical relationship developed between Latoya and myself.

This case study then sums up what this book has being saying throughout: that the musical relationship between a music therapist and an adoptee has similarities between that of a mother and infant. As such, music therapy can evoke and enable reparative experiences of attunement that have been lost to adoptees. These relational, musical experiences can be internalised by adoptee children and thereby impact their relationships beyond the music-therapy room.

In this closing chapter, I shall offer some conclusions that I have drawn from much experience within adoption, and also from my Ph.D. research, especially research arising from the deep analysis of casework with Jack, which has led to subsequent reflections on other related casework. This book has described my practice and subsequent research as a music therapist-researcher evolving an approach that I have come to describe as adoption-specific, and I have outlined what this term might mean for those in the adoption community seeking post-adoption support. I have acknowledged the difficulty of simultaneously being therapist for and researcher of this work. Indeed, Gadamer (1996, p. 34) writes, 'Both therapy and research inevitably invoke a mutuality in which there is a "fusion of horizons" of client-participant and therapist-researcher'. Aron (1996) also describes similar mutuality in the interaction between research participants as between therapist and client. However, I have described my attempts to mitigate against what Gadamer positions as an inevitable fusion and mutuality, as the responsibility falls clearly upon myself as therapist-researcher to maintain boundaries.

Interrogation of lived experience has been a research method I drew upon in order to describe working within the adoption community, which I am a member of, and a therapist to and now which have researched. I came close to using autoethnography as a methodology at times, thinking that what Etherington (2004, pp. 140–1) writes matches my work:

> Autoethnography . . . requires us to write about ourselves . . . and has provided a methodology that legitimises and encourages the inclusion of the researcher's self and culture, as an ethical and politically sound approach that takes into consideration the complex interplay of our own personal biography, power, and status, interactions with participants, and written word.

As much as I have valued autoethnography, I have been slightly more cautious in how much of my self has been shared and instead returned to an interrogation of lived experience. As Finlay and Evans (2009, p. 121) write: 'The researcher needs to avoid undue navel-gazing, and preoccupation with their own experience or the research will be pulled in unfortunate directions.' I have also taken care with how much of my experience is retold in consideration that potential adoptee clients and their families can access published work (and are most welcome to do so), and any of my self-revelations could potentially impact future music therapy (for example, transference and countertransference may be impinged upon if a client already has substantial knowledge of their therapist). It may not be helpful for my own identity within the adoption community to be fully revealed, therefore, while it is at the same time imperative that I disclose this identity because of its link to music therapist and researcher bias. Also, for potential future clients, there may be something reassuring in knowing I am a member of the adoption community, via lived experience, without a necessity to know precisely what that experience may be.

Theoretically, then, I have drawn upon in this book the British object-relations school of psychoanalysis (specifically Winnicott), and inter-subjective developmental theory (specifically Stern). I have also considered relational psychoanalytic theory, especially as this is interpreted and used by the music therapist Trondalen. My practice, research and other writing are therefore comprised of an integrative frame of reference, which draws on other related theories as required. My aim has first been to carve out with my clients and their families an appropriate needs-led practice, upon which a body of theory has been built. I continue to make this my endeavour in the music therapy room and would encourage other music therapists to embark on similar journeys. Then, client-led approaches of the type I described may continue to emerge and evolve, in order to best serve individuals and families presenting with specific needs. New music therapy approaches should come to exist between other music therapists and their clients, in a synthesis of practice, theory and our own research.

I continue this closing chapter then, with a revisiting of the major themes this book has explored.

Recapitulation and reiteration of main themes

Part I: Holding

The notion of a 'musical holding' is something I describe using predominantly Winnicott's concept of holding and discussing its application in music therapy. Winnicott (cited in Wilberg, 2002, p. 63) writes that the analyst holds the patient by 'conveying at the appropriate moment something that shows that the analyst knows and understands the deepest anxiety that is being experienced'. I have argued that the listening music therapist might provide something akin to this holding in their musical responses to an adopted child.

Winnicott describes how the mother/caregiver is tasked with holding the baby in order to keep it safe from unpredictable (or traumatic) events that may interrupt a state of going-on-being. Such unpredictable, traumatic events are called impingements by Winnicott. If maternal holding is lost to the child in this sense (which always occurs in adoption), then the infant experiences environmental unreliability and will react to external impingements and ultimately to what feels like the threat of annihilation. The case-study chapters in this book have described my experience of the effect of the loss of maternal holding with various adopted clients, and especially my client Jack. For some, the loss came early in the form of separation when they may have been just moments old. Others who had a longer time with their first mother may or may not have had a good experience of being held. Jack appeared to have at least experienced some good early holding experience, which became evident within his musical relationship with me.

I have described how an infant is utterly unable to respond to early experience, other than in embodied states. They will lack conscious memory of their loss of the mother but store feeling states about it unconsciously. Older children placed for adoption have additionally experienced traumas of emotional, physical and psychological abuse, which are certainly impingements in the extreme. I have illustrated from casework how a musical holding environment must reduce the number of impingements that an adoptee has to react to. Within the case study of Jack, it was necessary for me to first provide Winnicottian holding in order that he may then become able to play in an intersubjective relational way within Winnicott's potential space. We were then able to play in ways that allowed him to enjoy experimenting with both musical and relational experiences while he felt held enough to do so. Working at times with his adopted mother present in the room provided her also with a sense of musical holding by me, which enabled her in turn to hold Jack (both physically and psychologically). A musical relational holding must first be provided before any other work can occur in music therapy with adopted children. In common parlance, we refer to holding someone in our gaze. Similarly, I have presented a discussion on how it is possible to hold someone in our listening, which might become a sort of 'aural gaze', and I am continuing to think of this as a concept for future work.

Part II: Attunement

I have defined attunement simply as a shared relational process or event occurring between two individuals, resulting in one feeling understood by the other. I described how interactions that occur between music therapist and client can be described as attuned because of their similarity to interactions that occur in mother–infant attunement (Stern). I therefore have developed my argument that the musical, relational experience of music therapy is rooted in the proto conversation of mother and infant. I described how opportunities for attunement are denied to the infant who is removed from their mother and subsequently placed for adoption. A fundamental principle then of offering music therapy within the adoption community is that music therapy can offer these infants (and also older children) new opportunities for attuned experiences, which have a beneficial impact for the adoptee themselves, but also impacting relationally within their adoptive families.

I have also drawn upon Trevarthen (and other developmental theorists such as Malloch et al.), who argue that human musicality originates from the core impulses and relating that goes on between a mother and infant. Malloch named such early relating 'communicative musicality', and this theory influences the thinking of music therapists (evidenced in its inclusion on training courses). Darnley-Smith (2018) describes the value of a musical relationship because of the way it might replicate the rhythms, forms and affective qualities of mother–infant vocal communication. I have discussed that mother–infant interaction and music improvisation are not completely equivalent (as written about by Rolvsjord, 1996; Tønsberg & Hauge, 1996). They can, however, be seen as parallel and complementary processes (as written about by Johns, 1993; Smeijsters, 2012). Darnley-Smith (2018, p. 142) utilises Trevarthen and Malloch's work, defining specific musical elements such as pulse, pitch, etc., that precede verbal communication as being key to relating where 'words cannot play a role and are due to the infants and parents desire to attune to one another'. Mother and infant interactions, therefore, provide a model for musical interactions in music therapy, where, within a musical relationship, the therapist seeks to elicit and extend this relational quality. I have illustrated from close analysis of casework how musical and emotional attunement can result in moments of embodied synchronisation that simultaneously affect regulation in states which are pervaded with a sense of emotional sharing. From this, an emerging shared narrative can grow.

I have described how embodied synchronisation of affect states has been termed cross-modal attunement by Stern. In 2010, Stern differentiated what he called categorical affects from vitality affects. Both are crucial for attunement. Categorical affects are the earliest emotional communications of a baby (which Stern conceives of as being innate from birth). Vitality affects occur later and are not themselves emotions but are more like ways of being in the world and projecting feelings out. Stern uses words such as 'bursting', 'floating', 'falling' to describe how vitality affects show feeling states. The vitality affects of the baby, or indeed the client, can be met in the response of the mother or therapist in cross-modal attunement. I have argued that this is a response that is not merely imitation but reflects a feeling state, recast in another form. Stern argues that both categorical and vitality affects can be attuned to, but attunement occurs more with the latter. Cross-modal attunement behaviours 'recast the event and shift the focus of attention to what is behind the behaviour, to *the quality of feeling that is being shared* . . . attunement is the predominant way to commune with or indicate sharing of internal states' (Stern, 1985, p. 142; my italics).

I have argued that attunement is a process worth observing in music therapy with adoptees where it may become possible for internal states to be shared. This was illustrated with Jack's case study, wherein I felt and experienced that unconscious, embodied states from his infancy, which would be remembered wordlessly, could be recast in a symbolic musical form.

Illustrations from other case studies have shown that working with processes of attunement is not age-dependent. Music therapists work with a range of clients spanning the entire life span, and yet Stern's thinking is still applicable. We can draw upon Pavlicevic's (1997) concept of dynamic form, which offers an application of Stern's concepts to music therapy generically. Here, dynamic form corresponds to Stern's vitality affects but is explicitly musical in character. Pavlicevic describes how a musical process, akin to attunement, occurs in intersubjective moments of intensity, timing and shape. Joint improvisation in music therapy, therefore, enables the therapist to tune into the client's early dynamic form as it was created with their mother. It is possible then that the process of attuning gives the music therapist some sense of the quality of an adopted child's first relationship(s) and how this/these may be impacting upon relating in their here-and-now adoption placement.

Part III: Intersubjectivity

The music therapist Gro Trondalen (2016, p. 14) writes: 'A main goal for music therapy is to expand the client's lived experience and intersubjective awareness through new ways of relating through music.' Her framing of expansion of new experience as a 'goal' for therapy differs to my own as I do not necessarily always have to identify goals for my work. Instead, I describe how relational experiences of intersubjectivity, including attunement, might be made available in a needs-led music therapy based completely in free improvisation. Trondalen (2016, p. 14) continues, describing what the music therapist might bring to therapy: 'The therapist's emotional availability and responsiveness, in addition to attention, regulation of emotions, and reflexivity, are of vital importance in such a musical approach.' This recognises that intersubjectivity is a two-person experience, and throughout my work I have considered both the adoptee client and the music therapist, what each contributes, and how this can be made sense of. I follow Atwood's (2012, p. 83) thinking:

> the idea that the clinician unilaterally, uni-directionally heals the patient is medical model thinking . . . what Stern (2012) referred to as 'an internists view' . . . Cure is in some sense a mess, but a mess from which we can extract meaning and a measure of human dignity, as we create a space in which the truth about someone's life can find a home.

Finlay and Evans (2009, p. 124) write that the therapeutic relationship should be co-created 'as an interactional event, a constantly evolving co-constructed relational process to which client and therapist, participant and researcher contribute alike and impact on each other in an ongoing way'.

By engaging in freely improvised co-created music, the adopted client and music therapist are simultaneously evolving the relational processes that Finlay and Evans advocate. I have drawn upon Stern's theory of 'now-moments' describing how present now-moments occurring in the musical relationship can be illuminated by past experience. Then, new experiences in both music and relationship can offer an adopted child possibilities for exploring new ways of being with others, especially their adoptive family, in the wider world. Thus, music therapy has the potential to modify a child's internal working model, and this is a hopeful reality for any music therapist working in adoption. Erskine (2015, p. 321), similarly to Trondalen, views this as a goal of therapeutic work, writing, 'My therapeutic goal is to stimulate and enhance the client's sense of visceral arousal and awareness so that he has a new physiological-affective-relational experience.'.

This revisiting of the major themes of this book leads me back to how first my research then this second book came about as I wanted to think more deeply about the usefulness for work with adoptees of experiencing what I was calling 'micro-moments of attunement' in music therapy. Throughout, I have been arguing that there is significance in offering something in music therapy, which is akin to a Winnicottian holding, and which in turn enables Sternian experiences of attunement (especially cross-modal) to occur between music therapist and client. It is by offering an adopted child a potential space to play, being within the presence of a music-mother, that they might be enabled to experience new relational ways of being. Such newness encountered within the therapeutic relationship that music therapy provides can then lead to the child experimenting relationally outside of the music-therapy room (especially, it is hoped, with their adopted family) and no longer being influenced solely by traumatic internal-world early experience. If it is traumatic re-enactments of early experience within adoptive families that lead to the potential breakdown of an adoptive placement, then music therapy has a special role in lessening the impact of early trauma and offering hope for future relating. This is what I hope writing about my approach contributes to future work of music therapists within this specialist area of adoption-specific music therapy.

Key findings and messages

Perhaps the most obvious finding from my work is summed up by this statement by Trondalen (2016, p. 39): 'Music therapy offers relational experiences through music. These experiences sometimes prompt changes in the client's life, and even in the therapist's life as well.' I very much like her loose style of both language and attitude here when she states experiences 'sometimes' prompt change. I have found in my own work that I need to keep the process soft and open, without any pressure from fixed goals or outcome measures. There is no guarantee that the approach I offer will actually bring about change. However, I can recognise that no adoption that I have worked with at threat of breakdown has yet disrupted. Also, all adoptive families I have worked with have described gaining a better understanding of one another through having received music therapy. This is not 'hard data' as such, and these findings could, in fact, be called incidental. However, they are consistent. My case study of Jack evidenced this. He and his adoptive mother were able to have musical relational experiences together, and this helped give meaning to Jack's early experience and enabled his adoptive mother to understand how that could be impacting still, here and now.

I have discussed that free improvisation in music therapy seems to me to be the best way of enabling clients to reveal unconscious feelings. It is working with the unconscious and bringing early trauma to consciousness that my work shows is so important for adoption music therapy. Music does not depend on words and can thereby bypass verbal functioning. Stern (2010, p. 102) validates the use of the creative-arts therapies when he writes, 'It is no longer true that you have to talk about it to get any good out of it. You don't have to make it conscious – it can become part of implicit knowledge.' Real deep work can happen within the musical relationship, as my work with Jack and other adoptees has illustrated. Although I may work with a client and have an interpretation of what might be going on for them within my own mind, I do not have to translate music back into words. Music can simply do its job, and we can allow this to happen by playing in an attuned, sensitive manner with clients.

Evans and Gilbert (2005, pp. 74–5) write that it is necessary to meet clients as 'the sum total of who they are in all their complexity and with their own individual histories and ways of organising their experience *and their unconscious processes*' (italics mine). In other words, then, the music therapist is 'faced with the challenge of meeting the other in all his/her complexity' (Evans & Gilbert, 2005, pp. 74–5). However, as Jaenicke (2015, p. 8) writes, this is 'a joint enterprise . . . a system comprised of two transferences, as well as the level of implicit relational knowledge', and this has implications for the music therapist. Winnicott writes about the analytic/therapeutic relationship in terms of what happens when maternal provision is lost and how the therapist might work to understand the impact of early loss. I have also drawn upon the interpersonal and relational contemporary school of psychoanalysis, which considers the therapeutic relationship less as developmental processes being reworked by the client within the holding of the therapist and more as an intersubjectively shared process. Levinson et al. (1972) especially argues that the analyst/therapist will inevitably be embedded within the transference–countertransference.

My findings from my reflections upon case studies and subsequent research show that the music therapist is both within the music by contributing to playing it themselves and also within the relating and will therefore experience transference and countertransference in both music and relationship. Consequently, it seems inevitable that, as the interpersonal/relational school argues, the music therapist will definitely be in a shared musical relationship with their clients. It is though a position I have described as being like having one foot in the river but the other firmly on the riverbank. The music therapist must be able to step back so the client's experience is privileged and we are not unhelpfully embedded. Then, as Mitchell (2020, p. 96) writes, 'The expansion of the qualities of intersubjectivity between us provide . . . different sorts of attachment experiences than early life had allowed.'

My findings have also shown that the adopted clients I have worked with have first needed a felt sense of being held in a music-therapy relationship before they can use an intersubjective relationship. Therefore, I am conflating approaches within my work that at first might not seem entirely congruent theoretically but which have made sense in practice of my client's material. Fonagy and Target (1998) have similarly explored ways in which secure attachment experiences occurring within therapy can then engender a complex sense of intersubjectivity between therapist and client through which they argue the client comes to sense himself as an agentic subject by experiencing himself in the mind of the therapist. However, Trondalen (2016), drawing on the work of Brantzaeg et al. (2011), argues that it is, in fact, an experience of intersubjectivity that should be considered as crucial before attachment can be experienced. I conclude that, whether attachment or intersubjectivity come first, both are necessary.

In the work described with my research client Jack, I experienced he and I together in a shared process of forming a sense of his early life experiences. These endured in an embodied way and could be experienced in his body within a music therapy that offered time, space and relationship and that utilised musical elements such as rhythm, which are similar to the elements of communication in early life between a mother and infant. Trondalen, as a music therapist, argues that music therapy 'works' because it is possible for early mental states to be shared musically without needing any translation into language. The philosopher Susanne Langer (1942; cited in Nagel, 1943, p. 323) takes a similar view and argues that the specific function of music is 'to serve as conceptualisations and articulations of forms of feeling, forms which are incapable of formulation in ordinary language'. In her own words, Langer (1942, p. 328) sums this up in the simplest of language writing, 'Music sounds the way emotions feel.'

This, then perhaps, is the benefit of all the creative-arts therapies: 'Creativity is one way out of simultaneous feelings of being and nothingness' (Jaenicke, 2015, p. 2). The music therapist Rachel Darnley-Smith (2018, p. 136) draws upon and elaborates Jung's notion that art-making enables a 'conscious waking attitude directed to the perception of unconscious contents'. Thus, emotional disturbance can be worked with 'not by clarifying it intellectually, but also by giving the mood an external visible shape through art media . . . as a way of giving fantasy free play' (Darnley-Smith, 2018, p. 136). She argues that the 'domain of art' gives a 'visible shape' to emotional disturbance (Darnley-Smith, 2018, p. 138). I have shared my idea that the music of music therapy provides an audible shaping of adoptee's early emotional experience.

This translates into practice then in the music-therapy room into a need to consider not only what is being played in a session but also how that music is played (including the embodiment of both players and ways in which both music and relationship develop). Darnley-Smith (2018, p. 139) cites Priestley's statement that 'the patient explores new pathways symbolically in the world of the imagination but with the bodily expressed emotion in sound which gives her a safe toehold in the world of everyday life'. I also cited this quotation in Chapter 1 and think it is a useful summary of what music therapy provided for my research client Jack. He was able to play his own music and then have this met by mine so we could share a felt experience. This experience was more than just musical as the music carried an emotional meaning. As we playfully improvised together, unconscious aspects of Jack's early life emerged and could be safely played with. Together, in music, we were then 'working out something related to distance and intimacy, presence and loss, that was not unrelated to . . . early traumas and deprivations, but that was happening in a very lively way between us now' (Mitchell, 2020, p. 97).

Communications of the unconscious then within music therapy are important (in fact I would say essential) for adoption work. Winnicott departed from a classical psychoanalytic theory of the unconscious, describing instead how the unconscious is comprised of the ego's inability to encompass intense emotional experience. Experience from early life especially is likely to become unconscious because trauma is not remembered as either explicit or symbolic memory. More contemporaneously, Erskine (2015, p. 61) defines the unconscious in the following way: 'Most of what we colloquially refer to as 'unconscious' may best be described as pre-symbolic, sub-symbolic, symbolic non-verbal, implicit, or procedural expressions of early childhood experience that are significant forms of memory.'

He is stating clearly that early childhood experience is contained within the unconscious. He also describes how the unconscious is stored and manifest and why it is inaccessible through language: 'Early childhood memory is pre-symbolic and non-linguistic. It is not available to consciousness through language because the experience is pre-verbal. Such memory may be expressed in self-regulating patterns, emotional reactions, physiological inhibitions, and styles of attachments and relationships' (Erskine, 2015, p. 61).

I suggest then that if the preverbal unconsciousness is non-linguistic then it might not be accessed through verbal means. This then is the role of the creative-arts therapies, and certainly music therapy especially, in adoption-support work. Early life experiences are what need to be addressed in this work, and music therapy, as a non-verbal modality, offers a safe, playful, creative way of working with these, as my case study Jack has illustrated.

The future

Part I: Future work for the music-therapy profession

In this section, I consider how my research that informs this book might in turn inform future work for music therapists and others who work therapeutically within adoption support. I have always described a music-therapy approach rather than a method. I advocate that others interested in working within adoption support take care not to limit themselves to the use of any one particular adoption music-therapy theoretical position but rather stay fluid and flexible in both practice and in theorising that arises out of practice. By doing so, we remain open to whatever the client brings to us while also remaining open to searching out other ways of thinking that help us to make sense of what they bring. Mitchell (2000, p. xiii) writes that psychoanalysts should 'feel quite comfortable with a loose eclecticism, in which drive, object relations, interpersonal, ego, and self-psychological principles all coexist and are called into service by the clinical problem that emerges'. His loose eclecticism is, of course, not theory-less but rather has the capacity to draw upon several theories while not being in thrall to any particular one.

I have also shown that the sort of presence' we bring to our work is fundamental. As a music-therapy educator, I know this is much trickier to teach than 'techniques'. However, 'practising presence and inclusion, committing to the between and engaging reflexivity can all be immensely meaningful and rewarding, but they may also be challenging and uncomfortable' (Finlay & Evans, 2009, p. 124). In order to work in the ways I have described, it is imperative that music therapists are supported by their own clinical supervision and, at times, personal psychotherapy. Additionally, if music therapists have their own personal histories and lived experience of adoption, then care should be taken to ensure client material remains privileged and personal material utilised in a way that benefits both.

My work also raises issues for the future training of music therapists. Wilberg (2002) has argued that a focus on measurement and competence has become a problem in the institutionalisation of counselling training. He maintains that such standardised training can teach counsellors (or similarly music therapists) to 'describe what gathers in terms of nameable emotions or thoughts, or to challenge . . . with questions which, however open, can . . . *foreclose our listening*' (Wilberg, 2002, p. 32; my italics). In his view, training in listening skills (which encourages an emphasis on verbal echoing, mirroring, summarising and questioning) is based on a negative definition of listening. Music therapists also are trained similarly to match and mirror their clients playing and to musically converse in questioning and answering phrases, and so on. These techniques, though undoubtedly requiring listening skills, do not equate to the sort of deep embodied listening that is necessary to attune to the emotional referent in an adoptee's music. A client who plays a phrase which is immediately musically copied might feel that they have just been exposed or even mocked (especially if their level of musical skill is significantly below the therapists). Wilberg's (2002, p. 32) negative definition of listening is described as such because it emphasises *what is not done*, i.e., 'not interrupting, not giving advice, not answering questions, etc.'. By taking this focus, he argues, there is 'no positive understanding of what listening itself really is – of the wordless activity of attuning and gathering' (Wilberg, 2002, p. 33).

This deeper sort of listening is possibly something that could become a focus in music-therapy training. It is possible to play music with a client without truly being with them emotionally and psychologically, and music therapists might instead, in Wilberg's (2002, p. 34) terms, engage in a 'hearkening to the wordless questing of each other's being'. Indeed, training in this sort of listening is relevant for all music therapists not just those working in adoption.

Part II: Future work for other research and practice

Earlier in this chapter, I described some of the tensions that exist between the theoretical elements that are combined in my music therapy approach in adoption. Mace and Margison (1997, p. 213) write: 'There have been tensions within contemporary attachment literature between a cognitive effort towards understanding of the unsatisfactory working model, and a fundamental attempt to offer recapitulation through a positive attachment experience.'

These tensions can develop into splits between differing ways of thinking about and working with early material. Yet, an adopted child in music therapy can present material that needs thinking about from different perspectives. Bowlby's (1998) early descriptions of attachment theory were accompanied by his account of internal working models, which, he suggested, came into being through early attachment experiences. I have described how the residue of early attachment and subsequent loss for the adopted child results in 'not simply cognitive working models of the interpersonal world, but affective states of undifferentiated connection with attachment figures, organised around both positive affects . . . and negative affects' (Mitchell, 2020, p. 91). It seems necessary then to find ways of integrating ways of thinking about early life material, which Mitchell (2020, p. 83) argues is timely: 'The development within the attachment tradition, together with the turn towards relationality in the psychoanalytic tradition, makes this a particularly appropriate time to explore the convergence between these quasi-independent lines of theory making.'

This could be the work of future research that attempts to find ways of making sense of adopted children's presentations and their difficulties expressed in the here and now of daily life within their adoptive families. As Finlay and Evans (2009, p. 194) write: 'phenomenological researchers should acknowledge multiple levels of empathic engagement as they strive to understand the lifeworlds of others and contribute to hermeneutic phenomenological knowledge'.

Other spaces and places to continue the dialogue: Music and brain science

In this penultimate section, I will consider briefly another arena where my work may be of interest and have impact, and that is the growing area of music and brain science. This is an area I have not explored here (other than acknowledging its presence in the literature), but one in which music therapists increasingly are becoming involved.

Alanne (2010) cited the period 2000–9 as a decade when much new thinking about music and the brain was published. During this period, interest seemed to have increased in the ways in which music is processed and experienced within the physical brain. Also, this decade saw a huge output of research and publishing about trauma and the brain. The theory that early experience impacts on brain development is now frequently discussed in the popular media and often seems to have been accepted as fact. Secure attachment has been shown to affect the social brain, and, therefore, failed attachments (especially traumatic experience of loss, including adoption itself without any additional trauma) can lead to epigenetic changes, such as a poor capability for affect regulation and many disorders in later life. Music has been shown to create well-being in the brain, and it is possible it may have evolutionary importance in creating secure attachments. Brain science is currently exploring this territory.

That decade also bought significance discoveries of brain functions such as an awareness of the existence of mirror neurons, which show the physiological value of sharing musical elements such as rhythms and harmony, etc. Brain science might well be able, therefore, to describe, for example, in terms of the effects on mirror neurons, how musical matching and mirroring work. However, in my opinion and drawing from my research, I suggest that it is not the application of musical technique that is significant when music therapists seek to consciously musically match and mirror. Rather, it is the *felt* experience that is important, and there may yet be ways in which the brain science can begin to explore this territory.

Rose (2004) has shown how music affects the same brain systems as trauma. He argues that musical knowing and experiencing are equal in impact to language upon these systems, but I have argued further than this that music has particular value when working with adoption trauma. Rose describes the very first memories human beings experience as not being verbal but rather amodal feelings embodied in the self. This concurs with my work and research. These ambient experiences and mutual affect attunement are internalised from the mother–infant dyad rather than verbal memories. Rose proposes the name 'concordance' for his theory of isomorphism in psychoanalysis in order to synthesise psychoanalysis and developmental psychology and its relationship to neuroscience and neurobiology. The idea that Rose's amodal feelings might be retained in embodied form relates to my discussion of the significance of embodied states in music therapy. There is then some crossover between my work within adoption-specific trauma and current work in brain science. Perhaps this could be a fertile ground for further research? However, I would still agree with Erskine (2015, p. 43) that 'In this era of industrialisation of psychotherapy it is essential for psychotherapists to remain mindful of the unique interpersonal relationship between therapist and client as the central and significant factor in psychotherapy.' There are some aspects of human relationship that I hope may remain forever mysterious.

Final words

To end, I will now offer some brief reflections on what it has meant to my practice to engage in research. I earlier wrote this about the importance of needs-led music therapy in adoption, stating:

> 'Needs-led', that is without any 'goals' or 'aims' imposed . . . instead, the client has a relational experience within the music therapy room that cannot be prescribed as an aim . . . neither can . . . it be taught as a 'technique' to enable intersubjective experience.

Research has, I believe, served to help me make further sense of what has emerged from my practice and has enabled me to value my eclectic, melded approach. I have been reminded by doing the research that being needs-led in adoption-specific music therapy means that I need to come to each client anew and not to assume I am doing something called 'adoption work'. My research client Jack taught me again the significance of doing this and of the importance of allowing his story to unfold as he musically shared it. I take encouragement from both Yalom and Brodie in this quote:

> As with Winnicott's mothering, this, I believe, cannot be taught. To try to teach a therapist how to act with certain types of clients is to teach a programmed response that is inevitably artificial and inhuman . . . Irvin Yalom (1997) virtually shouts out his credo, 'Create a new therapy for each patient.'
>
> (Brodie, 2020, p. 21)

This is what I have attempted to do, and my research shows how a body of theory relevant to adoption-specific music therapy has gradually arisen out of each new music therapy with each client. I am sure and certain that this should continue to evolve in my own practice because, as Orcutt (2021, p. xi) writes, 'theory, especially as it strives to understand and promote the growth of human personality, must itself grow and change'.

In Chapter 1, I cited Darnley-Smith's (2018, p. 143) argument that, 'for the music therapist whose approach is rooted within a psychoanalytic paradigm, a good improvisation is concerned with care for others, in this case, care for the therapeutic quality of the relationship'. She states that this is because 'in following our client's direction, we have the greatest hope of gaining understanding of their inner worlds' (Darnley-Smith, 2018, p. 146). This echoes Brodie's argument above and Yalom's argument contained within it. When we follow the client, we are being needs-led. This, in turn, can, I think, ensure that our work becomes what Wilberg (2002, p. 36) describes as a 'good therapy': 'To help another person to be led on their own way of being means helping them to be led by a listening that hearkens to their own being.'

My therapeutic approach is rooted in both psychoanalytic thinking and intersubjectivity theories. As I hold loosely to established theoretical positions informing my work, I also hope to keep the work fresh and alive. This entails *both* the client and me being prepared to explore new and uncertain territory at times and Jaenicke (2015, p. 5) encourages me in this:

> If I don't believe therapy is something that I do to you, but rather that we change and become who we are through one another, then who we aren't and can't be is as important as who we are and can be.

This quote of Jaenicke values the intersubjective experience but also recognises its limitations. Aspects of my research show how careful and considered music therapists need to be in our therapeutic relating. Our clients will only be able to go so far as we have the capacity to take them.

I end this section with a comment by the psychotherapist Erskine (2015, p. 319) who describes having his own experience of music therapy. Afterwards he wrote:

> The safety and nonverbal aspect of the music therapy made it possible for me to reexperience a trauma that had previously not been available to my consciousness. Music therapy is but one way of working with pre-symbolic and procedural memories.

Here was a verbal adult who was able (because of his own qualification as a therapist) to make sense of his own experience. He clearly identifies how music therapy made unconscious memory and trauma accessible. His statement supports my work and my research. I could not ask Jack verbally how he experienced music therapy because he would not be able to conceive of this, nor have the verbal capacity to tell me. However, I do conclude that music therapy might provide an analogical structure that can both evoke and contain early traumatic experience of adopted children. Therefore, there is significant evidence for the argument that music therapy is a modality well suited for working within adoption support. This is because my research has shown that micro-moments of attunement that occurred with my research client Jack evidenced the significance of therapeutic holding and attunement and that this has implications for the practice of music therapy within the adoption community.

By explicating therapeutic experiences in the music-therapy room (such as described at the opening of this chapter and elsewhere throughout this book), I have sought to explore, theorise and communicate such experiences using psychological, psychoanalytic and philosophical theories. It is not possible, given the number of theoretical reference points there are to my music therapy in adoption-specific trauma approach, to ensure that all the ends tie up neatly, as it were. This is important because my approach continues to evolve and will do so if I continue to allow the therapeutic experience to lead the development of this work. I have detailed some of the primary and secondary themes that have become important in this work, though, obviously, there is not enough space here to describe every concept that I use in detail. As I stated in Chapter 1, this work has been a journey that I began without a map, and it is the experiences with clients that have become both territory and map. The multiplicity of ideas which I now hold in my mind can be accessed at any point in a client's music therapy as part of the attempt to give meaning to where there has been none. In work that I describe as being 'needs-led' by the client, I expect and indeed hope that this integrated body of (at times) disparate thought surrounding my approach will be challenged. This book and my previous book extend an invitation for others to go on a sense-making journey in their own music-therapy practice. Meanwhile, I continue to interrogate both my therapeutic practice and approach and my lived experience and hope that other music therapists will join me in the journey.

Hope

As I write these closing words at the end of 2025, the Adoption Support Fund (ASF) in England has been through a crisis. The fund has usually been renewed every five years by the government. The current government delayed their response to renewing the ASF from the years 2024–5. Although a decision about any continuation of funding was supposed to be in effect from the end of March 2025, no decision had even been reached or confirmed by this date. Nationally, therapists working with adoptees and their families were informed that ASF funding for therapeutic work could not continue beyond the end of March. Many therapists were informed that work had to end. Others decided to end work themselves ahead of this date, for the ethical reason that a child's therapy should not be left hanging until the last moment with a decision to continue or end work. Certain therapists felt that ending prematurely was so detrimental to therapy that they continued to work unpaid.

Having had no funding secured by 1 March, local authorities could no longer guarantee any future funding, and talk in the professional community was darkening, with a growing sense that the fund would stop. However, on 3 April, a decision was made to continue the fund, albeit with significant reductions. The professional community was devastated as an enormous amount of work had ended. Also, some therapists had gone and got new jobs as their future in adoption work was so insecure. Therapists who had ended work prematurely were unable to simply restart as families were told they had to reapply (a process which itself can take months). It was not helpful for children, who had been given endings in their therapy to be told it would begin again. There has resultingly been enormous anger expressed by the adoption community to the government about the lack of consideration for their adopted children's needs, and for family needs.

The ASF is currently continuing until spring 2027. This is little more than a year away. Yet, it can take a considerable amount of time to set up new work, likely leaving less than a year for the actual therapy to take place. I hope that my research illustrates that, almost entirely, short-term work is not best practice for adoptees who present with complex needs, which will not be resolved in a few months. I hope this book inspires other music therapists to hold out and argue for our clients' deepest therapeutic needs. I have recently been involved in a research 'think tank', the results of which will be presented to the government, which argue for adequate therapeutic provision. If, as a society, we continue to believe that adoption is a preferred form of family-making, then we must also commit to the resourcing of adoptions. Otherwise, we leave adopted children and adopters to puzzle out their conflictual relationships alone. This is likely to result in more children having no opportunity to process their experiences, and, continuing to live with enduring trauma impacting on their relating, they will likely become involved with either adult psychiatric or prison services.

It is my hope that as we place some of the most complex and troubled children into new families, there is an understanding of what is needed to support contemporary adoption. I also hope that this book has provided a coherent rationale for us as a profession of music, arts and other therapists to argue for the best of therapy in collaboration with the adoption community.

References

Alanne, S. (2010). *Music psychotherapy with refugee survivors of torture: Interpretations of three clinical case studies*. Picaset Oy.

Aron, L. (1996). *A meeting of minds: Mutuality in psychoanalysis*. Analytic Press.

Atwood, G. E. (2012). *The abyss of madness*. Routledge.

Bowlby, J. (1998). *A secure base: Clinical applications of attachment theory*. Routledge.

Brantzaeg, I., Smith, L., & Torsteinson, S. (2011). *Mikroseparasjoner: Tilknytning og behandling*. Fagbokforlaget.

Brodie, B. R. (2020) *Object relations and intersubjective theories in the practice of psychotherapy*. Routledge.

Darnley-Smith, R. (2018). Jung and the transcendent function in music therapy. In S. Wilson (Ed.), *Music–psychoanalysis–musicology* (pp. 136–150). Routledge.

Erskine, R. (2015). *Relational patterns, therapeutic presence: Concepts and practice of integrative psychotherapy*. Karnac.

Etherington, K. (2004). *Becoming a reflexive researcher: Using ourselves in research*. Jessica Kingsley.

Evans, K. R., & Gilbert, M. (2005). *An introduction to integrative psychotherapy*. Palgrave Macmillan.

Finlay, L., & Evans, K. (Eds.) (2009). *Relational-centred research for psychotherapists: Exploring meanings and experience*. Wiley-Blackwell.

Fonagy, P., & Target, M. (1998). Mentalization and the changing aims of psychoanalysis. *Psychoanalytic Dialogues*, *8*, 87–114.

Gadamer, H.-G. (1996). *Truth and method* (2nd rev. ed.). Sheed & Ward. (Original work published in 1965.)

Jaenicke, C. (2015). *The search for a relational home: An intersubjective view of therapeutic action*. Routledge.

Johns, U. (1993). Intersubjektivitet som grunnlag for utvikling. *Spesialpedagogikk*, *3*, 41–46.

Kramer, R. (2025). *Otto Rank and the creation of modern psychotherapy*. Oxford University Press.

Langer, S. K. (1942). *Philosophy in a new key: A study in the symbolism of reason, rite and art*. Harvard University Press.

Levinson, H., Molinari, J., & Spohn, A. (1972). *Organizational diagnosis*. Harvard University Press.

Mace, C., & Margison, R. (1997). Attachment and psychotherapy: An overview. *British Journal of Medical Psychology*, *70*, 209–215.

Mitchell, S. A. (2000). *Relationality: From attachment to intersubjectivity*. Analytic Press.

Nagel, E. (1943). Review of Philosophy in a new key by S. K. Langer. *Journal of Philosophy*, *40*(12), 323–329.

Orcutt, C. (2021). *The unanswered self: The Masterson approach to the healing of personality disorders.* Karnac.

Pavlicevic, M. (1997). *Music therapy in context: Music, meaning and relationship.* Jessica Kingsley.

Rolvsjord, R. (1996). Et interaksjonsperspektiv på musikkterapi: Hva vil et interaksjonsteoretisk perspektiv bety for å forstå musikken og småspillets funksjon i musikkterapi? *Musikkterapi, 1*, 15–31.

Rose, G. J. (2004). *Between couch and piano: Psychoanalysis, music, art and neuroscience.* Brunner-Routledge.

Smeijsters, H. (2012). Analogy and metaphor in music therapy: Theory and practice. *Nordic Journal of Music Therapy, 21*(3), 227–249.

Stern, D. N. (1985). *The interpersonal world of the infant.* Basic Books.

Stern, D. N. (2012). Lecture. SGAPS-Annual Conference. Brunnen, Switzerland.

Stern, D. N. (2010). *Forms of vitality: Exploring dynamic experience in psychology, the arts, psychotherapy, and development.* Oxford University Press.

Tønsberg, G. E., & Hauge, T. S. (1996). The musical nature of prelinguistic interaction. *Nordic Journal of Music Therapy, 5*(2), 63–75.

Trondalen, G. (2016). *Relational music therapy: An intersubjective perspective.* Barcelona.

Wilberg, P. (2002). *Being and listening: Counselling, psychoanalysis, and the ontology of listening.* New Yoga Publications.

Index